Farm accounting and management

Farm accounting and management

Seventh edition

Ford Sturrock
PhD MA BSc

lately Director
of the Agricultural Economics Unit
University of Cambridge

Pitman

PITMAN BOOKS LIMITED
128 Long Acre, London WC2

PITMAN PUBLISHING INC
1020 Plain Street, Marshfield, Massachusetts

Associated Companies
Pitman Publishing Pty Ltd, Melbourne
Pitman Publishing New Zealand Ltd, Wellington
Copp Clark Pitman, Toronto

© Ford Sturrock, 1967, 1971, 1982

First published in Great Britain, 1947
Seventh Edition, 1982

British Library Cataloguing in Publication Data
Sturrock, Ford
   Farm accounting and management.—7th ed
   1. Farm management   2. Agriculture—
   Accounting
   I. Title
   630′.68   S567

   ISBN 0–273–01788–8
   ISBN 0–273–01765–9 Pbk

Text set in 10/12 pt Linotron 202 Times, printed and bound
in Great Britain at The Pitman Press, Bath

Contents

Preface
to seventh edition

The opportunity has been taken to revise the text thoroughly. This has been necessary to take account of metrication and price rises but, of more importance, to allow for the many improvements that are taking place in farming. Higher productivity is evident in livestock production in the use of feeding-stuffs and labour. It is no less evident in crop production as larger machines and fields increase the amount of work a man can accomplish. To deal with the latter, a new chapter on mechanization has been included with separate standards for large, medium and small farms. Indeed, if productivity levels in industry were as dynamic and flexible as in farming, Britain would be a more prosperous country.

A second innovation has been the replacement of the chapter on program planning with one on planning with a computer which, for teaching purposes, gives a valuable insight into the way that farming enterprises can be combined to maximize the farmer's income.

A third innovation is the inclusion of a chapter on farm planning in the tropics. At first this may seem out of place in a book devoted almost entirely to British agriculture. There are two compelling reasons for including this material. The first is that about 30 per cent of the readers are located in the tropics and it seems reasonable to devote five per cent of the book to their interests. The principles of farm organization are the same everywhere and the techniques of analysis explained throughout this book can be used equally well in the tropics. Nevertheless there are problems that require special treatment. These include the opening up of new areas, either cleared in the jungle or irrigated in the desert. Decisions have to be made on the choice of farming systems, size of holdings and credit requirements. Textbooks deal with these matters in general terms but often tend to ignore the financial implications. There is room for only a few examples, but the reader should have no difficulty in adapting them to suit local conditions.

The second reason is that British graduates take posts or have to travel overseas on business. The first contact with tropical agriculture can, however, be disconcerting when one moves from a country where

30 hectares is a small family farm, to another where three hectares is a large one. It is hoped that this brief account may give them some insight into these very different conditions.

The remainder of the book has been revised but has the same general structure as before. A survey of lecturers has shown that this is the course they prefer.

The book is intended primarily for students of agriculture in colleges and universities—particularly for those that intend to join advisory services here and abroad or who intend to become management consultants. It should also be helpful to accountants, who wish to do more for their clients than provide a statement to satisfy the Inspector of Taxes.

Care has been taken to provide realistic examples and there is nothing to prevent a farmer from using the instructions given as a 'do it yourself' kit to assess his own performance and plan for better results in the future.

The book is divided into three parts. Part 1 describes the cash analysis system of accounting which is the one used by most farmers. The student is introduced to the subject by following the accounts of a farm over three years. This is the minimum necessary for anyone who wishes to use farm records to advise farmers or replan his own farm.

Part 2 deals with the business side of farming and covers matters such as partnerships, limited companies, valuations, banking, credit and running the farm office.

Part 3 gives a detailed account of the newer techniques of farm planning. Gross margin analysis was first advocated in Britain by the author's department at Cambridge and has since become widely accepted by advisory services and management consultants both here and abroad. Chapter 13 deals with the analysis of past records and measures of efficiency. Chapters 14 to 18 describe gross margin analysis. Chapter 19 deals with starting a farm and Chapter 20 with capital investment and the appraisal of projects. Finally Chapter 21 deals with farm planning in the tropics and Chapter 22 with taxation. Although none of the examples is that of an existing farm, each has been designed to illustrate problems observed on a number of farms.

The author is indebted to Messrs J B Finney, M C Murphy, J S Nix, J R Stansfield and many others for helpful comment and information. Suggestions for improvements that can be incorporated in a future edition will be welcomed.

November 1981   *Ford Sturrock*

Part 1 Cash analysis method of book-keeping

1 The value of keeping accounts

This book covers two subjects—farm accounting and farm management. At first sight these two may seem to be unrelated but, as will be shown, the one subject leads on to the other and both are necessary for success in modern farming.

Why, it may be asked, should a farmer be expected to study accounting? Can he not leave it to the accountant? The following are a few of the reasons.

(1) It is in the farmer's own interest to keep a systematic record of his transactions so that an accurate statement can be prepared at the end of the year with a minimum of queries and expense.

(2) During the year, the farmer should keep a close check on the cash flow. If he is operating on an overdraft, he may, for example, have to plan the timing of purchases to avoid over-stepping the limits set by the bank.

(3) The farmer should be able to understand the statements the accountant provides. It is not enough to see that the profits are rising or falling. He should also be able to identify the reasons for changes taking place in costs, receipts, assets or liabilities. These are worth careful scrutiny because they may reveal trends that should be corrected while there is still time. Not only so, but he should ensure that the accounts are analyzed to provide the information he needs for management control.

(4) The Inland Revenue expect a set of accounts at the end of the year to assess taxes. When preparing it, the accountant may draw the farmer's attention to alternative (and legitimate) methods that might be used to reduce the burden of taxation. The farmer should have enough knowledge to appreciate the implications of the advice he receives.

An even more important reason for keeping accounts is that they provide invaluable material for improving the organization of the farm. Essentially, farm management has three functions.

(1) Day to day labour management of cultivations, livestock feeding etc. This can be learnt from long experience.

(2) Technical knowledge of the use of seeds, fertilizers, feeding stuffs, pesticides and other requirements. This can be learnt from textbooks or tuition in agronomy.

(3) The choice and planning of crop and livestock enterprises of the right size and type to suit the farm and changing conditions.

All these functions are essential. On a small or medium-sized farm, the farmer will perform all three. On a large farm, (1) will be largely delegated to an experienced foreman. (2) and (3) will be kept in the hands of the manager.

So far as functions (1) and (2) are concerned, the purpose is to show how to assess the efficiency of crop and livestock production on the farm. This is a matter of vital importance because surveys show that while some farmers can make twice the average profit or more, others make losses. Sometimes the reasons for losses are quite obvious and due to bad husbandry. More often, however, the causes are more subtle and farms that at first sight appear well managed may be unprofitable. Even high yields are not a passport to success because they may be purchased at too high a cost in feeding stuffs, labour, machinery or other inputs.

It is sometimes the case that the profit of a well-run farm is dissipated by one single enterprise that is losing money. To detect such weaknesses, the farmer needs efficiency tests. This is particularly important if the farmer leaves the day to day management of a livestock enterprise to a specialized stockman.

So far as function (3) is concerned, the purpose is to show how changes can be planned—the replacement of one crop with another, the introduction of a machine to save labour or buildings to house a new enterprise. This requires a plan and a first budget to decide whether the change, if carried through, is likely to be profitable. If the answer is favourable but heavy capital expenditure is required, a second budget will be required to plan the transition to the new system and the repayment of capital. It should be emphasized that a farmer that omits the second stage could find himself with serious cash flow problems that could bring his plan to a standstill before it was completed.

Planning and budgeting are obviously required by a new farmer when he starts operations. They are equally necessary for an established farm. Prices and markets alter and new techniques are introduced. In consequence, the farming system must be adapted to take advantage of these changes.

The close relationship between accounting and management can be seen in practice on large farms where computers have recently been introduced. Financial data are fed in each week and at the touch of a button the manager can use them to produce a trading account, a budget or an assessment of the feeding efficiency of the dairy cows or pigs. The same results and many others, can be achieved by the reader without a computer but the arithmetic will take longer.

It is thus obvious that management is not simply a matter of knowing how to grow crops and tend livestock. Technical skill is of course essential but financial management is equally necessary if the farm is to be productive and profitable.

2 The cash analysis account book

The farmer who has decided to keep accounts can select one of a number of different systems. The one to be described here is known as the *Cash Analysis System*: it has the merit of being simple and will give clear and accurate results with the minimum of labour. A number of other methods are in common use, and their merits are discussed in a later chapter.

The cash analysis system of farm accounts depends, as its name implies, on the keeping of an account book in which all the cash transactions are recorded and analyzed. The way in which accounts are kept under this method is best illustrated by taking an imaginary example.

Mr John Ford entered Manor Farm as a tenant on 1 April, 1980. The farm comprised 120 hectares, mainly arable, with buildings for 50 dairy cows. The agreed rent was £6000. When he took the farm, Mr Ford had £37 000 in cash with which to finance the farm and this is his capital.

On taking over the farm, he had to pay £8000 for growing crops and tenant right (the value of manurial residues, cultivations, and other items left by the previous tenant). He also bought £20 000 worth of tractors and implements (partly new and partly second-hand from the dispersal sale) and 40 down-calving heifers (£16 000) to start the dairy herd. During the year, he paid the following expenses

	£
Wages	9 000
Fuel	2 800
Feeding-stuffs	8 000
Seeds	3 200
Fertilizers	4 800
Rent	6 000,
Other costs	2 200
	£36 000

His receipts during the same period were

	£
Wheat	10 000
Barley	8 000
Potatoes	5 000
Milk	20 000
Other receipts	1 000
	£44 000

These transactions were all recorded in a cash analysis account book (*see* pages 6 and 7).

Entering the transactions

When the cash analysis book is opened, sales and receipts are entered on the left-hand page, which contains columns for the Date, the Name and Details, and a number of cash columns. The first of these cash columns is headed 'Total received', and is followed by columns for the main products sold, in this case Cereals, Potatoes, Milk, and Other receipts. The right-hand page, for Purchases and Expenses, is similar. The first cash column is headed 'Total paid' and is followed by columns for Cattle, Wages, Feeding-stuffs, etc. These columns are provided so that transactions can be classified as they are entered. The farmer can thus see at any time of the year not only the total spent or received up to that point but also the separate amounts for the purchase or sale of milk, seeds, feeding-stuffs, and other purposes.

At the beginning of the year, Mr Ford paid the £37 000 he owned into the farm bank account ready to start business. As the farm had received this sum, the £37 000 was entered as a receipt in the Total received column and called Opening Balance, being Cash in Bank. During the year, he entered the transactions detailed above, each item being entered twice, once in the total column and once in the appropriate analysis column. The completed cash book is shown in Fig. 1.1.

Checking the entries

At the end of the year the columns were totalled. If correctly carried out, every item (with the exception of the opening balance) should have been entered twice. The totals of the analysis columns, together with the balance at the beginning of the year, should thus agree with the Total paid or Total received columns. In this example, the checking was done as shown on page 8.

Sales and receipts

Date	Name and details	Total received	Cereals	Potatoes	Milk	Other receipts
		£	£	£	£	£
1980–81						
	Opening balance, being cash in bank	37 000				
	Wheat	10 000	10 000			
	Barley	8 000	8 000			
	Potatoes	5 000		5 000		
	Milk	20 000			20 000	
	Other receipts	1 000				1 000
		81 000	18 000	5 000	20 000	1 000
		£81 000				
1978–80						
	Opening balance, being cash in bank	1 000				

Purchases and expenses

Date	Name and details	Total paid	Cattle	Tenant right	Wages	Feeding-stuffs	Seeds and ferti-lizer	Rent	Fuel	Imple-ments	Other costs
		£	£	£	£	£	£	£	£	£	£
	Tenant right	8 000		8 000							
	Implements	20 000								20 000	
	Dairy heifers	16 000	16 000								
	Wages	9 000			9 000						
	Fuel	2 800							2 800		
	Foods	8 000				8 000					
	Seeds	3 200					3 200				
	Fertilizers	4 800					4 800				
	Rent	6 000						6 000			
	Other costs	2 200									2 200
		80 000	16 000	8 000	9 000	8 000	8 000	6 000	2 800	20 000	2 200
	Closing balance, being cash in bank	1 000									
		£81 000									

Fig. 1.1 Receipts and expenses for the first year

Sales and receipts

Analysis columns	£
Cereals	18 000
Potatoes	5 000
Milk	20 000
Other receipts	1 000
Total receipts	£44 000
Add opening balance	37 000
Agrees with Total received column	£81 000

The total of £81 000 agreed with the Total received column, showing that the items have been correctly entered and totalled. The 'Purchases and expenses' columns were similarly added and were shown to agree with the total, £80 000 in the Total paid column.

A second check can now be carried out. The bank account received, at the beginning and during the year, a total of £81 000. As £80 000 had been paid out, there should be a balance of £1000 left in the bank. From the bank statement, this was found to be correct, thus proving that no transactions had been omitted from the accounts.* This assumes that all transactions have been made through the bank account—payments being made by cheque and receipts being paid into the banking account. This is a practice to be commended.

Ruling off the cash book

To complete the account book for the year, the closing balance of £1000 was entered in the Total paid column. Both sides then had the same totals, which were entered level with each other and ruled with a double line. This shows that the account is completed. Finally, the balance was carried down and entered on the opposite left-hand page in the Total received column, ready to start the accounts for the next year.

In this case, Mr Ford finished the year with a cash surplus or *credit balance* of £1000. If he had spent another £1300, he would have finished up with a *bank overdraft* or debit balance of £300. The final lines of the

---

*It is assumed for the present that all payments are made by cheque, and all receipts paid into the banking account. From the point of view of accounting, it is a practice to be recommended, and students should be accustomed to think in these terms from the beginning. The use of a petty cash box replenished by cheques drawn on the bank is explained in Chapter 9.

cash book would then have appeared as follows

1980–81

	Total received £	Total paid £
	81 000	81 300
Closing balance	300	
	£81 300	£81 300

1981–82

Opening balance, being bank overdraft		300

There should be no difficulty in recognizing whether the balance at the end of the year is a credit or a debit. If the Total received column is the greater, the balance must be a credit. If the total paid is the greater, the balance must be a deficit, which in this case means a bank overdraft.

Rules for writing up the cash analysis book

(1) Enter the balance at the beginning of the year—a credit balance in the Total received column and a debit balance or overdraft in the Total paid column.

(2) Enter receipts and payments throughout the year—once in the Total received or Total paid column and once in the appropriate analysis column.

(3) Total all columns at the end of the year.

(4) Add the analysis columns (together with the balance, if any, at the beginning) and check with the Total paid and Total received columns.

(5) Enter the closing balance and check it with the bank passbook.

(6) Transfer the balance to the opposite page ready to begin the next year.

Questions

1. You take over a farm of 80 hectares and open a banking account with £50 000. You start by buying cattle (£25 000), and you pay the outgoing tenant £15 000 for implements and £8500 for tenant right and crops. During

the year you pay

	£
Wages	7 600
Feeding-stuffs	12 000
Machinery	8 300
Seeds and fertilizers	4 200
Rent	4 000
Other expenses	5 000

during the year, you receive for

	£
Crops	7 200
Cattle	2 500
Milk	35 200

Write up the cash analysis account book, following the procedure given above. What is the bank balance at the end of the year?

2. You have been farming for some time and start the year with a bank overdraft of £5000. Payments during the year were as follows

	£
Feeding-stuffs	11 000
Rent	3 000
Fertilizers	3 500
Cattle	6 300
Weaner pigs	5 000
Seeds	1 500
Calves	1 200
Wages	4 000
Rent	3 000

receipts for the sale of farm produce were

	£
Fat cattle	12 000
Pork pigs	2 000
Store cattle	3 000
Bacon pigs	8 000
Crops	20 000

Write up the cash analysis account book. Is the balance at the end of the year a credit balance or overdraft?

3. After writing up the cash analysis book, a farmer found that the total of the receipts analysis columns plus the opening balance did not agree with the Total received column. What mistake would you expect to find?

4. In another case, the account book was checked and found to be correct, but the balance at the end of the year did not agree with the balance in the bank statement. What mistake had been made?

3 Simple form of balance sheet and trading account

Having completed the cash analysis book, Mr Ford was ready to draw up a final statement to see whether he had made a profit or loss. During the first year, he had spent considerably more than he had received, and his bank balance had dropped from £37 000 to £1000. On the other hand, the farm was then in full operation and by 31 March, 1981, when he had been farming for twelve months, he possessed a dairy herd, crops, and implements. Thus before he could ascertain his financial position at the end of the year and find out whether he was better or worse off as a result of the year's farming, a valuation of his farm stock was necessary. On that day, therefore, he went round the farm and made a list, or inventory, of the livestock, crops, and implements on the farm. Their value was as follows

	£
Tenant right (including cultivations and growing crops)	8 000
Implements	15 000
Dairy herd	18 000
	£41 000

Thus, if he had sold up and left the farm on 31 March, he could (if his valuations are correct) have realized £41 000.

Preparation of trading account

The next step was to prepare the trading account (or, as it is sometimes called, the Profit and Loss account). As we have already seen, Mr Ford spent £80 000, and received £44 000 during the first year. At the end of that time, however, he had stock and crops on the farm valued at £41 000. The question now arises: had he made a profit during the year? Assume for a moment that he had sold up at the end of the year, realizing £41 000. If to this is added his receipts, £44 000, he would have received a total of £85 000. Total expenditure, however, was only £80 000, leaving a margin or profit of £5000. To show this in detail, a trading account was drawn up as follows.

Trading account for year ending 31 March, 1981

Purchases and expenses	£	Sales and receipts	£
At the beginning of the year		During the year	
		Cereals	18 000
Tenant right	8 000	Potatoes	5 000
Implements	20 000	Milk	20 000
Dairy cows	16 000	Other receipts	1 000
	44 000		44 000
During the year		Closing valuation	
Wages	9 000	(31 March, 1979)	41 000
Feeding-stuffs	8 000		
Seeds and fertilizers	8 000		
Rent	6 000		
Fuel	2 800		
Other costs	2 200		
	80 000		85 000
Net profit	5 000		
	£85 000		£85 000

All the items have been copied from the analysis columns in the cash book (except that Tenant right and Implements have been given separately). It is customary to put *Purchases and expenses* on the left and *Sales and receipts* on the right. The closing valuation is also on the right and the opening valuation (there is none in this case) on the left. Having totalled the columns (£80 000 and £85 000), the difference (£5000) is the profit. This is written in on the Purchases and expenses side, making the totals the same on both sides.

At the end of the first year, the farmer did not in fact give up farming, but the trading account is more easily understood if that assumption is made. The fact that Mr Ford spent considerably more money than he received was inevitable during the first year, when he had to buy implements, livestock, and tenant right to start the farm as a going concern. But it will be clear that this does not mean he had made a loss.

Preparing a balance sheet

He then drew up a balance sheet, which is a statement showing his financial postion at the end of the year.

On the right-hand side is a list of the farmer's possessions or assets, which in this case consisted of stock and crops valued at £41 000 and £1000 in cash in the bank. On the left-hand side are placed the liabilities, or debts, owing by the farm. In this case there were none, and the balance sheet was completed as shown, the balance—£42 000—being the amount of capital invested in the business at 31 March, 1979. It is called the *Net capital*. The appearance of the net capital as a liability in the balance sheet may seem strange, but can be explained if the farm and farmer are regarded as two separate units. It can therefore be said that at the end of the year the farm 'owed' the farmer £42 000, the amount that was invested in the farm at that date.

Balance sheet at 31 March, 1981

Liabilities		*Assets*	
	£		£
Net capital	42 000	Valuation	
		Tenant right	8 000
		Implements	15 000
		Cattle	18 000
			41 000
		Bank balance	1 000
	£42 000		£42 000

Questions

1. Draw up a balance sheet from the following information

Valuation	
	£
Cattle	5 123
Sheep	3 468
Pigs	6 420
Crops	12 642
Implements	14 983
Tenant right	7 414

There is also a credit balance at the bank of £1549.

2. A White took over Woodgate Farm on 1 October, 1980. The account book was written up during the year and at 30 September, 1981, the Purchases and

expenses totals were

	£		£
Wages	10 042	Feeding-stuffs	6 045
Seeds	3 841	Pigs	3 402
Fertilizers	7 482	Implements	21 400
Rent	8 000	Tenant right	7 840
Fuel	2 145	Other costs	3 420

Receipts were: wheat £19 081, barley £10 423, pigs £7 423. The closing valuation was £40 400

Has he made a profit or a loss?

3. On 1 January, 1981, a tenant took over Church Farm. At that time he had £30 000 in the bank. To start the farm, he purchased

	£
Dairy cattle	8 360
Implements	13 204
Crops and tenant right	3 320

Other expenses during the year were

	£		£
Wages	5 520	Machinery repairs	4 623
Fertilizers	5 254	Service fees	210
Fuel	3 624	Rent	6 500
Seed	996	Other costs	4 563
Feeding-stuffs	7 506		

Receipts were: wheat £6804, barley £12 721, cattle £3704, milk £14 562.

At the end of the year his valuation was as follows

	£
Dairy cattle	9 405
Implements	10 563
Crops and tenant right	3 450

Prepare a trading account and closing balance sheet.

4 Classification of receipts and payments

In the previous chapter, we saw how the cash analysis book was completed for the first year and how the balance sheet and trading account were drawn up. Mr Ford is now well established at Manor Farm. He is anxious, however, to start a pig herd. Existing buildings could be converted to take the sows, and the landlord agreed to erect a fattening house for an additional £800 rent. He started the herd by buying twenty gilts. They cost only £1600 but there was soon heavy expenditure on feeding stuffs to rear the first batches of pigs. In addition to this, the second-hand combine harvester proved unsatisfactory and a new one had to be purchased. For these reasons, expenditure outran receipts by £10000. As the farmer started the year with only £1000 in the

Sales and receipts	£	Purchases and expenses	£
Barley	9 040	Wages	7 400
Wheat	16 250	National Insurance	1 480
Potatoes	6 621	Workers income tax	1 085
Milk	18 295	Electricity	654
Calves	1 100	Fuel and oil	2 106
Cows	343	Repairs	2 010
Fat pigs	6 040	Small tools	240
Grazing let	126	Cattle	1 430
		Gilts	1 600
		Feeding-stuffs	12 337
		Seeds	3 208
		Fertilizers	2 731
		Sprays	2 185
		Rent	6 800
		Combine harvester	18 000
		Fire insurance	496
		Rates	243
		Accountant and valuer	174
		Stamps and stationery	43
		Telephone	110
		Other expenses	1 243
		Private drawings	3 000

bank, it was obvious that he would have either to slow down the expansion of the pig herd, or borrow money. He decided to go ahead with his plans but first of all he had an interview with his bank manager. He produced a programme and was able to convince the bank manager that a loan was justified.

Choice of headings for cash analysis columns

To assist in classifying items under the analysis columns, some further explanation is necessary.

Normally, each column of the cash analysis book furnishes one item for the trading account. Therefore, the greater the number of columns, the more detail can be given in the final result. On the other hand, if the number of columns is too great the account book becomes rather large and clumsy. The choice of headings naturally depends on the type of farm. The following are a few suggestions on the choice of column headings.

Sales and receipts

(1) A column for total received.

(2) A column for each of the main types of livestock and livestock products sold, e.g. cattle, milk, pigs, sheep, wool, poultry, eggs.

(3) A column for each of the main cash crops, e.g. wheat, barley, potatoes, sugar beet, fruit, vegetables.

(4) A column for miscellaneous receipts, e.g. minor enterprises and other sources of revenue such as receipts for seasonal grazing or work done on contract for a neighbour.

(5) A spare column for capital items (e.g. sale of land or implements) or for private receipts (e.g. dividends on shares) paid into the farm bank account. These items are kept separate because they are either omitted from the trading account or require special treatment for tax purposes.

With the tendency towards simplification, there are seldom more than four or five major enterprises. For this reason, eight or nine columns may be quite sufficient on the sales and receipts side of the account.

Purchases and expenses

(1) A column for total paid.

(2) A column for each of the main types of livestock for which purchases are made, e.g. cattle, sheep, pigs, poultry.

Purchases and expenses

e	1 430
	1 600
...ing-stuffs	12 337
...lizers	4 916
...ds	3 208
...es	9 965
...l and oil	2 106
...airs and small tools	2 250
...nt	6 800
...er overheads	2 963
...lements purchased	18 000
...vate drawings	3 000
	£68 575

...his total similarly agrees with the Total paid column.

The second check on the accuracy of the cash analysis book can now ...e carried out. The difference between the total received and the total ...aid columns should equal the bank balance, as follows

...otal paid column	£68 575
...otal received column	58 815
...ifference	£ 9 760

...Mr Ford had therefore spent more than he possessed and, as already ...nentioned, had been compelled to borrow money from the bank. On ...onsulting his bank statement he found that the bank overdraft was ...ndeed £9760, thus confirming the result shown above. After proving ...he entries in this way, the deficit of £9760 was entered on the receipts ...age as 'Balance being bank overdraft' and the two sides totalled and ...led off as shown in the example.

...ivate drawings and unpaid accounts

...the records, two new items arise in this second year which are treated ...the following way.

...vate drawings

...ring the first year, Mr Ford drew out no money for private expenses. ...t during the second year he spent £3000 on living expenses. As this ...drawn from the farm bank account, it was entered as an expense in ...cash analysis book. But as it is not part of the cost of running the ...n it is not transferred to the trading account.

(3) Columns for the chief livestock variable costs, e.g. feeding-stuffs, AI and other livestock costs.

(4) Columns for the main crop variable costs, e.g. seeds, fertilizers and sprays.

(5) Columns for the main common or fixed costs, e.g. wages (including casual labour, workers' income tax paid to the Collector of Taxes, employers' liability insurance, and wages paid to the family for work done on the farm), repairs and small tools, fuel and electricity, rent and rates, other overheads (telephone, stationery etc.).

(6) A column for capital items (such as land purchased) that do not appear in the trading account and implements that require special treatment for tax purposes.

(7) Private drawings (farm cash spent by the farmer on himself and his family, and his own income tax).

When deciding on whether or not to open a column for some item, the *number* of items rather than their size should be the criterion. Egg sales, for example, may have weekly totals and be worth a column even if only a minor enterprise. By contrast, two large capital items could easily go in the same column. They can easily be separated again if necessary.

Checking the entries

At the end of the year, the columns were totalled and checked as in the previous year.

Totals of analysis columns

Sales and receipts

Milk	£18 295
Cattle	1 443
Pigs	6 040
Cereals	25 290
Potatoes	6 621
Miscellaneous	126
Total receipts	57 815
Add opening balance	1 000
	£58 815

The final total, £58 815, agrees with the Total received column and shows that the items were correctly entered.

Sales and receipts

Date	Name and details	Total received	Milk	Cattle	Pigs	Cereals	Potatoes	Miscellaneous receipts
		£	£	£	£	£	£	£
1981–82	Opening balance, being cash in bank	1 000						
	Wheat	16 250				16 250		
	Barley	9 040				9 040		
	Potatoes	6 621					6 621	
	Milk	18 295	18 295					
	Calves	1 100		1 100				
	Cows	343		343				
	Fat pigs	6 040			6 040			
	Grazing let	126						126
		58 815	18 295	1 443	6 040	25 290	6 621	126
	Add debts receivable at end		1 905					
			20 200	1 443	6 040	25 290	6 621	126
	Closing balance, being bank overdraft	9 760						
		£68 575						

Purchases and expenses

Date	Name and details	Total paid	Cattle	Pigs	Feeding stuffs	Fertilizer and sprays	Seeds	Wages	Fuel and oil	Repairs and small tools	Rent	Other overheads	Implements purchased	Private drawings
		£	£	£	£	£	£	£	£	£	£	£	£	£
1981–82	Wages	7 400						7 400						
	National Insurance	1 480						1 480						
	Workers Income Tax	1 085						1 085						
	Electricity	654										654		
	Fuel and oil	2 106							2 106					
	Repairs	2 010								2 010				
	Small tools	240								240				
	Cattle	1 430	1 430											
	Gilts	1 600		1 600										
	Feeding-stuffs	12 337			12 337									
	Seeds	3 208					3 208							
	Fertilizers	2 731				2 731								
	Sprays	2 185				2 185								
	Rent	6 800									6 800			
	Combine harvester	18 000											18 000	
	Fire insurance	496										496		
	Rates	243										243		
	Accountant and valuer	174										174		
	Stamps and stationery	43										43		
	Telephone	110										110		
	Other expenses	1 243										1 243		
	Private drawings	3 000												3 000
		68 575	1 430	1 600	12 337	4 916	3 208	9 965	2 106	2 250	6 800	2 963	18 000	3 000
	Add debts payable at end				1 463	1 747	864							
			1 430	1 600	13 800	6 663	4 072	9 965	2 106	2 250	6 800	2 963	18 000	3 000

Unpaid accounts

The receipts and payments so far entered in the cash analysis book were those actually settled by cash or by cheque. At the end of the year, however, the farmer owed £1463 for feeding stuffs, £864 for seeds and £1747 for fertilizers. In addition, he had not received a cheque for £1905 for milk sold during March. Mr Ford will no doubt pay his bills during the next financial year and the Milk Marketing Board will certainly send him a cheque for his milk during April, 1982. As the feeding-stuffs had been used and the milk had been produced during the year ending 31 March, 1980, these transactions must be included in the accounts for that year. The amounts of these items were therefore added to the appropriate columns of the cash analysis book, as shown in Fig. 4.1.

It will be noted that purchases and sales on credit are not entered in the cash analysis book at the time when the goods are bought or sold but only when the money is actually paid or received. If, however, items are still owing at the end of the financial year, they must be added to the appropriate columns in the account book before these totals are transferred to the trading account. They are not, however, also included in the Total received and Total paid columns.

After the cash analysis columns had been completed for the year and ruled the Total received and Total paid columns were balanced. The difference between the two sides—in this case an overdraft of £9760—was carried down on the right-hand side as the first entry for the next financial year.

Question

The following is a list of receipts and expenses on a farm for a year. Write up the cash analysis account book. At the beginning of the year, the bank balance was £345.

Sales and receipts

	£		£
Wheat	4 820	Early potatoes	694
Calves	340	Milk	11 654
Turkeys	2 806	Old ewes	450
Lambs	650	Mustard seed	472
Barley	2 948	Main crop potatoes	14 723
Cocksfoot seed	262	Hay	44
Sugar-beet	13 806	Wool	278
Contract receipts	425	Old implements	733
Cottage let	175		

Purchases and expenses

	£		£
Fertilizers	2 648	Sprays and dusts	1 254
Electricity	368	Welding plant	670
Tyres and spares	463	Barley seed	544
NFU subscription	65	Sacks, boxes	207
Pest control	84	Dairy stores	456
Transport	215	Vet and medicines	317
Manure spreading	139	Holiday trip to Jersey	545
Milk recording	84	Employer's liability insurance	240
Casual labour	421	Wages	14 080
Telephone	362	Bank charges	95
County rates	258	Postage stamps and stationery	85
Fencing	221	Water rates	349
Fire insurance	445	Vehicle insurance	375
Accountant and valuer	400	Corn drill	3 400
Tractor	5 700	Irrigation equipment	2 783
Private drawings	7 998	Ram	65
Harrows	462	Motor van	4 660
Machinery repairs	1 248	Seed dressing	68
Tractor cab	860	Income tax (workers' deducted	
Income tax (farmers)	1 161	and sent to Inland Revenue)	1 245
Sheep dip	148		

At the end of the year, the farmer owed £371 for machinery repairs, £685 for ewes bought and £240 for water rates.

Add and check the analysis columns at the end of the year. What is the closing balance?

5 Completion of accounts for the year

In the previous chapter, Mr Ford's purchases and sales for the second year (1981–82) were classified and the columns adjusted for unpaid accounts. As in the first year, an inventory and valuation of live and dead stock on the farm was drawn up on the last day of the financial year (31 March, 1982) and all the necessary information was then available to complete the trading account and closing balance sheet.

Trading account for year ending 31 March, 1982

Purchases and expenses	£	Sales and receipts		£
Seed	4 072	Wheat		16 250
Fertilizers	4 478	Barley		9 040
Sprays	2 185	Potatoes		6 621
Feeding-stuffs	13 800			
Cattle	1 430			
Pigs	1 600			31 911
Labour	9 965	Milk	20 200	
Fuel and oil	2 106	Calves	1 100	
Repairs and small tools	2 250	Cows	343	
Rent	6 800			21 643
Overheads	2 963	Fat pigs		6 040
Combine harvester	18 000	Grazing let		126
	69 649			59 720
Opening valuation	41 000	Closing valuation		61 347
	110 649			
Net profit	10 418			
	£121 067			£121 067

One new feature will be noted in this trading account. The opening valuation is included on the left-hand side in addition to the closing valuation on the right-hand side. The presence of valuation in the trading account can be explained as follows. Assume that the farmer took over the farm at the beginning of the year at valuation, and sold out again at the end. His payments would be £41 000 for stock and crop at the beginning, and £69 649 for expenses during the year, giving a total of £110 649. Receipts would be £59 720, plus £61 347 for the sale of stock at the end, giving a total of £121 067. The difference—£10 418—is the Net Profit.

An alternative way of understanding the trading account is as follows. Receipts totalled £59 720 and expenses £69 649, leaving a deficit of £9 929. During the year, however, Mr Ford had started a new pig herd and had bought a new combine harvester. He also had some unsold crops on hand at the end of the year. The valuation had therefore increased by £20 347; in fact the farmer had invested the whole of his profit and a substantial sum borrowed from the bank in building up a larger farm business. There is a risk in incurring debt in this way, but the farmer is prepared to take it. The alternative would have been to wait (perhaps three or four years) until he had accumulated enough savings to finance the new pig herd without borrowing. He has chosen to do so on credit, hoping that the profits from the pigs will help to pay off the debt fairly quickly.

The profit can therefore be shown as

	£	£
Increase in valuation		20 347
Purchases and expenses	69 649	
Sales and receipts	59 720	
Deduct deficit		9 929
Net profit		10 418

Balance sheet

On this occasion the balance sheet is given in more detail and a further definition of a balance sheet is given.

A balance sheet is a statement drawn up to show the financial position of a business on a certain date. The business in this case is a farm, and on that day the farmer makes a list of all his possessions. These are called his *assets* and consist not only of cash, crops, and implements, but also of any money owing to him, or *debts receivable*. On the other hand, the farmer may owe money either to the bank or to private persons or firms. These debts, which he is liable to be called upon to pay at some future time, are called his *liabilities*, and are generally listed as *debts payable*, as *loans*, or, if owing to the bank, as an *overdraft*.*

* In some account books debts receivable are listed as *sundry debtors* or *accounts due to the farm*. Debts payable may also be called *sundry creditors* or *accounts due by the farm*.

The assets of a farm consist of the following
(*a*) The value of livestock, crops, stores, implements and machinery, and tenant right.
(*b*) Cash in hand and at the bank.
(*c*) Money owing to the farmer for goods sold or for services rendered, but not yet paid, i.e. debts receivable.
   Liabilities include
(*a*) Overdraft at the bank.
(*b*) Loans.
(*c*) Money owing by the farmer for unpaid accounts, i.e. debts payable.

After making a valuation of all his farm assets, Mr Ford drew up a balance sheet showing his financial position at 31 March, 1982. There are two new features in this balance sheet. As assets, he not only had livestock, crops, and implements, but a sum of £1905 due for milk. As liabilities, he had £9760 owing to the bank, £1463 owing for feeding-stuffs, £864 for seeds and £1747 for fertilizers.

Closing Balance Sheet at 31 March, 1982

Liabilities	£	Assets	£
Debts payable		Valuation	
Farm Supplies Ltd		Cattle	20 122
(feeding-stuffs)	1 463	Pigs	5 691
Robertson & Sons		Crops in store	984
(seeds)	864	Growing crops and	
Watson & Brown		tenant right	9 800
(fertilizers)	1 747	Implements	24 750
			61 347
	4 074	Debts receivable	
Bank overdraft	9 760	Milk (MMB)	1 905
	13 834		
Net capital	49 418		
	£63 252		£63 252

Thus the assets total £63 252 and the liabilities £13 834, leaving a balance of £49 418 which is the net capital. When the assets exceed the liabilities and the balance falls, as in this case, on the left-hand side, the business is said to be *solvent*. It means that if on this date the farm were sold up and all liabilities paid off, the farmer would be left with a surplus of £49 418 in cash and this is the amount shown as net capital. If liabilities exceeded assets, the balance would fall on the right-hand side, and the business would then be *insolvent*, meaning that if the farm were sold up, the assets would be insufficient to pay off the debts or liabilities, and the business might then be bankrupt.

Proving the accounts

After completing the trading account and balance sheet, the accuracy of the results is tested in the following way. In the closing balance sheet, the net capital—£49 418—was the surplus of assets over liabilities on the last day of the financial year. It is also possible to show this in another way. The net capital represents the amount of money invested by the farmer in the farm. If he makes a profit and spends it all on living expenses, it is obvious that the amount of money invested in the farm, or net capital, remains unchanged. If he does not spend all his profits, but leaves the remainder in the farm business, the net capital is increased. On the other hand, if he makes a loss, or spends more on private expenses than the net profit, the net capital decreases, and the farmer is said to be 'living on his capital'.

Mr Ford made a profit of £10 418, but spent only £3000 of this on private purposes, and the closing net capital should therefore show an increase of £7418. Looking up the balance sheets we find that the net capital at the beginning of the year was £42 000, and at the end £49 418—an increase of £7418. This result can be set out formally as follows—

	£
Opening net capital	42 000
Add net profit	10 418
	52 418
Deduct private drawings	3 000
Closing net capital	£49 418

This £49 418 agrees with the total in the closing balance sheet, and in this way the trading account and balance sheet are shown to be correct.

Lay-out of trading account and balance sheet

The general lay-out of the trading account and balance sheet should be carefully memorized.

Note that the *liabilities* are placed on the *left*. If the business is solvent, the balance falls on the left and is the *Net capital*. Should the liabilities exceed the assets, the business would be insolvent and the balance would fall on the right as the *Net capital deficit*.

Trading Account

	£		£
Purchases and expenses		Sales and receipts	
Opening valuation		Closing valuation	
Balance (if any) is the		Balance (if any) is the	
Net profit		Net loss	

Balance Sheet

Liabilities	£	Assets	£
Debts payable		Valuation of live and dead stock	
Bank overdraft			
Net capital		Cash in hand and at the bank	
		Debts receivable	

Questions

1. At Michaelmas you have £4242 worth of cattle, £6421 worth of pigs, £8432 worth of crops and £642 worth of feeding-stuffs and fertilizers. Parkinson & Co owes you £643 for pigs, you owe Mr Perkins £270 for ploughing and your bank overdraft is £1365. Prepare a balance sheet and show the net capital.

2. You have a bank overdraft of £5423 and a loan from Webster of £6200. Your cattle are worth £2433, sheep £3467 and implements £8423. You are owing £3680 for feeding stuffs and £682 for seeds. Is the financial position of the farm sound?

3. Prepare a Trading Account from the following information. Costs: seeds £930, fertilizers £5200, sprays £2700, feeding stuffs £15 500, wages £12 800, machinery costs £18 200, rent £6000. Receipts: crops £36 500, cattle £19 200, pigs, £9700. Opening valuation £105 400, closing valuation £94 500. Why is it particularly necessary to include the closing valuation in an example such as this?

4. Mr Robinson rents an arable farm of 230 ha. The soil is fertile but fairly heavy. The farmer concentrates on the growing of wheat with some barley and potatoes. He has no livestock.

Sales and receipts

	£
Wheat	85 850
Barley	10 800
Potatoes	23 750
Old Machinery	890

Purchases and expenses

	£		£
Seeds	11 216	Pest control	90
Fertilizers	13 754	Telephone	420
Sprays	13 540	Insurance	1 238
Other crop expenses	2 400	Machinery	21 300
Wages	14 642	Rent	16 000
Electricity	1 800	Rates	462
Fuel	3 590	Water charges	110
Repairs	4 107	Office expenses	300
Accountant	600	Miscellaneous	1 012
Valuer	30	Private drawings	10 000

Valuations	Opening	Closing
	£	£
Machinery and equipment	63 600	67 208
Crops	24 900	17 760
Tenant right	5 400	5 400
Stores	3 400	2 800

Owing at the end of the year

Fencing	£444
Sprays	£2 460

Overdraft at bank at beginning: £650

(a) Complete the cash analysis book; (b) prepare Opening and Closing balance sheets; (c) prepare trading account; and (d) prove the accounts.

6 Trading accounts in more detail

In this chapter, the accounts of Manor Farm are continued for a third year. While the general procedure is the same as before, more detail is given and certain new features are introduced.

It will be recalled that at the end of the second year, Mr Ford had an overdraft of nearly £10 000, the limit agreed with his bank manager and he also owed over £4000 to suppliers. During the year the farmer received a legacy of £2512, which he promptly paid into the farm account to help reduce the overdraft. Receipts from the expanded pig herd soon began to increase and there was a welcome rise in crop yields. After two years of expansion, the farmer was content to consolidate his position during the third year. The farm showed a good profit and, as it was not reinvested, farm receipts exceeded expenses by over £12 000. This enabled the farmer to pay off the bank overdraft as promised and he finished the year with a credit balance at the bank.

Details of receipts and payments

On 1 April, 1982 the third financial year began, and at the end of April Mr Ford was ready to write up the account book for the first month. He wisely decided, from the time he began farming, to pay receipts into the bank and pay accounts by cheque. It was thus a simple matter to write up the receipts from the counterfoils of the bank paying-in slips and the payments from the details on the cheque counterfoils.

Receipts during April (given on the paying-in slips) were as follows

1982,		£
April 9	11 pigs (Barr & Co.)	561
9	1 fat cow (Benchester Market)	257
16	20 tonnes wheat (Gavin & Co.)	1800
23	16 670 *l*. milk (MMB)	1834
23	Walker (ploughing)	142

Payments were

1982,

April	2	1 gilt (W Smith)	80
	2	1 heifer (B White)	320
	2	Wages	151
	9	Wages	154
	9	Small tools	5
	16	Wages	145
	23	Wages	152
	23	Accountant	145
	23	Feeding-stuffs (5 tons pig food, Simpson & Wheeler)	466
	23	Sprays (for cereals, Ace Chemicals Ltd.)	75

	23	Small expenses:	£	
		Petrol	6	
		Market	8	
		Nails, etc.	5	
		Miscellaneous	3	
				22
	23	Private		50

It will be noticed that Mr Ford does most of his business on a Friday. He visits the town on that day, pays receipts into the bank and cashes a cheque to pay the week's wages. On the last Friday of the month he pays outstanding bills and cashes a cheque for small expenses (£2). He also drew £50 for private expenses.

Details in the account book

When copying receipts and payments into the account book it is recommended that the following details should be given.

(1) Name of person or business firm concerned, for future reference.

(2) Numbers of livestock bought and sold, so that the totals can be checked at the end of the year.

(3) Quantities of produce sold and materials such as feeding-stuffs bought. This is helpful in calculating yields per cow or per acre and in estimating feeding efficiency.

Checking entries for the month

After entering the transactions for April, the columns were totalled and checked. It is desirable that this should be carried out every month, so that mistakes can be corrected without delay.

	£
Total Paid column	11 525
Total Received column	4 665
Difference which should equal bank overdraft at end of April	6 860

In other words, £4665 was received during the month and £1765 was paid out, leaving a surplus of £2900. This reduced the bank overdraft from £9760 to £6860.

For the remainder of the year, receipts and payments were entered month by month, as in April.

To save space the remaining transactions are given in a summarized form as follows

Receipts	£
Cattle	1 073
Pigs	16 352
Milk	19 390
Wheat	16 441
Barley	11 324
Potatoes	7 865
Miscellaneous	78
Private	2 512

Payments	
Feeding-stuffs	18 193
Seeds	5 184
Fertilizers and sprays	9 935
Wages*	9 912
Repairs and small tools	2 350
Fuel	2 834
Rent	6 800
Other overheads	3 667
Livestock expenses	2 904
Private drawings	3 950

* Including workers' Income Tax and National Insurance sent to the Collector of Taxes.

At the end of the year the Total received and Total paid columns were totalled and again checked with the bank balance, in this case a credit balance carried forward for the next year.

Sales and receipts

Date	Name and details	Total received £	Milk £	Cattle £	Pigs £	Wheat £	Barley £	Potatoes £	Miscellaneous receipts £	Private receipts £
1982										
April 9	11 pigs (Barr & Co)	561			561					
16	1 cow (Benchester Market)	257		257						
16	20 tonnes wheat (Gavin & Co)	1800				1800				
23	16670 l. milk (MMB)	1905	1905							
23	Walker (ploughing)	142							142	
		4665	1905	257	561	1800	—	—	142	—
	Cattle	1073		1073						
	Pigs	16352			16352					
	Milk	19319	19319							
	Wheat	16441				16441				
	Barley	11324					11324			
	Potatoes	7865						7865		
	Miscellaneous	78							78	
	Private	2512								2512
		79629	21224	1330	16913	18241	11324	7865	220	2512
	Less debts receivable at beginning		1905							
			19319	1330	16913	18241	11324	7865	220	2512
	Add debts receivable at end		2491							
		79629	21810	1330	16913	18241	11324	7865	220	2512

Purchases and expenses

Date	Name and details	Total Paid	Cattle	Pigs	Feeding stuffs	Seeds	Fertilizers and sprays	Wages	Repairs and small tools	Fuel	Rent	Livestock expenses	Other overheads	Private drawings
1982 April														
2	Opening balance being bank overdraft	9 760												
2	Gilt (W Smith)	80		80										
2	Heifer (B White)	320	320											
2	Wages	151						151						
9	Wages	154						154						
9	Small tools	5							5					
16	Wages	145						145						
23	Wages	152						152						
23	Accountant	145											145	
23	Feeding stuffs (5 T. pigs) (Simpson & Wheeler)	466			466									
23	Sprays (cereals, Ace Chemicals)	75					75							
23	Miscellaneous	22							5	6			11	
23	Private	50												50
		11 525	320	80	466	—	75	602	10	6	—	—	156	50
	Feeding-stuffs	18 193			18 193									
	Seeds	5 184				5 184								
	Fertilizers and sprays	9 935					9 935							
	Wages	9 912						9 912						
	Repairs and small tools	2 350							2 350					
	Fuel	2 834								2 834				
	Rent	6 800									6 800			
	Livestock expenses	2 904										2 904		
	Overheads	3 667											3 667	
	Private drawings	3 950												3 950
		77 254	320	80	18 659	5 184	10 010	10 514	2 360	2 840	6 800	2 904	3 823	4 000
	Less debts payable at beginning	—			1 463	864	1 747							
			320	80	17 196	4 320	8 263	10 514	2 360	2 840	6 800	2 904	3 823	
	Add debts payable at end				643	341	621							
			320	80	17 839	4 661	8 884	10 514	2 360	2 840	6 800	2 904	3 823	
	Closing balance being cash in bank	2 375												
		79 629												

Fig. 6.1 Receipts and expenses for the third year

Unpaid accounts

Details of unpaid accounts at the beginning and end of the year are given below

At 1/4/82	£	At 31/3/83	£
Debts payable			
Farm Supplies Ltd (feeding stuffs)	1463	Farm Supplies Ltd (feeding stuffs)	643
Robertson & Son (seeds)	864	Robertson & Son (seeds)	341
Watson & Brown (fertilizers)	1747	Watson & Brown (fertilizers)	621
Debts receivable			
MMB (milk)	1905	MMB (milk)	2491

Unpaid accounts are dealt with in the following way. Taking milk as an example, it will be recalled that the £1905 owing to Mr Ford at 31 March, 1982 was added to the receipts for the year ending 31 March, 1982. As the milk had been produced and dispatched from the farm before the end of the financial year, it was properly included in the accounts for that year. The cheque for this milk was received during April and was entered as a receipt in that month. To avoid including this sum in more than one trading account, the £1905 must be deducted from the receipts for milk in the accounts for the year ending 31 March, 1983. It may seem unnecessary to include this item in the accounts only to deduct it again at the end of the year. It is, however, essential to do so to ensure that the Total received column contains a complete list of all receipts that can be checked against the bank statement.

At the end of the year, £2491 was owing for milk dispatched in March and this sum was therefore added, giving a total of £21 810. As this is the precise value of milk produced during the year, this is the sum carried to the trading account. Other unpaid accounts were dealt with similarly.

Annual valuation

The next step was to take an inventory and valuation of livestock, crops, and other assets at the end of the year. Before completing the balance sheet, it is desirable to check the numbers of livestock to make sure that they have all been accounted for.

Check on livestock numbers
Take the total at the beginning of the year, add the numbers purchased or born, deduct those sold, died or used during the year, and the final total should agree with the numbers on hand at the end of the year.

The result for this farm was as follows

	Cattle	Pigs
Number at beginning	60	196
Number purchased	1	1
Number born	34	424
Total	95	621
Less		
Number sold	17	327
Number died	8	73
Number at end	70	221

Items shared between farm and private use

Before completing the trading account, there are a number of new items to be taken into consideration. It has already been pointed out that private expenses must be kept strictly separate from farm expenses. In some cases this may be found rather difficult. The farmer may use the farm car occasionally for private purposes. In addition he may use milk or other produce which would otherwise have been sold. Obviously, some allowance must be made in the trading account in such cases.

The following are the most important items to be dealt with in this way.

(1) Farm produce (such as milk or eggs) used in the house.
(2) The farm car or telephone when used partly for private purposes.
(3) Farm stores (e.g. fuel) used in the house.
(4) Value of the farm-house if included in the rent of the farm.

The dwelling-house is generally used partly as a private house and partly as a farm office, and the accepted rule is to charge two-thirds of the annual value of the house to private use and one-third to the farm.

On the other hand, the farmer may incur private expenses for the benefit of the farm. If he is boarding farm workers in his dwelling-house, he is entitled to charge the cost to the farm trading account.

When car, telephone, or similar expenses are shared in this way, the simplest method is to charge them to the farm in the first place and to make an adjustment to the trading account at the end of the year. If the accounts are to be used for the assessment of income tax, agreement should be reached with the inspector on the allowance to be made. All personal benefits, received from the farm, are added to Sales and receipts as if 'sold' by the farm. Similarly any benefits rendered to the farm are added to Purchases and expenses.

At the end of the year, Mr Ford made the following allowances: farm produce consumed £60, private use of farm car £100, and share of rent of farm-house £90. These were added to the Sales and receipts in the trading account.

Trading account

All information was then ready to complete the trading account which, given in detail, is shown below.

The lay-out should be studied and compared with that shown on page 23. In both cases, the purchases of livestock, and the sale of livestock and livestock products (e.g. milk) are given in a sub-total, and this is of advantage in calculating the livestock output—a term which will be explained later. Crop sales are also given a sub-total for a similar reason. It will be noted that the trading account for 1982–83 gives more

Trading account for year ending 31 March, 1983

Purchases and expenses	£	£	*Sales and receipts*	£	£
Seed		4 661	Wheat		18 241
Fertilizers		5 502	Barley		11 324
Sprays		3 382	Potatoes		7 865
Feeding-stuffs		13 545			37 430
Cows	9 850		Milk (200 090 *l.*)	21 810	
Pigs	7 989		Cows	460	
		17 839	Calves	870	
Gilt		80			23 140
Heifer		320	Baconers	16 503	
Livestock expenses			Sows and boar	410	
(AI, Vet, Stores)		2 904			16 913
Labour	10 514		Miscellaneous		220
Fuel and oil	2 840				77 703
Repairs	2 360				
Rent	6 800		Non-cash receipts		
Other overheads	3 823		Credit for private use of		
		26 337	Farmer's car	100	
			Farmhouse	90	
		61 025	Farm produce	60	250
Opening valuation		61 347			77 953
		122 372	Closing valuation		59 547
Net profit		15 128			
		£137 500			£137 500

detail. It is not for that reason any more accurate than the trading account for 1981–82, but while the inclusion of this additional detail is not essential, the accounts are of greater value as an aid to farm management.

At the end of each year, the farmer should examine his trading account and compare it with that of the previous year. He should note any increases or decreases and attempt to find the reason. If costs are rising, he should examine the items responsible and consider whether the increase is justified. They may be rising because of an increase in the production of livestock or crops, in which case the rise in costs should be balanced by an increase in sales or in the valuation. The rise may be due to an increase in prices over which the farmer has no control. But if no explanation can be found, the accounts may indicate where economies can be introduced.

Balance sheets

The *Closing balance sheet* was then drawn up, preceded by a shortened form of the *Opening balance sheet*, copied from the accounts for the previous year, as follows

Opening Balance Sheet at 1 April, 1982

Liabilities	£	Assets	£
Bank overdraft	9 760	Valuation	61 347
Debts payable	4 074	Debts receivable	1 905
	13 834		
Net capital	49 418		
	£63 252		£63 252

Closing Balance Sheet at 31 March, 1983

Liabilities	£	Assets	£
Debts payable		Valuation	
Farm Supplies Ltd		Cattle	23 100
(feeding-stuffs)	643	Pigs	6 744
Robertson & Sons		Crops in store	1 241
(seeds)	341	Growing crops and tenant right	9 900
Watson & Brown (fertilizers)	621	Implements	18 562
	1 605		59 547
Net capital	62 808	Cash in hand	2 375
		Debts receivable (MMB)	2 491
	£64 413		£64 413

Proving the accounts

The final step is to prove the accuracy of the accounts. At the beginning of the year the capital invested was £13 202. As a result of the year's trading this had been increased by the Net Profit, and there were some private receipts paid into the farm account. On the other hand, the capital had been reduced by private drawings, and by the value of farm produce used. Setting this out in tabular form it appears as follows.

		£
Net capital at beginning of year (per opening balance sheet)		49 418
Add	£	
Net profit	15 128	
Private receipts	2 512	
		17 640
	£	67 058
Less Private drawings	4 000	
Produce used	250	
		4 250
Balance agrees with net capital at end of year (per closing balance sheet)		£62 808

It will be seen that this statement has been inserted in the closing balance sheet showing that the accounts have been correctly completed.

Questions

1. The following is a very simple account to be used as a drill of general procedure

Opening Balance Sheet

Liabilities	£	Assets	£
Debts payable		Valuation	32 000
Feeding-stuffs	640	Debts receivable:	
Net capital	34 960	Milk	2 800
		Cash in bank	800
	£35 600		£35 600

(a) Enter in the account book   Private drawings £10 000
opening bank balance £800

Receipts	£	Payments	£
Cereals	2 400	Wages	6 000
Milk	32 800	Feeding-stuffs	12 000
		Rent	3 200
		Seeds and fertilizers	400
		Other costs	4 000

Deduct amounts owing at the beginning (*see* balance sheet above) and add those owing at the end

Owing to the farmer: milk £2600

Owing by the farmer: feeding-stuffs £800, seeds £160.

(b) The closing valuation is £30 000; complete the Trading Account, allowing £50 for produce used in the farmhouse.

(c) Complete the closing balance sheet and prove the accounts.

2. Mr Adams has an arable farm of 70 hectares. He grows cereal crops and sugar beet and fattens a few cattle.

His receipts during April were

		£
April 3	Midland Grain Co. 72 tonnes Wheat	7 043
18	Midland Grain Co. 9 tonnes Barley	894
25	Barton Market, 2 fat cattle	706

Payments in April were

April 3	Wages	84
	Smith & Co., wire netting	19
11	Wages	91
	Campbell, Vet.	18
	Acorne Garage, spares for tractor	45
18	Wages	90
	Midland Electricity	35
	Farm Supplies Ltd, fuel	120
	Barton Market, 10 store cattle	1 624
25	Wages	88
	Broadacre Estates, rent	2 500
	Water rates	15
	Vehicle taxes	53
	Clark and Scrivenor, Accountant	180
	Bunthorn, Estate Agent, valuation	30

Receipts for the rest of the year were

Wheat	7 827
Barley	8 902
Sugar-beet	9 340
Cattle	4 056

Payments for the rest of the year were

	£		£
Seeds	2 392	Office expenses	30
Fertilizer	2 214	Telephone	82
Sprays	1 489	Pest control	24
Other crop costs	488	Bank charges	79
Feeding-stuffs	96	Rates	110
Other livestock costs	18	Water	16
Wages	4 237	Fencing, etc.	451
Repairs (machinery)	629	Insurance	300
Rent	2 500	Vehicle insurance	110
Electricity	123	Implements	6 570
Fuel	616		

Creditors: at beginning, £155 for sprays, £19 for wire netting, £35 for electricity and £31 for telephone; at end, £321 for seeds, £44 for electricity, £39 for telephone.

Debtors: at beginning £894 for barley, £706 for cattle; at end, £1244 for wheat, £803 for cattle.

Opening valuation £52 986, closing valuation £48 907.

Private use of car, farm house, telephone, etc. £700.

Overdraft at beginning of year £843.

Private drawings £8000.

(a) Write up cash transactions for April, total the columns; (b) write up transactions for the rest of the year; and (c) prepare trading account and opening and closing balance sheets. Prove the accounts.

7 Summary of procedure

The accounts for Manor Farm have now been dealt with for three years, further details being added at each successive stage. In practice, very few accounts would be run in the simple form shown for the first year, but the method shown for the third year would be used throughout. The simpler method of presentation has been given to show how accounts are continued from year to year—the closing balance, valuation, and balance sheet for one year becoming the opening cash balance, valuation, and balance sheet for the next year.

To summarize the method of keeping accounts by means of a cash analysis account book, a brief outline of the procedure is given below.

(1) Take a valuation of live and dead stock and prepare an opening balance sheet (if not already carried out at the end of the previous year).

(2) Copy the opening bank balance into the account book.

(3) Enter receipts and payments throughout the year, checking the totals once a month with the analysis columns and the bank balance.

(4) Total the account book at the end of the year, carrying the balance forward.

(5) Make a list of unpaid accounts and adjust the analysis columns.

(6) Make an inventory of live and dead stock and draw up the closing valuation, checking the livestock numbers.

(7) Complete the trading account, adding the value of produce used, etc., to the receipts.

(8) Complete the closing balance sheet.

(9) Prove the accounts. Taking the net capital in the opening balance sheet, add—

net profit (if any)
private receipts paid into the farm account

deduct—

net loss (if any)
private drawings
value of produce, etc., used.

The result should equal the net capital in the closing balance sheet.

In the next section we shall deal with some of the practical details in keeping accounts—the use of a petty cash book and other records, valuations, banking, and income tax—but before doing so, it is important that the general principles of accounting laid down in the preceding chapters are thoroughly understood.

Questions

1. Mr Jones is a tenant on a 50 ha dairy farm. He specializes on milk production with 60 cows, but rears a few calves for sale as beef stores or dairy heifers. The following is a list of his payments during the year.

	£		£
Feeding-stuffs	18 098	Wages	8 784
Veterinary charges	632	Rates	112
Accountant	403	Water rates	766
Valuer	58	Fencing, etc.	477
Telephone	345	Machinery purchased	1 853
Bank charges	157	Repairs	1 874
Pest control	43	Fertilizer	1 583
Electricity	1 276	Other livestock expenses	1 793
Fuel	964	Miscellaneous	1 554
Seeds	141	Insurances	583
Sprays	36	Private drawings	7 000

Valuations	Opening £	Closing £
Dairy cattle	14 283	17 250
Young stock	3 220	4 485
Beef cattle	14 328	9 482
Machinery and equipment	14 158	15 185
Tenant right	700	700

Sales	£
Milk	29 366
Cows	1 981
Beef stores	23 877

The Milk Marketing Board owed him £2216 at the beginning and £2362 at the end of the year. At the beginning of the year he owes the Wessex Feeding Co. £1264 for feeding stuffs and £1010 at the end. He owes Turners & Twist £540 for fertilizer at the end and the vet £160 at the beginning. He owed Wilkinson and Co. £391 at the beginning and £264 at the end for machinery repairs and spare parts.

Prepare: (a) cash analysis; (b) opening and closing balance sheet assuming a bank balance of £945 at the beginning of the year; (c) trading account allowing £250 for private use of the car and £250 for private use of the farm house; and (*d*) prove the accounts.

2. Mr Burton rents a farm of 160 hectares. His main crops are cereals and sugar-beet. He also has a small sheep flock that uses by-products. His receipts are as follows.

Wheat (206T) £20 136, barley (126T) £11 592, sugar-beet (899T) £20 712, peas (54T) £8041, lambs (95) £2850, combine sold £6405. His payments are—electricity £202, fuel and oil £2060, repairs £3455, office expenses £181, telephone £805, subscriptions £151, bank charges £753, insurance £355, seeds £4315, fertilizers £6622, sprays £3228, other crop expenses £2134, feeding-stuffs £1781, other livestock expenses £156, wages £8588, rent £8920, new combine harvester £24 305, private drawings £8000, private use of car, etc. £400. £1120 was owing for fertilizer at the beginning and £298 was owing for the vet at the end. Receipts for 35 tonnes of wheat (£3290) were owing at the beginning and for 44 tonnes (£4424) at the end. Bank balance at beginning £1000.

Valuations	Opening	Closing
	£	£
Machinery	27 510	38 729
Sheep	4 400	4 200
Stores	3 900	3 490
Tenant right	4 420	4 420

Prepare: (*a*) cash analysis and trading account; (*b*) opening and closing balance sheets; (*c*) after seeing the accounts, Mr Barton makes the comments. 'The accounts show a profit of over £13 000. I have spent far less than that on myself and yet my bank balance has become a large overdraft. Where has the profit gone?' How would you explain the position to him?; (*d*) ewes at beginning 110, at end 105, born 95. How many died?

Part 2 The business side of farming

8 Banking and credit

Every farmer should have a banking account, and payments and receipts should, so far as possible, be made through it.

The advantages are

(1) money is safer in a bank than in the farm office, and the use of cheques avoids the need for carrying large sums of money;

(2) a bank cheque can be used as evidence of payment if a dispute should arise;

(3) it is easier and quicker to write a cheque than to count out a large sum of money;

(4) money may be borrowed from a bank in the form of an overdraft;

(5) a banker's reference may at times be useful as evidence of financial standing, as, for example, in leasing a farm when the applicant is not known to the landlord, or in obtaining credit.

Opening a banking account

When opening a banking account, a person unknown to the bank manager may be asked to produce references. Generally, however, an introduction by some responsible person—preferably one who deals with the same bank—is sufficient. The prospective customer makes his first deposit of money, gives a specimen of his signature, and receives a cheque book and a book of paying-in slips. The bank will record the cheques he draws and the money he pays in on statements that he can examine any time he wishes. Alternatively, the statements will be sent to him as each sheet is filled or at regular intervals according to his instructions.

Cheques

A cheque is an order to a banker to make a payment of money. The person who writes the cheque is the *drawer* and the person or firm who is to receive the payment is the *payee*. The drawer fills in the date, the name of the payee, the sum of money, and signs his name. It will be noted that the amount of money is given in both words and figures, and to avoid fraud, care should be taken to leave no gaps where additions can be made afterwards. To assist in book-keeping, the name of the payee and a few details should be entered in the cheque book.

If a customer wishes to draw cash for his own use, he writes *self* or *cash* in the line reserved for the name of the payee and signs the cheque in the ordinary way.

Crossed cheques

If two parallel lines have been printed or drawn across the cheque, it is said to be 'crossed' and must be paid into a banking account. An 'open' cheque with no crossing can be cashed (at the customer's bank only) by anyone, e.g. a farm worker with no bank account. Open cheques, however, are not safe if lost or stolen and are discouraged by the banks. The usual crossing consists of two plain lines with or without the words '& Co.,' but as a precaution against theft, the words 'Not negotiable,' 'Account payee only,' or the name of payee's bank may be added. A borough or county council may request that the cheque for a car licence be marked 'Motor Taxation A/c,' and the cheque must be paid into that account in the bank. Today, most cheques have a crossing printed on them. If the drawer wishes to make one of these open (e.g. to draw out cash) he can write 'Pay cash' in the crossing and sign his name.

Paying in a cheque

On receiving a cheque, the payee completes a paying-in slip. These slips may be obtained in book form or as loose forms. The cheque and the paying-in slip are handed to the bank cashier who initials the entry (and in the case of a book, returns it to the customer).

Instead of paying in a chque, the payee can endorse it (by signing it on the back) and pass it to someone else to pay into *his* bank account. A shopkeeper, for example, might take such a cheque to oblige a customer who was short of cash or had no bank account of his own.

Forgery

A bank has to be satisfied that the signature to a cheque drawn on them is genuine before cashing it. If money is paid against a forged signature, the bank may be called upon to make good the loss, unless it can be proved that the customer by carelessness or other circumstances contributed to the forgery.

Errors

If when writing a cheque the drawer finds that he has made an error, he may correct it and sign or initial the alteration. It is more satisfactory, however, to destroy the cheque and make out another.

Stopped cheques

The payment of a cheque can be stopped on the intruction of the drawer in writing. Notice of his death or bankruptcy acts similarly. It is advisable, therefore, to present cheques at the bank without delay. If kept too long, the cheque becomes 'stale,' and will not be paid without reference to the drawer. The usual limit is six months, but some public bodies specify that their cheques must be cashed within a much shorter interval.

Dishonoured cheques

If a cheque is not properly completed, or if the drawer has insufficient money in his account, it may be dishonoured by the bank and returned to the payee.

Post-dated cheques

If the drawer does not wish a cheque to be cashed immediately, he may post-date it. For example, if a cheque is written on 7 January and dated '21 January', the payee cannot obtain payment until 21 January. This practice is not favoured by the banks.

Bank Giro

The normal way to pay a bill is to send it with a cheque to the creditor. He then sends it to his bank which collects the money from the farmer's bank. This procedure can be shortened, however, if the farmer instructs his bank to pay money straight into the creditor's bank account. Some large firms and public bodies encourage their customers to pay bills in this way. The farmer can fill out a form (or use the one on the back of the bill) and send it with a cheque to his own bank. If he pays several bills at a time he can make a list and send one cheque to cover them all. Unless the firm states the name of their bank, however, this method cannot be used.

To avoid writing cheques for regular payments such as subscriptions or hire purchase repayments, the farmer can give the bank a *standing order*. The bank will continue payments until instructed to stop.

In place of a standing order the payee can take the initiative. A firm asks its customers to authorize a *direct debit*. This allows the firm to collect payment from the customer's account. This is obviously very convenient for the firm concerned and can be used, for example, to collect life insurance premiums. A farmer should, however, be cautious about authorizing any outside body to change the amount charged without his prior knowledge.

Paying wages and salaries

A farmer can pay his employees by cheque if they agree. He can go a step further and ask his bank to pay wages directly into the men's bank accounts. This system is more likely for salaried foremen or managers. The system is spreading and the employer can avoid carrying large sums of cash.

The use of more than one bank account

To avoid filling the farm account books with private receipts and payments, some farmers keep two accounts at the bank. Private receipts are paid into a personal account, and to cover living expenses the farmer transfers a sum from the farm account at monthly or three-monthly intervals. The practice has much to commend it. If this method is adopted, the name of the account—'Private a/c' and 'Farm a/c,' or 'No. 1 a/c' and 'No. 2 a/c,' is entered below the signature when the cheques are written, and on the credit slips when money is paid in.

Bank charges

Most banks charge for keeping customers' accounts. The method of calculating this varies slightly between different banks, but the amount generally depends on the number of cheques drawn, the number of items paid in and the size of balance kept. In some cases, no charge is made, if the customer keeps an agreed minimum balance.

Bank charges are deducted from the customer's account at quarterly or half-yearly intervals and should be copied into the Cash Book as a payment when checking the bank pass-book or statement.

Current and deposit accounts

The banking account from which cheques are paid is known as a 'current' account. If a large balance has accumulated, it may be transferred to a 'deposit' account. On this interest is allowed, but cheques are not expected to be drawn on it. To withdraw money from a deposit account, the bank may require a few days' notice, but in practice payment can generally be arranged on request.

General rules

From the book-keeping point of view, the following rules concerning the use of banking accounts should be remembered.

(1) When cheques are received, they should be paid into the bank *promptly* lest they become stale or be stopped for some reason.

(2) To assist in writing-up the account book, the name, date, and a few details of each transaction ('12 bullocks,' 'feeding-stuffs,' etc.) should *always be entered on the counterfoils* of cheques and paying-in slips.

(3) All cheques and cash received should be paid *into the bank account*. Any cash required to meet expenses should be obtained by a separate cheque drawn to 'self' or 'cash.'

In this way, all receipts and payments are recorded in the counterfoils of the cheque book, or on the paying-in slips, as well as in the bank statement. If these rules are strictly adhered to, book-keeping is greatly simplified.

Cheques should not be cashed over the counter or passed on to some other person in payment of a debt. Otherwise there is no record of such transactions, and they may be omitted from the account book.

Some further advantages of having a banking account may be mentioned here. If a farmer is selling goods to a stranger from another part of the country, he may hesitate to accept a cheque until he is sure that the payment will be met. In such a case he may ask his own bank to make a confidential inquiry as to the standing of the person with whom he intends to do business.

In many cases, arrangements can be made that regular receipts, such as cheques from the Milk Marketing Board, and dividends on shares, can be paid directly into a bank account. This saves time in paying in cheques, and avoids the risk of their being mislaid or overlooked. Large sums of money should not be allowed to accumulate on the farm, but should be banked as soon as possible. It is also prudent to deposit securities and insurance policies in a bank strong-room, which is proof against theft or fire damage.

Credit

Unless he has large resources at his disposal, the farmer may at times find that he has insufficient money to meet immediate expenses and he may be compelled to borrow money to meet a temporary shortage. He may need a loan to carry out permanent improvements, such as a scheme of drainage or the building of a new cowshed. The borrowing of money does not imply that the farm is showing a loss, and even an efficient farmer may find himself so placed. Credit, or the borrowing of money for business purposes, may be placed in two categories— long-term and short-term—depending on the purpose for which it is required.

Short-term credit

The need for temporary loans depends on the type of farm. The dairy farmer whose receipts are spread over the year and who receives regular monthly cheques for milk is perhaps in the most favourable position in respect of ready cash. On an arable farm, however, expenses for seed, manures, and feeding-stuffs have to be met throughout the spring and summer when very little money is coming in from sales. By June or July, cash is running short, and it may be necessary to borrow until after the harvest. The same may also be true of a hill sheep farmer, the bulk of whose receipts come once a year at the autumn lamb sales. A short-term loan may also be required to buy store bullocks, which will be sold fat three to six months later.

Two main sources of short-term credit are open to the farmer: a bank overdraft, and credit from merchants and auctioneers. An overdraft is arranged by interview with the bank manager, the farmer giving an estimate of the amount required and his reasons for borrowing. The bank may require the borrower to deposit securities to cover the loan, usually one of the following

(1) title deeds of the farm if the farmer is an owner-occupier;
(2) life insurance policies;
(3) Stock exchange securities;
(4) collateral security. If the farmer has no possessions of his own to offer, a friend or relative may be willing to deposit securities on his behalf or give a guarantee which is acceptable to the bank.

In some cases the bank manager, if he is satisfied as to the integrity of the borrower, may be prepared to advance money without formal security. In this case, the farmer may be asked to fill out a form, similar to a balance sheet, giving a list of his possessions and if the net capital (assets less liabilities) is substantial, the bank manager will feel fairly safe in granting an overdraft.*

When arrangements satisfactory to the bank manager are concluded, the farmer may borrow up to the specified amount. Interest is charged quarterly or half-yearly at a rate which varies from time to time but is usually $1\frac{1}{2}$ to three per cent above the base rate. (Set by the Bank of England).

A bank overdraft is a useful form of short-term credit to cover a seasonal shortage of cash lasting a few months. For intermediate term loans (e.g. for three to eight years to buy livestock, erect a building) the bank may be willing to continue an overdraft against security. The bank may, however, prefer a Development Loan. This is a kind of short-term mortgage with regular repayments. The interest is often a flat rate on the *whole* sum borrowed. (A flat rate of eight per cent is equivalent to nearly 16 per cent on the diminishing unpaid balance.)

Apart from this, the farmer will find that many feeding stuffs, seeds, and manure merchants and other tradesmen are prepared to allow their bills to remain unpaid for several months. In return, the farmer must expect to pay a somewhat higher price than if the bills were paid promptly. Sometimes the invoice states formally that interest will be charged after a certain interval, or alternatively, an addition for credit may already have been made, discount being given for prompt payment. In some parts of the country, an auctioneer may allow a customer to buy store cattle or sheep on credit, the debt being settled when the livestock are sold. In such cases, however, the livestock may remain the legal property of the auctioneer. In addition, after a poor harvest or during a time of agricultural depression, a landlord may allow a hard-pressed tenant extra time to pay his rent, thus giving him a form of short-term credit.

Another form of credit is *hire purchase*, which is sometimes used for large implements (such as tractors, combine harvesters) or motor cars. Occasionally it is used for livestock such as cows or store cattle. The operation is as follows. Assume that a farmer buys a tractor for £10 000 and pays a deposit of £2500, leaving £7500 to be paid over two years. The hire purchase company is charging 12 per cent.

	£
Sum borrowed	7500
Interest 12% of £7500 × 2 years	1800
	£9300

Monthly repayments $\frac{9300}{24} = £387.50$.

---

* A farmer can pledge live and dead stock by signing an 'agricultural change'. This has the disadvantage that if it becomes known, other creditors will press for settlement. It is hardly ever used.

It will be noticed that 12 per cent is charged on the whole amount borrowed for two years, although the amount owing is being reduced month by month. The effective rate is thus nearer 24 per cent. The term 'hire purchase' means that the implement (or other asset) bought with the money borrowed remains the property of the finance company and is theoretically on hire to the farmer until the last instalment is paid. If the farmer fails to pay the instalments, the property can usually be taken back and used to repay the balance outstanding. Before this happens, however, a farmer in temporary difficulties should come to some arrangement with the company, e.g. postpone an instalment until after harvest. It is also possible to hire machinery from a finance company. A cheaper form of credit for buying machinery is to join or organize a machinery syndicate. These are sponsored by the NFU and can obtain bank loans on very favourable terms.

On the whole, a bank overdraft is usually the cheapest form of short-term credit and will be preferred by the farmer. There are times, however, when the bank refuses a loan, either because the bank manager does not recommend it or because there is a 'credit squeeze' and the bank is reducing loans on government advice. The farmer must then turn to other sources of credit. Merchant credit varies but is usually rather more expensive. This is not unreasonable because the farmer is using the merchant's capital and the merchant in turn may have to borrow from the bank or elsewhere. Hire purchase is often used by farmers who have difficulty in obtaining a bank loan. A small proportion of such clients have difficulty in repaying their loans and this raises the costs of the finance company; hence the higher charges.

Much criticism has at times been levelled against credit given by merchants and auctioneers. The disadvantages are that the farmer is not in a strong position to drive a bargain with a merchant to whom he owes money and may feel obliged to buy his supplies from him. Moreover, if he has obtained livestock on credit he is expected to sell again through the same auctioneering firm when he might prefer to dispose of his stock in some other way. On the other hand, men who have started farming with insufficient resources, and without security on which a bank is willing to grant an overdraft, have often been helped over a difficult period by a merchant who had faith in their ability and wished to earn their future goodwill.

Long-term credit

Various forms of long-term credit are available to the farmer to carry out permanent improvements to the farm. Loans may be raised by private arrangement or though one of the officially approved schemes. As the usual form of security is a mortgage on land or buildings, this form of credit is available only to landowners and owner-occupiers.

Advances may be obtained under the provisions of the Agricultural Credits Act of 1928 and 1932 for the erection or reconstruction of farm buildings and workers' cottages, the provision of water supplies, farm roads, and the drainage of land. Agricultural mortgage corporations exist for this purpose and arrangements can be made to pay off loans over periods of up to forty years, each instalment consisting partly of interest and partly of repayment of the original loan. Annual repayments depend on the rate of interest when the loan is arranged. The following repayments per £1000 borrowed are typical.

| | 10% | 14% | 18% |
	£	£	£
Over 10 years	163	192	223
Over 20 years	117	151	187
Over 40 years	102	141	180

This represents the cost of the improvements to the farmer. Before carrying out a programme of erecting new buildings, for example, he will weigh up the benefits—the saving in labour, the bonus for better quality milk, the increased output by keeping a pig herd—which he expects to gain, and if the increased profit is likely to cover the interest by a comfortable margin, then the farmer is justified in borrowing.

Lease-back

An owner-occupier short of capital to improve his farm or buy more land may sell his farm to an investor (e.g. insurance company) and stay on as a tenant. He may gain by operating on a larger scale; he will lose any rise in value of the land sold.

Conclusion

In many countries, the State has taken elaborate measures to provide credit facilities for farmers, by encouraging the formation of special agricultural banks and co-operative credit societies of various kinds. Attempts to introduce similar methods in Great Britain have not met with much success, and the banks and the merchants remain the normal sources of credit. It will be seen that when borrowing from the bank, the owner-occupier or the man who is fortunate enough to possess stocks and shares seldom has difficulty. The established farmer, who has carried on business with success over a number of years, can secure a loan on his personal reputation without formal security. But, the tenant farmer who is not well known and whose need is primarily for short-term credit may have difficulty in borrowing at the beginning of his career when his need for such facilities is greatest.

In practice, the chief source of short-term credit is the bank and much depends on the local knowledge of the manager and his ability to distinguish between the farmer who needs credit to expand his enterprise on sound lines and the man who wishes to borrow to stave off bankruptcy. The farmer who can present a convincing plan (on the lines recommended later in this book) showing the purpose, the amount required and the period over which he can be repaid, is more likely to receive sympathetic consideration on questions of credit and borrowing.

Questions

1. What advantages are there to the farmer in having a banking account?
2. Explain briefly what you understand by the following
   (a) crossed cheque; (b) Bank Giro; (c) lease-back; (d) stale cheque; (e) deposit account; (f) agricultural charge.
3. What sources of credit are available to a farmer who needs ready cash
   (a) to tide the farm over from June until his crops are ready for sale in October; (b) to build a brick piggery costing £20 000?

9 Running the farm office

To carry out a system of farm accounts on the lines recommended the following books and records are essential.

(1) Cash analysis account book.
(2) Petty cash book.
(3) Wages book.
(4) Cheque book counterfoils and receipted accounts.
(5) Paying-in slips.

The cash analysis account book

The cash book contains a record of receipts and payments with analysis columns to classify them. Space can be provided for the opening and closing valuations, balance sheets and trading accounts. Such annual statements may be included in the account book or kept separately. Some account books are stoutly bound and large enough to last several years. But where the accounts are audited, book-keeping may be held up until the cash book has been returned. For this reason, it is convenient to use a fresh book each year.

Petty cash book

As already emphasized, payments should, so far as possible, be made by cheque. There are, however, many small items paid in cash. In many cases no proper record is kept, and small payments, which may add up to a considerable sum, are omitted from the accounts. However, if they were all entered in the account book it would be filled with innumerable small items, greatly increasing the task of auditing. In practice it is more convenient to enter them in a petty cash book or note-book from which the totals can be copied into the account book once a month.

One of the following methods should be adopted.

(1) A definite sum, say £20, is drawn by cheque (the counterfoil being marked 'Petty cash') and put in a cash box from which small payments are made. When spent, a further £20 is drawn. At the end of each month, cash in hand is checked against the payments shown in the petty cash book.

(2) The second method, the 'imprest' system, is widely adopted by business firms. As before, a lump sum of, say £40 is drawn and put in the cash box. Suppose that at the end of the month, payments amount to £26·02. After checking the balance (which should be £13·98), a cheque is drawn for £20·02, and the money put in the box, bringing the total back to £40.

When payments are made by a foreman or clerk who must account for money placed in his charge, one of these two methods should be used. A petty cash book is kept in the cash box and if the farmer makes payments from his pocket when away from the farm, he should draw the amounts from the cash box. Strict care should be taken that the cash box is kept only for business purposes.

(3) If the farmer makes his own payments and does not wish to keep a cash box, a third method is suggested. This is less accurate, but is frequently adopted in practice. When the farmer needs cash he draws a cheque for say £40, marking the counterfoil 'Private and petty cash'. He keeps a note of small farm expenses and totals them at the end of the month. If he has spent £26·02 for farm purposes, he assumes that the balance (£13·98) has been spent on private expenses. The cheque for £40 is entered in the account book as: £40 in the total paid, £13·98 in the private expenses, and £26·02 in the other expenses or other appropriate columns.

A further point is the method of entering the details in the account book. Assume that the petty cash payments for one month were

January	£
Market expenses	10·42
Carriage	4·60
Postage stamps	2·40
Petrol and oil for car	7·20
Nails	1·40
	£26·02

In order to classify these, the note-book may have columns corresponding to the headings in the account book. This entails using a fairly large book, and is hardly necessary. Apart from small repairs, which come under 'Repairs and small tools', the balance generally consists of 'Other expenses'.

In this particular case, the farmer was using the imprest system, and he entered the cheque for £26·02 in the account book as shown below, the more important items being entered separately.

Payments

Date	Name and details	Total paid	Repairs and small tools	Other expenses
January 31		£ 26·02	£	£
	Petty cash	26·02		
	Car expenses			7·20
	Small expenses		1·40	17·42

Wages book

In order to calculate deductions for insurance stamps, workers' income tax, etc., a separate wages book should be kept, only the weekly total being transferred to the account book. Given below is a suggested appropriate ruling for such a book.

Week ending . . .

Name of worker	Total earnings	Deductions			Paid to worker
		Workers' share of National Insurance	Rent, milk, etc.	Income tax	
	£	£	£	£	£
J Brown	90·00	5·87	—	17·55	66·58
A Hendry	95·00	6·19	2·50	17·25	69·06
T Armstrong	97·00	6·32	—	16·95	73·73
	282·00	18·38	2·50	51·75	
Total paid to workers (transferred to account book)					£209·37

In the example, J Brown's regular weekly wage was £85·00 and he received £5 extra for overtime, making a total of £90·00 as Total Earnings. Out of this he was liable for £5·87 for national insurance, and £17·55 for income tax, leaving £66·58 which was paid to him in cash. The total wages for the week (£209·37) were transferred to the wages column of the Account Book. National Insurance and workers' income tax are also entered in the wages column when forwarded to the Collector of Taxes.

Some employers of large staffs issue time sheets to the men, who fill in details of the time of starting and finishing and time off.

As wages are paid in cash, a cheque is usually drawn weekly to cover the cost. The best method is to draw a cheque for the exact amount of the wages—say £209·37. Alternatively, if the wages book is not made up at the time, a lump sum of £250 can be drawn and the remaining £40·63 carried over for the next week's wages.

Counterfoils of cheques and paying-in slips

The counterfoils in the cheque book and the paying-in slips give a list of receipts and payments transacted through the bank, and they are the chief sources from which the cash book is written up.

While the records mentioned are the minimum required, there are others which may be necessary.

Livestock movement book

To assist in tracing outbreaks of disease, farmers are under a statutory obligation to keep a record of the movement of livestock to and from the farm.

Invoice book

When goods are sold on credit, an invoice book should be used. Each invoice is completed in duplicate, one copy remaining in the book, giving a convenient list of unpaid accounts for use at the end of the year. The other copy is sent as a bill for payment.

Record of cropping

It is useful to keep a record of the manuring and yields in various fields on a farm. This is often written in a diary, but details are difficult to trace when mixed up with a mass of other notes. A better method is to have a special book with a page for each field, noting crop, yield, manuring, and other details year by year, thus building up a history of each field and of the results obtained.

It is useful to have a map of the farm. The best maps are those published by the Ordnance Survey Department. The 1:10 000, formerly the 6-inch map (6 inches to the mile) shows field boundaries, and the larger scale, 1:2500, formerly the 25-inch map gives, in addition, the reference number, and hectares and acres of each field.

Files

Business papers should be stored so that they can be traced, and receipts should be kept for seven years in case any dispute of payment should arise. Invoices, receipts, and correspondence should be stored in files neatly labelled, and a new set should be started each year. Box-files are satisfactory, or, if accounts are numerous, concertina files with pockets lettered in alphabetical order.

Some practical details about running the farm office

The amount of book-keeping required in a farm varies according to its size and the method of selling the produce. On large specialized farms where fruit and vegetables are dispatched daily to shops or markets, accounts must be attended to daily, and a full-time office staff is required. On most farms, however, produce is sold in bulk and the number of receipts and payments is generally not more than about 20 or 30 per month. Indeed, on some of the more remote hill-farms, the business transactions for a year could be written on one sheet of note-paper.

On an ordinary medium-sized farm, the office routine might be as follows. The majority of payments are made by cheque, the exceptions being wages and petty cash. For small expenses a petty cash box is kept. Wages are drawn by cheque weekly, and any surplus is put in the wages box for use the following week. Most of the money received is in the form of cheques, but cash received is set aside and paid into the bank.

At least once a week a period is allotted for office work, for filling in the wages book and writing cheques for accounts due for payment. A visit can then be paid to the bank to draw cash for wages and if necessary for the petty cash box. Cheques and cash received during the week are paid in at the same time.

At regular intervals the account book is written up. This is done by copying details from the counterfoils of the cheque book and paying-in slips which should contain a complete list of all payments and receipts. The columns are then totalled and the balance checked with the bank pass-book. It is advisable to check the entries at least once a month.

The routine outlined above is simple and foolproof, and on all but a few exceptional farms there should be no difficulty. If, however, it is impracticable to avoid using cash receipts to make farm or private payments, a separate cash account will be necessary. Further details are given in Chapter 11.

Checking cash book with bank balance

If all receipts and payments are passed through the banking account, the cash book and bank pass-book will be identical and the balance in both should be the same at all times. If they do not agree, it will probably be found that the discrepancy is due to one of the following causes

(1) bank charges and interest on an overdraft have been omitted from the account book. They are deducted periodically from the banking account, and care should be taken to copy them into the cash book as a payment;

(2) when a farmer sends a cheque in payment of a bill, the recipient may not present the cheque for payment at once, and when he does so, there may be a slight delay before the farmer's own bank is notified. If the farmer pays in a cheque, his account is usually credited on the same day. Nevertheless, if the bank pass-book is not up to date, it may be reconciled with the cash book as follows.

On 30 November, a farmer found that the balance in the bank pass-book was £91·23 and in the account book £110·25. On checking the entries, he found that a cheque for £12·13 sent to R Johnson had not been deducted from his account, and a cheque from C Barker for £31·15 and paid into the bank had not then been credited.

Reconciliation statement

	£
Balance in bank pass-book	91·23
Add cheque paid in bank not credited	31·15
	122·38
Less cheque sent but not presented	12·13
Total agrees with account book	£110·25

(3) The bank pass-book is a record of the current account, and if money has been paid directly into a deposit account it will obviously not

appear in the bank balance. Deposit receipts should therefore not be overlooked when balancing the accounts.

If a farmer accumulates a large bank balance in his farm account, he may decide to invest the money in shares or other securities. In this case, it is best to withdraw this money from the farm accounts altogether: e.g. if a farmer bought 12 per cent defence bonds costing £2000, this would be shown under payments in the account book as 'Private expenses'. Similarly, if a farmer cashed private securities and intended to use the proceeds to buy farm stock, the amount would be entered under 'Private Receipts'.

Contra accounts

Occasionally a transaction such as the following occurs. A farmer bought a cow on credit from J Allan for £350. Later he sold 2 tons of hay to the same man for £120, giving him a cheque for the difference (£230). If the payment of £230 were entered under Cattle, the sale of the hay would be completely unrecorded, and the cattle column would not show the full value of cattle purchased. The two transactions should be regarded as separate items and entered in the Account Book according-ly. As a reminder that they were settled in this way the items may be marked 'contra account'.

Under *Sales and receipts*:
    Feb. 20. J Allan—2 tonnes hay (Contra account)   £120

Under *Purchases and expenses*:
    Feb. 20. J Allan—1 cow (Contra account)   £350

Questions

1. A farmer tells you that he has difficulty in dealing with petty cash payments. What advice would you give to him?

2. Assume that you have taken a farm of 80 hectares. What account books and records would you consider necessary?

3. Assume that you have just taken an appointment as manager on an 800 hectares arable farm with two foremen. Describe the office organization and record books you would consider necessary.

10 Valuations

As already stated, a valuation of assets is made on the date when book-keeping is first begun, and at the end of every year afterwards, the closing valuation of one year serving as the opening valuation of the next.

Date of valuation

The date on which accounts begin and end is a matter of secondary importance, provided that the same date is used each year. In some cases, the calendar year is chosen and accounts run from 1 January to 31 December. More commonly, book-keeping begins on the date of entry to the farm. In England, this is either at Lady-day (25 March) or at Michaelmas (29 September) and in Scotland at Whitsun (28 May) or at Martinmas (28 November). Where there is a choice of dates, a spring valuation is often preferred, particularly in arable districts. In the autumn, the bulk of the year's crops are still on hand, and any error in calculating the weight or value of stacks of grain, clamps of potatoes and other produce will have a marked effect on the trading account and give a misleading result. In the spring, the bulk of the crops have been sold or used, and although some of the spring crops are sown, the valuation generally stands at its lowest point for the year, thus leaving a smaller margin of error. The valuation on a hill sheep farm is more easily taken in autumn after the lambs and 'cast' ewes have been sold. In spring, particularly during the lambing season, the number of lambs and their value is difficult to estimate.

Market value or cost of production

In making valuations, two methods are possible, one based on market value and the other on cost of production.

When a farm changes hands, the valuation of live and dead stock which the incomer takes over is based largely on market values. But when valuations are made for book-keeping purposes, cost of production is generally the more satisfactory basis. This can be shown in the following way. Assume that a farmer bought five store pigs at £20 apiece, and that the cost of fattening them was £14 each. When the accounts were closed, their market value was estimated at £50 each in the closing valuation. In the form of a miniature trading account the result would be as follows.

Trading Account for year ended 31 December, 1980

	£		£
Purchase (5 pigs at £20)	100	Closing valuation (market	
Expenses	70	value, 5 pigs at £50)	250
	170		
Net Profit	80		
	£250		£250

The pigs were sold during January, but they realized only £44 each. The result during the second year would be as follows

Trading Account for year ended 31 December, 1981

	£		£
Opening valuation	250	Sales, 5 pigs at £44	220
		Net Loss	30
	£250		£250

Using the 'market value' method, the farmer showed a profit of £80 in the first year, but it was only an 'anticipated' profit. In this case, he was too optimistic and the account for the following year showed a loss.

It is a sound maxim in book-keeping not to anticipate a profit before it is realized, and if the pigs had been valued at the cost of production, or £34 apiece (£20 purchase price plus £14 for expenses), the two trading accounts would have been as follows

Trading Account for year ended 31 December, 1980

	£		£
Purchase (5 pigs at £20)	100	Closing valuation (cost of	
Expenses	70	production 5 pigs at £34)	170
		Net Loss	—
	170		
Net Profit	—		
	£170		£170

Trading Account for year ended 31 December, 1981

	£		£
Opening valuation	170	Sales of pigs	220
Net Profit	50		
	£220		£220

By using the latter method, the accounts showed no profit or loss on the pigs until they were sold and the profit realized in the form of cash.

Occasionally, the farmer may find that some of his crops or livestock are not worth the money he has spent on them. Crops may fail through attack by pests, or livestock may be injured, and in these circumstances, there is nothing to be gained by showing crops or stock in the valuation at a price which they would not realize if sold. The valuation should be reduced to the market value, and the expected loss written off during the year in which it occurred.

As a general rule, therefore, *valuations are based on cost of production or market value, whichever is the lower*.

Inventory and valuation

To make a valuation for book-keeping purposes, the farmer goes round the farm with a note-book making a list or inventory of the crops, livestock and dead stock.

For convenience, the items may be classified under four headings

(1) livestock;
(2) harvested crops;
(3) growing crops, and tenant right;
(4) implements and stores.

The first three groups are valued at *cost of production* as explained above.

Implements are dealt with in a slightly different way which will be explained later.

Valuation of livestock

For valuation purposes, livestock may be divided into two classes: *Trading stock* and *Productive stock*.

Whereas trading stock is valued at 'cost of production,' productive stock is valued at a fixed price termed the *Standard value*.

Trading stock
Under this heading are included all livestock intended primarily for sale, e.g.
Cattle. Bullocks for sale fat or as stores, pedigree cattle reared for sale as breeding stock.
Sheep. Lambs or hoggs for sale fat or as stores, and temporary or 'flying' flocks of ewes.
Horses. Horses reared for sale.
Poultry. Fattening cockerels, pullets reared for sale.

As already stated, these should, so far as possible, be valued at 'cost of production'. The value of purchased livestock, (e.g. store bullocks) is the buying price plus an allowance for their keep up to the date of valuation. If the livestock are home bred, the cost of production is less easily ascertained. When cost accounts are kept, the farmer can calculate the cost of rearing livestock; but if no such records are kept, an estimate must be made. On the whole, it is reasonable to asssume that the cost of production is normally a little less than the market value, and at the time of writing the Inland Revenue Department is prepared to accept a valuation of homebred cattle at 60 per cent of market price and sheep and pigs at 75 per cent. Thus, a home-reared bullock whose market value was estimated at £200, could be valued at £120.

Productive, or fixed, stock
Under this heading come all livestock that are not primarily intended for sale, e.g. cows kept to produce milk or calves for rearing, permanent ewe flocks, breeding sows, and laying hens. Working horses, stock bulls, rams, and boars are also placed in this category. Productive livestock, must be sold when old or otherwise unsatisfactory, but this is an incidental receipt and not the chief object for which they are kept. This distinction between trading and productive livestock is of considerable importance in drawing up valuations.

The method of valuing productive livestock is as follows.* A dairy herd that is to be valued for the first time would be valued at the estimated cost of production, which would probably be slightly less than market value. The valuation might be as follows

	£
20 dairy cows at £400	8 000
5 heifers in calf at £420	2 100
5 heifers (1 to 2 years) at £200	1 000
6 calves at £80	480
	£11 580

* An alternative method of valuing productive livestock for income tax purposes is explained in Chapter 22.

Having once adopted this basis of valuation, the farmer should not change it except under exceptional conditions, and should continue every year to value cows at £400, heifers in calf, £420, and so on, ignoring small fluctuations in market values. A fixed conventional price of this kind is known as a standard value.

To show the importance of keeping such values constant, assume that, a year later, the herd still consisted of 20 cows. Market values had increased temporarily and similar dairy cows were selling for £450 each. If the valuation were increased to this figure, the herd would appear in the closing valuation as 20 cows at £450—£9000. The herd therefore appeared in the opening valuation at £8000 and in the closing valuation at £9000—an increase of £1000. But an increase in valuation means an increase in profit; and by writing up the value of the cows, the profit would have been increased by £1000. The herd was the same as before, the cows had not been sold, and the increase in market values had produced no real benefit to the farmer. This £1000 profit is therefore fictitious and is known as a 'paper profit'. If by the end of next year, market values had fallen to £350, the accounts for the next year would have shown a 'paper loss' of £2000. Juggling with valuations in this way is undesirable and defeats the object of accounting—which is to show the genuine profit or loss on the year's trading.

If prices continue to rise over a long period, allowance must be made for the increased cost of rearing young stock. Old cows retained in the herd should remain at their former value because they were produced at lower costs, whilst newly calved heifers drafted into the herd, having cost more to rear, are shown at an increased value.

Assume that at 29 September, 1981, a farmer had 20 cows valued at £400. During the next year, five old cows were sold and replaced by five home-bred heifers valued at £420. The valuation at 29 September, 1982, would be

	£
15 cows at £400	6 000
5 cows at £420	2 100
20	£8 100

If, in the following year, four more old cows were replaced by heifers valued at £440, the valuation at 29 September, 1983, would be

	£
11 cows at £400	4 400
5 cows at £420	2 100
4 cows at £440	1 760
20	£8 260

In this way, allowance would be made for the extra cost of rearing replacements but no 'paper profit' would be shown on the old cows retained in the herd.

The disadvantage of this system is that, unless the farmer values the cows individually, he may not know the price group of any cow he sells. A slight modification could be made in the following way. The valuation at 29 September, 1982, was: 20 cows, £8100, and is equivalent to £405 per head. The cows would be carried forward at this value and the valuation at 29th September, 1983, would be

	£
16 cows at £405	6 480
4 cows at £440	1 760
20	£8 240

The average value is now £412 per head and this is used in the succeeding valuation. If falling costs appear likely to last for a considerable period, the value of replacements should be reduced in a similar manner. Other classes of breeding stock, such as ewes or sows, should also be valued at standard prices.

Stock bulls, rams, and boars

The value of young stock animals is increased until they come into service and written down thereafter until sold. For example, a bull purchased for £800, and expected to be in use for three years, and then sold for £200, would have a depreciation of £200 per year. The value after one year will be £600, and after two years, £400.

Valuation of harvested crops

Harvested crops, which include crops in the stack or in the granary, clamps of potatoes, and other root crops, will be dealt with in two groups.

Crops for sale

Crops such as barley, wheat, or potatoes, should be valued on 'cost of production' in much the same way as livestock for sale. If no costing records are available, the valuation is taken as a little less than market price (say 15 per cent less). Quantities of crops are estimated from the cubic capacity of stacks and clamps, with due allowance for tail corn and waste. In assessing the price, a deduction should be made for any costs to be met before the crop is marketed for threshing corn crops, riddling potatoes, and the cost of transport.

Fodder crops

Fodder crops include beans, peas, oats, and other grains grown for feeding, and hay, straw, silage, mangolds, turnips, and other root crops grown for fodder. When a farm changes hands, a professional valuer is usually called in to value such items according to the custom of the district. Fodder crops harvested, or ready to be harvested, may be valued by one of two methods—by market value or by feeding or consuming value.

Market values of hay, oats, beans, and peas are easily ascertained. Mangolds, turnips, kale, and the like are normally grown for use on the farm, and there may be no recognized market value. The valuer therefore uses conventional prices settled by the local valuers' association.

A farmer valuing fodder crops for book-keeping purposes can draw up a list of 'standard' values per ton or per hundredweight. These can be based in the first instance on the estimated average cost of production on his own farm or upon published reports of the agricultural economists. As already stated, when dealing with productive livestock these values should be altered only when the general level of costs changes.

Growing crops, cultivations and manures

In addition to harvested crops, crops in preparation must also be valued. This heading, therefore, includes cultivations, growing crops, and manures in the soil which will benefit future crops.

Cultivations are valued at cost, and if the farmer is making his own valuation, he can base it on contractors' prices or, better still, calculate average costs for his own farm. Professional valuers use conventional rates calculated by their associations, modified where necessary to suit local conditions. It is now the rule that cultivations are valued as if done by tractor unless there is good reason (e.g. on a small farm or in an awkward field) for using horses.

Growing crops are valued at the cost of seed, fertilizers and cultivations to date. The cost of carting and spreading manure should also be included.

The last items are farmyard manure and unexhausted manurial residues. When a farm is let to a tenant, the farmyard manure as such usually belongs to the landlord. The tenant, however, is entitled to compensation for the manurial residues of purchased feeding-stuffs and corn fed to the animals producing the manure. The right of a tenant to claim compensation for manurial residues, growing crops, cultivations and the like is known as 'tenant right'. Formerly the rate of compensation depended on local custom which varied from county to county; but under the Agricultural Holdings Act 1948, a greater degree of uniformity has been introduced.

The law governing tenant right is too complex and in some respects too rigid to be used in ordinary farm accounting. For accounting purposes, therefore, a tenant farmer would be well advised to accept the figure paid on entry for manurial residues and carry it forward unaltered as one of his assets. If he believes that the value has altered materially and wishes to show the change in his accounts, he should consult a professional valuer.

'Unexhausted manurial residues' is a term used to cover the unexhausted value of manures applied in previous years. For example, the beneficial effects of a dressing of lime or slag may be visible for several years after application. Such residues are of two kinds—those derived from artificial fertilizers and those from cake and other feeding-stuffs fed to livestock. Schedules of prices for manurial values have now been prescribed officially in regulations under the Agricultural Holdings Act 1948. A professional valuer, making a valuation for a farmer who is entering or leaving a farm, goes through the receipts for feeding-stuffs and manures purchased and records of home-grown corn fed during the previous two or three years and calculates the residual values.

When a farm is changing hands, the calculation of the value of tenant right is a matter of great importance. For book-keeping purposes it is not generally necessary to revalue these residues each year. In most cases the amount of farmyard manure and other residues changes little from one year to another, and the same value can be used each year. Valuers frequently give little detail in their statements; and when taking a farm, a farmer would be well advised (after the valuation has been completed) to ask for further particulars. This will not only furnish information for drawing-up future annual valuations, but will be of advantage should the farmer ever leave the farm in ensuring that he obtains the same treatment on quitting as on entering the farm.

If the farming system is radically altered or the numbers of livestock greatly increased or decreased, due allowance must be made in the valuation of farmyard manure and other residues.

It should be noted that when the valuation of farmyard manure and manurial residues is retained at the same figure in the opening and closing valuation, the profit would be unaffected if omitted from the valuations altogether. This fact is generally recognized and for income tax purposes the following arrangement has been made after discussions between the Inland Revenue Department, the Agricultural Department, and the Farmers' Unions.

Where the normal value of tillages, unexhausted manures and growing crops does not exceed £700, and a detailed valuation is not available, a certificate that the value at the beginning of the year did not differ materially from that at the end of the year will usually be accepted.

Even where the normal value exceeds £700 a valuation will not be pressed for in every case, and a similar certificate may be accepted after any inquiry necessary to establish its reasonable accuracy.

The object of the above arrangement is to assist farmers by enabling a detailed valuation to be dispensed with in such cases.

This arrangement, which is limited to cases where detailed valuations are not available, does not prevent a farmer, who so desires, from bringing into his accounts a full detailed valuation of tenant right or waygoing rights and liabilities at the beginning and end of each year. Any farmer who makes a detailed valuation is at liberty to put in that valuation and should in fact do so. The valuation should be made on precisely the same basis as if valuing an outgoing tenant. In other words, the valuation should, in the case of a tenant, be based upon the actual tenancy agreement, and in the case of an owner-occupier, be based on the custom of the country which would, in the absence of a written agreement, be applicable if a tenancy existed.

In spite of these concessions, it is recommended that tillages, unexhausted manures, and growing crops should be valued. Otherwise, although the effect on the profit may be slight, the list of assets would be incomplete and would not indicate the total sum of money invested in the farm.

Valuation of implements and fixtures

When a farm implement is in use on the farm, it gradually wears out, and in course of time, is replaced by a new one. The value of the implement falls from year to year and to allow for this it is usual to write off a proportion of the cost each year known as a 'wear and tear' allowance. For example, assume that an implement is valued at £1600 and that the rate of depreciation is 25 per cent. The method adopted is to calculate the depreciation of wear and tear allowance as a percentage of the written-down value at which the implement stands at the beginning of the current year, as follows

	£
Opening valuation	1 600
Less depreciation: 25 per cent of £1600	400
Value at end of 1st year	1 200
Less depreciation: 25 per cent of £1200	300
Value at end of 2nd year	900
Less depreciation: 25 per cent of £900	225
Value at end of 3rd year	£675

It will be noted that, in the example given, the depreciation is greatest during the first year (£400), gradually diminishing (£300 and £225 in the second and third years) as the implement becomes older. In practice, new implements do lose value more rapidly than old.

In making these calculations, it is generally sufficient to give the result to the nearest £.

To show how depreciation can be calculated, take a farmer whose implement valuation at 1 January, 1980 was as follows

	£
Motor car	5 000
Tractors	14 000
General implements	24 000
Small tools	500
	£43 500

During the year, he purchased a tractor for £7000 and sold the old one for £1000. He bought implements worth £500 and sold the old ones for £800. The general implements were valued at £24 000 at the beginning of the year and small tools at £500.

Depreciation allowances for year ending 31 December, 1981

Implements	Value at 1 Jan., 1980	Add Pur- chases	Less Sales	Sub total	Less Depreciation at 25 per cent	Value at 31 Dec., 1981
Motor car	5 000	—	—	5 000	1 250	3 750
Tractors	14 000	7 000	1 000	20 000	5 000	15 000
General implements	24 000	5 000	800	28 200	7 050	21 150
Small tools	500	—	—	500	—	500
Total	43 500	12 000	1 800	53 700	13 300	40 400

Fig. 10.1. Depreciation record for implements

Under the present rules for taxation (*see* Chapter 22), the cost of purchased implements can be written off in the year of purchase. Motor cars are depreciated by 25 per cent every year. It is nevertheless advisable to keep a record of depreciation allowances as shown in Fig. 10.1. The existing motor car, tractors and implements are each depreciated by 25 per cent after deducting the sales of old implements (which may have been traded-in when replacements were purchased). After this calculation has been made, the new valuation (at 31 December, 1981) totals £40 400.

No depreciation allowance is made for small tools (hand hoes, forks, spades, brushes, tools). They wear out rapidly and, as the cost of renewing them is charged under 'Repairs and small tools' and not 'Implements bought', the cost of buying small tools does not appear in the wear and tear calculation. In practice, their numbers vary little and unless there is some substantial change, the same value can be carried forward unaltered from year to year.

Stores including feeding-stuffs, fertilizers, seeds, and fuel stored on the farm are valued at cost.

A valuation in detail

It may seem from the foregoing account that the drawing up of a valuation is a complicated task. In practice, it is less difficult than might be supposed. The description of the methods used by valuers has been given so that, whether the farmer employs professional assistance or carries out his own valuation, he may understand the principles involved and the implications of the method adopted. In the valuation of crops, there are two points that should be borne in mind.

In the first place, the methods of valuation, particularly of fodder and growing crops, vary to some extent from district to district. Indeed two persons using different methods might produce different estimates of the total valuation of the same farm. So far as the trading account is concerned, however, it is not the total valuation but the *difference* between the opening and closing valuation that affects the profit. It is of the greatest importance to make the opening and closing valuations by the same methods.

To illustrate this, assume that a farmer had 40 tons of hay at the beginning of a year and 45 tons at the end, both used for feeding. Valuer A considers that the hay was worth £45 per ton.

	£
Opening valuation 40 tons at £45	1 800
Closing valuation 45 tons at £45	2 025
Increase in value	£225

The £225 represented an increase in production of hay and would increase the profit to that extent. Valuer B took a different view and assessed the hay at £50 per ton.

	£
Opening valuation 40 tons at £50	2 000
Closing valuation 45 tons at £50	2 250
Increase in value	£250

Although the two estimates were entirely different, the profit in the second case would be only £25 greater than in the first. On the other hand, if the hay were valued at £45 at the beginning by A and at £50 at the end by B, the effect would be as follows

	£
Opening valuation 40 tons at £45	1 800
Closing valuation 45 tons at £50	£2 250
Increase in value	£450

In this case, the profit would be increased by £450, a result that is entirely misleading. Every care should be taken to adopt a correct basis in drawing up valuations, but it is even more important to use the *same* methods at the beginning as at the end of the year.

In the second place, the farmer should follow the terms of his contract, and show straw and farmyard manure in the valuation only if paid for at entry. Nevertheless, in valuing fodder crops standard values are to be preferred to market prices for the same reason as was recommended for productive livestock. For example, a farmer, who used all his straw for litter, had 10 tons at the beginning and 10 tons at the end of the year. The market price had increased from £20 to £40 per ton. If he valued this at £200 in the opening and £400 in the closing valuation, the accounts would show a 'paper profit' of £200, which the farmer was unlikely to realize.

Unless there are reasons to the contrary, it is suggested that a valuation should be drawn up as follows

Trading livestock: actual cost of production if known, or 60 per cent of the market value for cattle and 75 per cent for pigs and sheep.

Productive livestock: standard value.

Crops for sale: actual cost of production if known, or 85 per cent of market value.

Growing crops and tillages: cost of cultivations, seeds and fertilizers up to the date of valuation.

Fodder crops: standard values.

Implements: original cost less depreciation.

Stores: at cost.

Farmyard manure and unexhausted manurial residues: cost at entry, adjusted, if necessary, where the value has increased or decreased since that date. Figure 10.2 is an example of a valuation drawn up in accordance with these principles.

Inventory and valuation of live and dead farming stock,
tenant right, etc. taken for the purpose of stock-taking
as at 31 March, 1982

	£	£
Cattle		
93 cows—in milk	400	37 200
4 cows—dry	400	1 600
34 heifers—in calf	270	9 180
1 Hereford bull		300
40 buds	30	1 200
15 calves	80	1 200
15 steers	180	2 700
14 steers and heifers	160	2 240
20 steers	240	4 800
26 steers	280	7 280
11 heifers	200	2 200
37 steers and heifers	180	6 660
		76 560
Pigs		
60 sows	45	2 700
124 pigs	5	620
3 boars	40	120
10 gilts—in pig	60	600
165 pigs—2–4 months	17	2 805
180 pigs—4–6 months	38	6 840
		13 685
Poultry		
10 hens		12
Corn and seeds		
350 tonnes wheat	85	29 750
400 kg grass seed	0·5	200
		29 950
Hay		
Quantity of clover bales		
25 tonnes	60	1 500
Straw		
Quantity of wheat and barley bales		
30 tonnes	15	450

Feeding-stuffs	£	£
90 tonnes beans	80	7 200
25 tonnes feed barley	70	1 750
11 tonnes feed oats	70	770
Other feeding-stuffs (given in detail)		1 260
		10 980

Roots	£	£
70 tonnes King Edward ware	60	4 200

Silage	£	£
50 tonnes silage	8	400

Manures	£
35 tonnes 20:10:10	4 200
30 tonnes Nitram	3 120
Manure in heap, 200 tonnes	200
	7 520

Fuel and oil, etc.	£
3370 litres diesel	450
220 litres petrol	60
650 litres lubricating oil	225
	735

Cultivations and cropping	£
Fertilizers	8 423
Seed	7 590
75 hectares wheat	
Cultivations thereon	1 512
20 hectares	
Farmyard manure applied thereon	500
12 hectares oats	
Cultivations thereon	240
50 hectares barley	
Cultivations thereon	992
10 hectares tic beans	
Cultivations thereon	322
19 hectares potatoes	
Cultivations thereon	470
19 hectares sugar-beet	
Cultivations thereon	624
38 hectares rye grass	
Cultivations thereon	576
3 hectares 4-year ley	
Cultivations thereon	48
	21 297

Summary—March, 1970

	£
Cattle	76 560
Pigs	13 685
Poultry	12
Corn and seeds	29 950
Hay	1 500
Straw	450
Feeding-stuffs	10 980
Silage	400
Roots	4 200
Fuel and oils, etc.	735
Manures	7 520
Cultivations and cropping	21 297
	167 289

We value the items contained in the foregoing Valuation at the sum of One hundred and sixty-seven thousand, two hundred and eighty-nine pounds (£167 289).

Signed...
Valuers and Surveyors.

Fig. 10.2 Farm valuation in detail

Questions

1. Explain the following terms. (*a*) Standard value; (*b*) tenant right; (*c*) productive livestock; and (*d*) wear and tear allowance.

2. You are a farm manager and decide to commence book-keeping from 1 January. Describe briefly how you would proceed to value (*a*) a herd of home-bred Friesian cows; (*b*) store cattle purchased on 15 December; (*c*) a clamp of potatoes; (*d*) a clamp of mangolds; (*e*) a field of winter beans sown in October; (*f*) ten bacon pigs almost ready for market; and (*g*) a combine purchased 12 months previously for £20 000.

3. What is a 'paper profit'? Give an example to show how a paper profit may arise through faulty methods of valuation.

4. When taking an annual valuation on 31 March, 1980, a farmer, by mistake, omitted a stack of hay worth £600. What effect is this likely to have on the profit of (*a*) the year ending 31 March, 1980? (*b*) the year ending 31 March, 1981? and (*c*) both years combined?

11 Other methods of book-keeping

In addition to the cash analysis system described, there are many other forms of book-keeping in use, and a brief account of some of the more important is given in this chapter.

Modification of the cash analysis system

It has been recommended in earlier chapters that all receipts and expenses should be passed through the bank account, and that small cash transactions should be recorded in a separate petty cash book for eventual transfer to the account book. If the farmer has a large number of cash transactions and does not wish to pass them through the bank account, he can record them direct in the account book. In this case it is desirable to separate cash and bank transactions, to simplify the auditing of the account book, and to allow the bank balance to be checked at any time.

To illustrate the method of using these modified cash analysis account books, the following examples are given, using first the account book already described (Method 1), and then two modified versions (Methods 2 and 3).

Method 1
Assume that at the beginning of a month a farmer has a balance of £250 in the bank and £50 in the cash box. During the month, the following transactions take place

	£
Paid miscellaneous expenses by cheque	10·00
Drew cash from bank for wages	190·00
Received for potatoes and paid into bank	250·00
Cashed cheque to cover miscellaneous cash expenses made from the petty cash box (bringing the balance back to £50·00)	15·00

The entry of these items is straightforward and is illustrated in Fig. 11.1.

Receipts

Name and details	Total received	Potatoes	(Other columns omitted)
	£	£	
Opening balance (in bank)	250		
Potatoes	250	250	
	500	250	
	£500		

Payments

Name and details	Total paid	Wages	Miscellaneous	(Other columns omitted)
	£	£	£	
Miscellaneous	10		10	
Wages	190	190		
Miscellaneous (per petty cash book)	15		15	
	215	190	25	
Closing balance (in bank)	285			
	£500			

Fig. 11.1 Cash analysis account book: method 1

Method 2

Assume that the farmer has the same balance at the beginning of the month. The payments and receipts are as before, but the farmer draws out and pays into the bank odd sums of money which do not necessarily correspond to his receipts and payments.

(a) He pays, as before, miscellaneous expenses by cheque (£10).

(b) He draws a cheque to self for £200. Of this he uses £190 for wages and £10 for miscellaneous cash expenses.

(c) He receives £250 for potatoes sold. Of this, he uses £5 for miscellaneous expenses and pays the £245 into the bank.

The list of transactions is therefore

	£
(1) Paid miscellaneous expenses by cheque	10·00
(2) Drew cash from bank	200·00
(3) Paid wages (cash)	190·00

(4) Paid miscellaneous expenses (cash)   10·00
(5) Received cash for potatoes   250·00
(6) Paid miscellaneous expenses by cash   5·00
(7) Paid cash into bank   245·00

In place of using a petty cash book, he opens separate 'Bank' and 'Cash' columns on the receipts and payments pages as shown in Fig. 11.2. First of all the cash and bank balances are entered on the

Receipts

Name and details	Cash	Bank	Potatoes	(Other columns omitted)
	£	£	£	
Opening balance	50	250		
Drew cash from bank	200			
Potatoes	250		250	
Paid cash into bank		245		
	500	495	250	
	£500	£495		

Payments

Name and details	Cash	Bank	Wages	Miscel-laneous	(Other columns omitted)
	£	£	£	£	
Miscellaneous		10		10	
Drew cash from bank		200			
Wages	190		190		
Miscellaneous	10			10	
Miscellaneous	5			5	
Paid cash into bank	245				
	450	210	190	25	
Closing balance	50	285			
	£500	£495			

Fig. 11.2 Cash analysis account book: method 2

receipts pages as shown, and the transactions are then completed as follows

Item 1. Payment by cheque for £10. This is entered on the payments page under the Bank and Miscellaneous columns.

Item 2. £200 drawn from the bank. This is a payment by the bank and a receipt of cash, and is entered by means of a 'cross-entry': in the Bank column on the payments page and in the Cash column on the receipts page. Being a transfer within the farm business, a cross-entry is not entered in any of the analysis columns.

Items 3, 4, 5, and *6* are all cash transactions and are entered in the cash column on the receipts or payments page and in the appropriate analysis column.

Item 7. £245 paid into the bank. This is another cross-entry and is entered as a payment by cash and a receipt by the bank.

At the end of the month the bank and cash columns are totalled, showing a bank balance of £285 and a cash balance of £50. Using this method, the farmer need not pay all receipts into the bank but may use them to make cash payments. But unless he records such cash transactions in the account book every few days (or keeps a record in a notebook) he may easily forget the details. Cross-entries are a further disadvantage: mistakes are easily made, and as they are not entered in the analysis columns, these columns cannot easily be checked against the totals columns.

Method 3

A third method has recently come into use and is shown in Fig. 11.3. It is a compromise between Methods 1 and 2 and is an attempt to avoid cross-entries. Briefly, the payments page with Paid in cash and Paid by cheque columns is similar to that described in Method 2 and (apart from certain of the cross-entries) is completed in the same way. On the receipts page, all receipts, whether in the form of cash or cheques, are entered in the Total received column and in the appropriate analysis column. All cash or cheques subsequently paid into the bank are entered in the Paid into bank column. Assuming the same transactions as for Method 2, the entries are made as follows

Item 1. Payment by cheque (£10) is entered in the Paid by Cheque and Miscellaneous columns.

Item 2. £200 drawn from the bank is entered in the Paid by Cheque column only. Such items should be marked to facilitate the checking of the columns at the end of the year.

Items 3 and *4.* These two cash payments are entered in the Paid in Cash and appropriate analysis columns.

Item 5. £250 received for potatoes is entered in the Total received and Potatoes column.

Item 6. Similar to *3* and *4* above.

Item 7. £245 cash paid into the bank is entered in the Paid into bank column only.

Receipts

Name and details	Total received	Potatoes	(Other columns omitted)	Paid into bank
	£	£		£
Opening balance	50			250
Potatoes	250	250		
Paid cash into bank				245
	300	250		495
				£495

Payments

Name and details	Paid in cash	Paid by cheque	Wages	Miscel-laneous	(Other columns omitted)
	£	£	£	£	
Miscellaneous		10		10	
Drew cash from bank		200*			
Wages	190		190		
Miscellaneous	10			10	
Miscellaneous	5			5	
	205	210	190	25	
Closing balance		£285			
		£495			

Fig. 11.3 Cash analysis account book: method 3

It will be seen that the Paid by cheque and Paid into bank columns correspond to the bank book and the balance should therefore agree with the bank balance. Cash transactions, however, are less easily checked, and for this reason Method 3 is generally used by farmers who employ professional assistance in completing their accounts. An accountant auditing an account book of this kind would check the cash transactions as follows

		£
Total received (including cash at beginning)		300·00
Add cash drawn from bank		200·00
Total receipts to be accounted for		500·00
Less paid into bank	£245·00	
paid in cash	205·00	
		450·00
Remainder (should agree with cash in hand)		£50·00

Short-cut method of cash analysis

The system of cash analysis using a columnar cash book is a clear and efficient system that can be recommended both for teaching and for use. To analyze individual items it is not, however, essential to have a series of columns. Indeed, many farmers merely make a list of receipts and payments and leave it to the accountant to do the analysis afterwards. The quickest way to classify the items for a year is to write a series of account headings on a sheet of paper as shown in Fig. 11.4 and enter the items under these headings. At the end of the year (or every month or three months) the individual accounts are totalled and checked against the total in the Total paid or Total received column. This method has the advantage that any number of accounts can be opened and the farmer is not restricted by the number of columns in the cash book.

After checking the totals at the end of the year, the usual additions and deductions can be made for debtors and creditors before transferring the totals to the trading account.

Other modifications of the cash analysis book have been suggested from time to time. Generally they are slight variations of one of the three methods illustrated above, and are designed to assist the farmer to record cash and bank transactions. Fundamentally, there is no essential difference between them, and in all cases the instructions given for completing the balance sheet and trading account are equally applicable.

Short cut method of Cash Analysis

(Manor Farm, year 1980–81, transactions for April, 1980)

Purchases and Expenses

Pigs	Cattle	Feeding-stuffs	Seeds	Fertilizers and sprays	Wages	Repairs and small tools	Fuel	Rent	Other overheads	Implements bought	Private drawings
80	320	466	—	75	151	5	6	—	145	80	50
					154	5			8	320	
					145	10		Monthly check April	3	466	
					152				156	75	
					602					10	
										6	
										156	
								Opening balance		50	
										1765	
										9760	
										11525 (agrees with total paid column)	

Sales and Receipts

Cattle	Pigs	Milk	Wheat	Potatoes	Misc. receipts	Private receipts	Implements bought
257	561	1834	1800	—	142	—	257
							561
			Monthly check April				1834
							1800
							142
							4594 (agrees with total received column)

12 Owner-occupiers and partnerships

While half the farmers in Great Britain are tenants renting land and buildings from a landlord, the others own the property they farm. As an owner-occupier, a farmer has certain advantages. He has security of tenure, and the knowledge that any improvements that he carries out will be entirely for his own benefit. One might also add that the possession of land gives a certain pride of ownership, which the farmer can never feel for property that belongs to someone else.

On the other hand, the tenant is now protected by law in many ways. If asked to quit, a tenant who has farmed according to the rules of good husbandry and carried out his other obligations can claim compensation for disturbance under the Agricultural Holdings Act, and secure payment for most forms of improvement carried out. A tenant, moreover, is less tied than an owner-occupier and if he prospers can move more easily to a larger farm. It must not be forgotten, however, that an owner-occupier requires a considerable amount of capital, and to buy a farm and stock it may cost five times as much as to stock it as a tenant. The man with a limited amount of money has a choice of purchasing a small farm outright or taking a larger farm as a tenant.

Owner-occupiers' expenses

It is always possible for a farmer with insufficient capital to buy a farm to borrow money by means of a mortgage, pledging the farm as security for the loan. He becomes the legal owner of the farm, and in place of paying rent, he pays interest on the mortgage (in addition to other ownership charges); in course of time he may be able to repay the sum borrowed. If, as has happened in recent years, land values rise, the owner can reap a substantial capital increment. On the other hand, if he buys the farm when land values are high, and this is followed by a period of falling prices he may be in a less happy position. A landlord might be prepared to forgo part of the rent at such a time, but the mortgage owner generally demands the payment of interest, and in default will have the farm sold to recover the value of his loan. A prospective buyer should be warned, however, that unless he can buy land cheaply he cannot expect to be able to buy a farm and repay the mortgage out of profits. For example, arable farms in the east of England have average farm incomes of about £170 before allowing for rent. If the land costs £3,500 per hectare, and the mortgage is as little as 12 per cent, the cost of 20 years is £469 per hectare or nearly three times the average income available.

Owners' rates and taxes

Before dealing with the method of keeping accounts as an owner-occupier, a brief explanation is given of the various taxes and levies charged on the ownership of land.

Tithe

Originally, tithe was a gift of a tenth of the produce of land, used for the maintenance of the Church. For many centuries, the produce itself was given, but after 1836 a money payment was substituted. From time to time there has been much discussion on this subject, and the payment of tithe has been represented as a heavy burden on agriculture as an industry. Finally, by a Tithe Act passed by Parliament in 1936, fixed annuities were substituted for tithe rent-charge and payments (with certain minor exceptions) will cease at the end of sixty years.*

Drainage rates

In certain areas subject to flooding, Drainage Boards have the power to levy rates to recover the cost of the construction and upkeep of drainage schemes. In some cases drainage rates are chargeable to the owner only; in others, both owner and occupier make a contribution.

Mortgage payments

An owner may have borrowed money on the security of his property, either to buy the farm, to erect buildings or to carry out other

---

* Strictly speaking, tithe rent-charge came to an end in 1936. The tithe owners received in compensation 3 per cent Government Guaranteed Stock. 'Tithe' paid by landowners is now devoted to redemption annuities, one-sixth of the annual payment being set aside to redeem the capital value of the Stock at the end of sixty years. For this reason, only five-sixths of the 'tithe' payment can be charged for income tax purposes.

improvements. Payments on a mortgage normally includes both interest and a gradual repayment of the original sum borrowed. (*See* Appendix 2 for details.)

Repairs

The final charge on land ownership is the cost of repairs and upkeep. When a farm is let, the landlord often agrees to bear a proportion of the cost of structural repairs. In some cases, he supplies the materials and the farmer supplies the labour. In others, the landlord is responsible for the maintenance of roofs and main walls and the tenant for the remainder. At the present time, there is a growing tendency for the landlord to pass the responsibility for repairs to the tenant. Whatever the arrangement, however, both parties will take the cost of repairs into account in negotiating the rent.

If a farmer is an owner-occupier, however, he must expect to pay for such repairs as would otherwise have been carried out by the landlord.

Book-keeping for owner-occupiers

When a farmer owns his farm, he pays no rent, but must meet the costs of ownership mentioned above. In making up his accounts, he can choose one of two methods. He may regard the ownership and tenancy of the farm as a single business, and show the profit on the business as a whole. Alternatively, he may arrange the accounts to give the profit he makes as an owner and as a tenant separately.

The two methods may be shown by means of an example. Take Mr Ford's farm for the year ending 31 March, 1981, as described in Chapter 6, assume that he was an owner-occupier and that the farm could be sold for £600 000.

As an owner, he did not have to pay the rent of £6800, but instead he would have paid £60 for tithe and £2463 on building repairs which would normally have been paid by the landlord. As an owner-occupier, the trading account would be as shown in Fig. 12.1 (some details are omitted to save space).

As an owner-occupier, Mr Ford would therefore have made a net profit of £19 405, in place of £15 128 as a tenant.

The alternative method is to arrange the accounts to show the profit made as a tenant separately from that made as an owner. In this, a column should be set aside in the account book for 'Ownership expenses'. A column for 'Ownership receipts' may also be required for sales of timber or gravel, the sale of parcels of land or cottages, and

Trading Account for year ending 31 March, 1981

Purchases and Expenses		£	Sales and Receipts	£
Seeds, fertilizers, sprays		13 545	Crops	37 430
Feeding-stuffs		17 839	Milk and cattle	23 140
Livestock		400	Pigs	16 913
Livestock expenses		2 904	Miscellaneous	220
Labour		10 514		
Machinery		5 200		77 703
Overheads		3 823		
			Private use of car,	
		54 225	produce, etc.	250
Ownership charges				77 953
Tithe	60		Closing valuation	59 547
Building repairs	2 463			137 500
		2 523		
		56 748		
Opening valuation		61 347		
		118 095		
Net profit		19 405		
		£137 500		£137 500

Fig. 12.1 Owner-occupier: simple trading account

rents received for property not included in the annual value of the farm. At the end of the year, an ownership account is drawn up similar to the trading account. After transferring ownership expenses to the ownership account and other expenses and receipts to the trading account, the rental value is added as an expense to the trading account and as a receipt in the ownership account as if paid by the farm to the landlord. The opening and closing valuations of live and dead stock are entered in the trading account. A trading account and ownership account for this alternative method are shown in Fig. 12.2, using the same figures as in the previous example.

The net result is thus

	£
Net profit as occupier	15 128
Net profit as owner	4 277
Net profit as owner-occupier	£19 405

By using the second figure, the farmer can see the profit which he would have made as a tenant farmer. This is useful because most reports on profits and farming efficiency published in this country assume that the farmer is a tenant. The profit as an owner is also of interest, as it

Trading Account for year ending 31 March, 1981

	£		£
Purchases and expenses	54 225	*Sales and receipts*	77 703
Transfer from ownership		Non-cash receipts	250
account—		Closing valuation	59 547
Rental value	6 800		
Opening valuation—			
(Tenant's assets)	61 347		
	122 372		
Net profit as occupier	15 128		
	£137 500		£137 500

Ownership Account

			£
Purchases and expenses—			
Tithe	60	*Sales and receipts—*	
Building repairs	2 463	Rental value	6 800
		(charged to tenancy	
	2 523	account)	
Net profit as owner	4 277		
	£6 800		£6 800

Fig. 12.2 Owner-occupier: trading account and ownership account

shows the return on the money invested in buying the farm. In this case, he received a return of £4277 on a capital sum of £600 000. The return per £100 invested was therefore

$$£ \frac{4277 \times 100}{600\,000} = 0.71 \text{ per cent.}$$

The corresponding return on the average of £60 447 invested as a tenant is

$$£ \frac{15\,128 \times 100}{60\,447} = 25 \text{ per cent.}$$

The return from money invested in the purchase of the farm is thus much poorer than from money invested as a tenant. The exact return varies widely according to circumstances, but a return of under one per cent for ownership and of 12 to 25 per cent as a tenant is quite typical. The return to an owner-occupier who had bought the farm for £600 000 would be less than 3 per cent. The return from land ownership also compares poorly with the annual return from investing in stocks and shares. This might lead one to the conclusion that rent and land values were out of step and that land ownership was a poor form of investment. Land, however, is bought for many other reasons than for the rent it can produce (or save in the case of an owner-occupier). A farmer might buy land to provide greater security and to satisfy pride of ownership. It may also be bought in the hope that land prices will continue to rise in value. A farm of this kind has probably increased in value tenfold in the previous twenty years. There is also the fact that land receives favourable treatment when being assessed for capital transfer tax.

Partnerships

When two or more persons agree to own and manage a business jointly, they are known as partners. There are a number of situations in which a partnership can operate very successfully.

(1) Two friends who wish to start farming may agree to go into partnership. There are a number of advantages. If the partners have only a limited amount of capital each, they may prefer to operate a large farm jointly rather than two small ones separately. They can divide responsibilities and each can become more specialized in one part of the business. When difficulties occur, one can turn to the other for help and advice. If one partner goes on holiday or is ill, the other can carry on the business until he returns.

(2) In some cases a father may take a son into partnership. Psychologically this is often a wise move. A son who must continue to take orders from his father well into middle age may feel frustrated but may be much more contented if recognized at least as a junior partner.

(3) A partnership can be used as a means of inducing a man with capital to invest in a farm. He might be unwilling to lend the capital but be willing to take a share in the ownership of the business. If he is content to leave the day-to-day management to his partner, he becomes a 'sleeping partner'.

(4) An experienced manager or foreman may become so useful that a farmer may be anxious to retain his services. One way of doing so is to make him a partner.

A partnership can be quite informal and two friends may carry on a joint enterprise for many years without any formal agreement. Unfortunately, such arrangements can lead to difficulties. The partners may disagree and, in the absence of formal rules, misunderstandings may arise. Worse still, if there is a quarrel and they wish to part company there may be disputes over the division of assets. Even when friends agree and have complete trust in one another, one may die and the other may find his partner's heirs much less sympathetic than was his partner. The heirs might, for example, insist on withdrawing their capital at an awkward time and cause acute difficulties for the remaining partner.

To avoid such difficulties, partners are strongly advised to obtain legal advice in drawing up a formal agreement or *deed of partnership*. This normally states

(1) The name and scope of the business.
(2) The amount of capital provided by each partner.
(3) The method of sharing profits.
(4) The terms under which the partnership can be dissolved.

Legally, all partners are equal and equally able to place orders or incur debts on behalf of the partnership. Indeed (apart from one exception mentioned later) each partner is personally responsible to the limit of his resources for the debts of the partnership.

In the absence of any other agreement, profits are assumed to be divided equally. It is, however, possible to make other arrangements.

(1) If one partner contributes more capital than another, each might receive interest on capital before the balance is divided.
(2) If one of the associates is a sleeping partner, the other might be paid a salary as manager before the balance is divided.

It is also worth noting that it is possible to arrange for a partner to have limited liability for the debts of the business. He must, however, be a sleeping partner who takes no part in the management of the farm.

Limited companies

Instead of forming a partnership, some farmers prefer a limited company. A *joint stock company* is the usual form of business organization. It is owned by the shareholders, who elect a Board of Directors to manage the business. Companies are of two kinds, each with its own set of rules: (1) the public company, often large in size, which raises capital from the public and has its shares quoted on the Stock Exchange, and (2) the private company, which raises its capital privately and is often (although not necessarily) smaller in size. Most farming companies are private. The business structure can be quite simple. A father and son or two friends farming as partners can turn themselves into a company—the partners becoming directors and also shareholders. Other members of the family or a manager or a sleeping partner can also be included as directors or shareholders. The profits of the company can be paid as fees to the directors or as a dividend to the shareholders, or can be retained in the business as a reserve, as the directors decide.

A limited company differs in a number of ways from a partnership.

(1) A limited company is a legal entity quite apart from its members. Directors and shareholders may change but the company, unless dissolved, can continue indefinitely.

(2) As its name implies, a limited company has limited liability. This means that if a company becomes bankrupt, the creditors can have the assets of the *company* sold to meet their claims but they have no claim on the personal property of the directors or shareholders. This provision protects the interests of anyone who invests in the company. He may lose his shares but that is all.* Firms dealing with the company must, however, be warned that liability is limited. It is for this reason that the title of the company, displayed on notepaper and elsewhere, always carries the word 'Limited' or 'Ltd'.

(3) A company allows the spreading of ownership without necessarily surrendering control. A farmer can, for example, give shares to his wife or family or to his manager but, if he retains 51 per cent or more of the shares in his own hands, he can retain control.

(4) Unlike a partner, a director cannot incur debts on behalf of the company unless the rules of the company authorize him to do so. If he goes bankrupt, this need not affect the company.

(5) In a private company, the minimum number of directors is one, and of shareholders, two. The maximum number of shareholders is normally 50. A private company could thus consist at a minimum of the farmer (director and shareholder) and one share assigned to his wife or manager.

The following are the principal rules in forming and managing companies.

(1) An agreement is prepared stating that the company will take over the farm business in exchange for shares issued to the farmer and his associates. If he is an owner-occupier, the farmer may prefer to keep the ownership of the holding in his own name and lease the farm to the company. If the farm is tenanted, it will be necessary to obtain the consent of the landlord to the transfer or subletting of the tenancy to the new company.

---

* If the shares are not fully paid up, the shareholder may be required to pay the balance. This is not a common practice in private companies.

(2) A Memorandum of Association is prepared stating

The name of the company, e.g. Smith and Son Ltd, Smith and Jones Ltd, Willowbank Farms Ltd.
A declaration that liability of the members is limited.
The object of the company.
The amount of capital and the shares into which it is divided.

(3) Articles of Association are also prepared. These are the rules for conducting the company and refer to matters such as the holdings of meetings, powers to increase capital or borrow money and the payment of directors.

(4) A private company cannot invite the general public to buy shares. Individuals can, of course, be invited privately to do so.

(5) A company must have an auditor (usually an accountant).

(6) If the directors wish to dissolve a company that is solvent, they can do so. The directors then sell the assets and, after paying debts, can divide the proceeds among the shareholders. If the company is insolvent, a creditor who cannot get payment may get an order from the High Court. The company is then wound up by the Official Receiver and the proceeds are shared out amongst the creditors to pay the debts of the company.

(7) A company pays Corporation Tax on its profits; a partnership does not. (*See also* Chapter 22.) Directors' fees qualify for the earned income allowance, dividends do not.

The cost of forming a company is very variable, depending on its size and complexity. A small private company might cost around a hundred pounds or a little more.

At one time, there were substantial advantages from the point of view of taxation in forming a company. Most of these advantages have disappeared but some remain. Individuals may be paying higher rates of income tax but a company pays only the basic rate on profits that have not been distributed (unless they are excessive). On the other hand, a company with a large enough profit has to pay Corporation Tax whereas individuals and partners do not. A further consideration is that when a company is formed this is a new business and the tax rules for new businesses apply. If profits are below average at that point, the timing of the operation may affect tax liability (*see* Chapter 22). The subject is, however, complex, and as the rules are constantly being altered to deal with cases of tax evasion, a farmer would be well advised to obtain up-to-date advice from his accountant and his lawyer to find whether there would be any advantage, in his particular circumstances, in forming a limited company.

Succession to tenancy

When a tenant farmer dies, a close relative can apply for the tenancy. Under the Agriculture (Miscellaneous Provisions) Act 1976, the applicant must satisfy the following tests.

(1) He must be the child, brother, sister, husband or wife of the deceased. (This normally excludes nephews, nieces, in-laws and grandchildren).

(2) The farm must have provided the principal source of livelihood of the applicant for five of the last seven years. (A widow may find this a bar unless she has taken an active share in running the farm—housework does not count).

(3) The applicant must be 'suitable'. This includes knowledge of farming. (A college or university course in agriculture would be an advantage and up to three years study could be included in the five). The applicant must have the financial resources, health and fitness to manage the farm.

The effect of these provisions is that a son, for example, does not succeed his father automatically—he must be qualified and already working on the farm.

Provision is made for repossession of the land for certain special purposes, e.g. research or when withholding repossession would inflict greater hardship on the landowner than on the applicant.

As two successions are permitted, a landowner who lets a farm might have to wait three generations for its recovery. It is hardly surprising therefore that, if a farm falls vacant, the landowner is likely to farm it himself or sell it because a farm with vacant possession has a higher value than one with a tenant.

As a tenancy can provide an entry to farming for a man with insufficient capital to buy a farm, it is perhaps unfortunate that the supply of farms to let is dwindling. Some change in this legislation is possible.

Part 3 Farm organization and management

13 Improving farm efficiency

When a farmer has completed his accounts for the year, the figure likely to interest him most is the Net Profit, for unless he has an outside source of income, this is the sum on which he must live. The trading account shows the profit or loss but little else. The purpose of the remaining chapters is to show how the farmer can use these records to measure his success in the past and plan improvements for the future.

The first point to note is that the profit is the difference between two large totals. For this reason, a small change in either the output or the inputs can alter the profit quite drastically. In 1976–77 the average farmer in England and Wales obtained £120 output for every £100 spent on inputs—leaving a profit of £20. But this margin is very sensitive to changes in efficiency. A successful farmer obtaining 20 per cent more output for the same inputs would have had a profit of £44 or more than twice the average. The penalty for failure is equally sharp. A farmer obtaining 20 per cent less output per £100 input would have had a loss of £4. A 20 per cent increase in costs could produce nearly as much effect. Indeed a slight fall in output or increase in costs that might go unnoticed for months or even years could have a marked effect on the farmer's income. For this reason analyzing the past can pay large dividends for the time spent on it.

The extent to which profits vary in practice can be illustrated by the results of a survey given in Fig. 13.1. Medium-sized farms, for example, had an average income of £12 234 but nearly a quarter (24 per cent) had incomes below £5000 and nine per cent had losses. At the other end of the scale, nearly a fifth had incomes of £20 000 and one per cent had incomes over £50 000. A similar conclusion can be drawn from the other size groups.

Why are some farms so much less successful than others? The types of farms the adviser is likely to encounter can be classified under the following headings.

(1) The really badly managed farm. The faults in poor yields and unthrifty stock may be so obvious that no records may be necessary to

Per cent	Very small	Small	Medium	Large	Very large
Losses	7	5	9	8	5
Incomes					
0–£4999	61	26	15	10	10
£5000–£9999	26	38	18	16	9
£10 000–£19 999	5	26	39	28	24
£20 000–£49 999	1	5	18	32	41
£50 000–£99 999	—	—	1	6	10
£100 000 and over	—	—	—	—	1
	100	100	100	100	100
Average income	£4 266	£8 213	£12 234	£17 903	£24 154

Fig. 13.1 Range of net income per farm (Farm Incomes in England & Wales, 1976–77. MAFF)

bring them to light. If this is due to ignorance and incompetence there may be little that one can do. In these days of high costs and narrow margins, such a farmer is unlikely to survive long in business unless he has some other source of income.

(2) The reasonably well-managed farm that, because of some fault that may not be obvious, is less successful than one might expect. This is the type that the farm adviser usually has to deal with. An examination of records may be necessary either to find the faults or to confirm an impression of them gained from observation.

(3) The farm that looks impressive with high yields and thriving stock but with excessive costs. This type can deceive the inexperienced adviser. Records can be most useful in detecting excessive costs.

(4) The problem farm. It may be too small. If output is below a minimum of say £5000, then no matter how efficiently the farm is managed, a farmer would have great difficulty in obtaining a living. The farm may have very infertile soil or some intractable problem of drainage or lack of equipment. Even if a solution can be found, the capital costs of implementing it may be quite beyond the farmer's means. Sometimes there is no solution and the best advice may be to leave the farm.

(5) The above-average farmer who wishes to be even more successful. This can be disconcerting to an inexperienced adviser because the farmer may be more knowledgeable about his particular enterprises than the adviser. A comparison with averages—even premium standards—may be a waste of time, except to demonstate that the farm is above average. Replanning with the farmer's own high gross margins

and capital budgeting for expansion may be more to the point than an analysis of past results.

Efficiency factor analysis

If we are examining a farm's past records, we require a series of yardsticks or *efficiency factors*. The method of calculating these can be illustrated by taking the Trading Account of Farm A (Fig. 13.2).

Trading Account for year ended 31 December, 1980

Purchases and expenses	£	£	*Sales and receipts*	£	£
Variable costs			Cattle		4 800
Cattle	2 020		Wheat		6 392
Seeds	935		Barley		6 980
Fertilizer	1 463		Oats		1 200
Sprays	601				19 371
Feeding-stuffs	750				
		5 769			
Fixed or common costs					
Wages	4 144		Closing valuation		
Machinery and power	4 576				
Overheads	1 211		Cattle	1 080	
Rent	3 081		Barley	1 400	
		13 012	Other items	22 685	
		18 781			25 165
					44 536
Opening valuations					
Cattle	1 050				
Barley	1 500				
Other items	22 685				
		25 235			
		44 016			
Net profit		520			
		£44 536			£44 536

Fig. 13.2 Trading account for Farm A

Gross output

The output of a farm for any particular year is the value of production in that year. To estimate output, take the sales for the year and adjust for valuation changes. The reason is that sales for 1980 may include crops grown or livestock reared in 1979. The sales may also omit crops or livestock produced in 1980 but still unsold when the accounts are completed. In the present case, sales of barley were £6980. Of this, £1500 was in store at the beginning (opening valuation) and the remaining £5480 was grown in 1980. Another £1400 worth of the 1980 crop was in store ready for sale at the end of the year. The output was thus £5480 plus £1400 = £6880. Output can thus be calculated as Sales *less* opening valuation *plus* closing valuation or, more briefly

$$\text{Crop output} = \text{Sales} \; {+\text{ increase} \atop -\text{ decrease}} \text{ in valuation.}$$

With livestock, there is the complication that some of them may be purchased. If a farmer buys £1000 worth of cattle and sells them six months later for £1400, his output is £400—the gain in value while on his farm. The £1000 paid for the cattle is part of some other farm's output.

In this case, the livestock output is

		£
Livestock sales		4 800
Opening valuation	1 050	
Closing valuation	1 080	
Add increase		30
		4 830
Less purchases		2 020
Gross livestock output		£2 810

Milk, eggs and miscellaneous items need no adjustment (unless the farmer buys milk and eggs for resale).

The general formula for livestock is thus

$$\text{Gross Output} = \text{Sales} \; {+\text{ increase} \atop -\text{ decrease}} \text{ in valuation, } \textit{less} \text{ purchases of livestock.}$$

On the Input side, costs are grouped for convenience into *variable costs* (*see* gross margins below) and *fixed* or *common costs* (labour, machinery, rent and other overhead costs). The only other adjustment is an allowance for the farmer's *manual* labour (taken as £3000) added to wages. 'Machinery and power' comprises implement depreciation, repairs and fuel (including the electricity). *See* Fig. 13.3.

Net output

Net output is sometimes used instead of gross output

Net Output = Gross Output *less* purchased feeding stuffs, and
        seeds.

The justification for these deductions is that farmers who depend heavily on purchased feeding stuffs may appear to have a higher output per hectare than others who grow more crops for feeding. By deducting purchased foods, both types of farm are put on an equal footing. The same consideration applies to seeds. Net output is tending to give way to gross margin which has wider uses.

Efficiency ratios

The output shows the amount that the farm has produced. But output is economical only if produced at a reasonable cost in resources. The profitability thus depends on the output per unit of input. A good overall measure is *Gross Output per £100 of Inputs*. Another useful measure is *Output (gross or net) per hectare*. When comparing output per hectare with standards, allowance must of course be made for the quality of the land—a hectare of windswept moorland cannot be expected to produce as much as a hectare of fen. The output per hectare can also be increased by pigs and poultry that produce output but use little or no land.

Labour productivity

As wages are one of the largest items of cost, the productivity of labour is of vital importance. It is possible to calculate the output *per man*; but in practice this means translating wages paid to casual workers or women and overtime payments in fractions of 'men'. It is more convenient to calculate *Output per £100 labour*. 'Labour' in this case includes wages and an allowance for the farmer's *manual* labour.

As the farm worker and his implements can be regarded as a unit that does the work of the farm, there is some merit in calculating *Output per £100 labour and machinery*. Another justification for adding these two costs together is that labour and machinery are to an extent substitutes and a farmer who spends more on machines should spend less on labour and vice versa.

So far as the farmer is concerned, the most important measure of success is the profit and it is of interest to compare it with the average of other farms of the same kind. Profits, can however, vary for reasons which have nothing to do with the farmers' efficiency as a manager. One farmer is an owner with no debts, a second is a tenant with a very high rent, while a third is paying interest on a large loan. To make a fair comparison, therefore, the profit must be standardized.

Net farm income

The convention in this country is to express the profit as to a debt-free tenant farmer. Wages are charged for family workers (except the farmer and his wife) but interest charges are omitted. When dealing with an owner-occupier, an estimated rent is charged and expenses that would normally be paid by a landlord are omitted.

The farm income is expected to provide the farmer with

(a) a return on the capital invested;
(b) a wage for his manual labour (if any); and
(c) a reward for management.

It is, of course, possible to split the profit between these headings either by charging interest on capital* or by making a charge for the farmer's labour.

Management and investment income

Management and investment income has been shown in the modified trading account (see Fig. 13.3) by allowing the farmer £3000 for manual labour. On a small farm when the farmer does all the work, the profit per hectare should be greater than on a large farm where all the work is done by paid workers. The effect of charging a wage for the farmer is therefore to put large and small farms on a similar footing.

Return on capital

Return on capital is a useful measure of profitability.

$$\text{Return} = \left[\frac{\text{Management and Investment Income}}{\text{Tenant's Capital}} \right] \times 100.$$

Sometimes farm income is used instead of management and investment income. Tenant's capital in this case is the valuation not net capital.

---

* In the United States, it is usual to charge interest on capital. It is considered that a farmer who has invested heavily should obtain a larger profit than one who has not done so. If interest is charged, they are on an equal footing. This profit measure, called *labour income*, is not much used in this country.

Modified Trading Account

Inputs	£	£	Outputs			£	per ha
Variable costs			Cattle	(20 ha)		2 810	140
Seeds		935	Wheat	(16 ha)		6 391	400
Fertilizer		1 463	Barley	(20 ha)		6 880	344
Sprays		601	Oats	(4 ha)		1 200	300
Feeding-stuffs		750		(60 ha)			
		3 749					
Fixed or common costs			Gross output			17 281	
Wages	4 144						
Farmer's labour	3 000						
Total labour	7 144		Management				
Machinery	4 576		and				
Overheads	1 211		investment				
Rent	3 081		income				
		16 012	Loss			2 480	
Total inputs		£19 761				£19 761	

			This farm £	Local average £
Management and investment income per hectare			−41	115
Gross output per hectare:	$\frac{17\,281}{60}$	=	288	448
Gross output per £100 inputs:	$\frac{17\,281 \times 100}{19\,761}$	=	87	134
Gross output per £100 labour:	$\frac{17\,281 \times 100}{7\,144}$	=	242	774
Gross output per £100 labour and machinery:	$\frac{17\,281 \times 100}{11\,720}$	=	147	281

Gross output		17 281
Less feeding stuffs	750	
Less seeds	935	
	1 685	
Net output		£15 596

Net output per hectare $\frac{15\,596}{60}$ = £260

Return on capital = management and investment income per £100 capital:
Capital (including machinery and tenant right) £25 200

Return $\frac{-2\,480 \times 100}{25\,200}$ = −10 per cent   16 per cent

Fixed or common costs per hectare

	This farm	Local average
Labour	£119	£ 49
Machinery	76	102
Rent	51	56
Overheads	20	23
	£266	£230

Fig. 13.3 Modified trading account for Farm A

This ratio measures the return to all capital employed on the farm whether or not it belongs to the farmer.

Having calculated the efficiency factors, standards of comparison are required.

Interpretation of results

If the profitability of this farm were up to average, the management and investment income would have been £6900 (£115 per hectare) instead of a loss of £2480 (£41 per hectare). What short-comings in management can we detect?

(1) The output per £100 inputs is low, suggesting below average efficiency in production.

(2) The output per £100 labour is low, suggesting that either output is low or labour costs are too high. Both these conclusions appear to be true. Machinery costs are, however, quite modest.

(3) The output per hectare is far too low. Thus, however efficiently it is produced, an adequate profit is not possible.

Why is output too low? The crop outputs per hectare are quite reasonable but one-third of the farm is devoted to cattle with an output of only £140 per hectare. The real fault is that cereals and beef cattle are not a sufficiently intensive system for a comparatively small farm. If the farmer could do all the work himself, he might make a modest living. But if he carries a hired worker he must intensify. He could for example, put some of the grass land in crops if it is ploughable and introduce sugar-beet, potatoes or some other high-value crop. An intensive livestock enterprise is another possibility.

The ratios that we have been using are sometimes called *Efficiency Factors*. The faults in this example were fairly easy to diagnose, and the method proved quite useful in indicating in very general terms the remedies that might be adopted. To decide which of these is likely to be feasible requires the more detailed analysis discussed in the succeeding chapters.

There can be little doubt that efficiency factors, together with a few physical measures such as density of stocking, concentrates per litre and some specialized ratios such as food costs per £100 output calculated separately for pigs, poultry or cattle can help to highlight weaknesses in organization. The emphasis, however, is on tightening-up the efficiency of existing systems, rather than finding a better one.

One drawback of using ratios is that they often have more than one interpretation. If, as on Farm A, output per £100 labour is low, this may mean that labour costs are too high. On the other hand, if the output is very low (due to poor yields, for example) this depresses the output per man through no fault of the workers.

Another drawback of efficiency factors is that they compare the farm with an average. Thus while they are useful in showing how a badly managed farm falls below the average, this is of less use when dealing with above-average and unorthodox farms. It is, however, possible to compile 'premium' standards based on above-average farms. The lessons to be learnt from efficiency factors are also fairly general. A conclusion that 'output is low' does not carry any indication of which output is to be raised or how it is to be done. It does not allow for the fact that under the right conditions a low intensity system might be the most profitable. Nonetheless, in the hands of an experienced adviser who is well aware of their limitations, such tests can be useful.

They have the advantage of being easier to prepare than gross margins if the records give little detail. They were popular in the early 1950s when management advice first came into vogue but have since been largely replaced by gross margins.

Gross margin analysis

Gross margins for farm planning will be described in more detail in the next chapter. They are, however, equally useful for detecting faults in management. Gross margins are calculated by deducting variable costs from the output of each enterprise. For crops, the variable costs are fertilizers, seeds, sprays and dusts.* For livestock they are feeding-stuffs, veterinary expenses, medicines and AI. They are called variable costs because they vary directly with the acreage of crops or number of livestock. This being so, there are advantages in deducting such costs from output per hectare. If for example, the output of barley is £400 and variable costs are £100, then each extra hectare of barley will contribute £400 and incur £100 of such costs. It is thus convenient to deduct the one from the other and say that each hectare of barley contributes £300 gross margin.

There are, in addition, costs for labour, machinery, rent and over-heads. These costs, however, are incurred for the farm as a whole and are therefore named 'common costs'. Once a machine is bought, its depreciation will continue whether or not it is used. Once a regular

---

* In this chapter, casual labour is included with 'labour', to put farms using casual labour (e.g. for harvesting potatoes) on an equal footing with those that use only regular labour. When preparing budgets for an individual farm, however, casual labour is best treated as a variable cost.

worker is employed his wages will continue whether there is work for him to do or not. For this reason, common costs are sometimes called fixed costs. They are not, of course, unchangeable; but unless deliberately altered, they tend to continue. If a plan is changed, therefore, the point is not whether a few man hours are used on a particular crop but whether the labour and machinery can deal with the crops and livestock prescribed.

To take a very simple example, assume that a farmer has 100 hectares, cropped as follows

		£
70 hectares barley @ £300 (gross margin)		21 000
20 hectares potatoes @ £600 (gross margin)		12 000
10 hectares cattle @ £200 (gross margin)		2 000
100 hectares @ £350 (gross margin)		35 000
Less:		
100 hectares common costs @ £250		25 000
Net profit		£10 000

The reason for presenting the results in this form is that it is very much simpler to see the effect on profit of altering or improving the system of farming. Suppose that the farmer by applying £10 of fertilizer can increase the yields of barley by £30. The effect would be to increase the gross margin per hectare by £20. As there are 70 hectares, this would increase the total gross margin by £1400 and as common costs would be unchanged, the profit would also rise by £1400.

Suppose that the farm grew one hectare less barley and one more of potatoes. The effect would be a loss of £300 (barley) and a gain of £600 gross margin (potatoes), i.e. a net gain of £300. It may be asked, will this not change the man hours and tractor hours required? The answer is that if the change is not large, the regular labour force and machinery will remain virtually unaltered. There will be some changes—more fuel required in one month and less in another, more wear and tear of one machine and a little less of another, some change in overtime. But such changes are unimportant and partly self-cancelling if the work is done by regular staff.

If, on the other hand, the change in the farm programme is so large that an extra man is required, the common costs will rise but in one lump when the man is recruited. It is for this reason that common costs are treated separately from other costs.

Our concern now is to use these gross margins to identify weaknesses in farm organization. If farm income is too low, faults can be classified under three headings

(1) the gross margins per hectare or per unit of output may be too low—due to low yields, unthrifty stock, excessive variable costs, such as feeding-stuffs;

(2) the intensity may be too low—not enough high-value crops or types of livestock;

(3) the common costs may be too high—labour, machinery and power, rent or other overheads.

Each fault has different remedies and they are set out in summary form in Fig. 13.4. Such a diagnosis cannot, of course, determine precisely how the remedy is to be applied—that may be a technical matter beyond the scope of this book. But properly applied, the system can indicate the measures likely to solve the problem.

There is another matter that can be brought out clearly with the use of gross margins—the level of intensity at which the farmer should aim. Within limits, high output is associated with high income. What, however, are these limits? There are two ways in which output may be increased

(1) the farmer can increase crop yields, for example, by applying more fertilizer. But as more fertilizer is used, diminishing returns apply and the yield begins to fall off. If £1 fertilizer produces £1·50 of crop, it is worth applying. If the next £1 produces £1·10, it is just worth applying. If the next £1 produces £0·90, then the application has gone beyond the optimum point. It will be noticed that in this case, the output continues to increase as each extra dose of fertilizer is applied whether the application is justified or not. The gross margin (from which fertilizer cost is deducted) reaches a maximum when the optimum dose is applied and then declines. The size of the gross margin is thus quite a good measure of the extent to which the farmer has attained not the maximum yield but the most profitable one. The same consideration applies to feeding-stuffs. It will thus be apparent that a low gross margin can be due *either* to low yields *or* to excessive variable costs, e.g. overfeeding dairy cows.

(2) The second way is to add enterprises with a high gross margin or substitute enterprises with a high gross margin for those with a low one. What is the limit to this process? On well-equipped farms with good soil and ample capital, the limit may be quite high. On poor land or with limited capital resources, the limit may be much lower. But under the right conditions a low-output system can be successful. These conditions are that the land is cheap and that the common costs can be kept to a modest level. The profit will probably be lower per hectare than under

Gross margin	Normal		Fault 1 Low gross margins		Fault 2 Low intensity		Fault 3 High costs	
		£		£		£		£
Barley	70 hectares @ £300	21 000	70 hectares @ £200	14 000	50 hectares @ £300	15 000	70 hectares @ £300	21 000
Potatoes	20 hectares @ £600	12 000	20 hectares @ £500	10 000	10 hectares @ £600	6 000	20 hectares @ £600	12 000
Cattle	10 hectares @ £200	2 000	10 hectares @ £150	1 500	40 hectares @ £200	8 000	10 hectares @ £200	2 000
Total GM	100 hectares @ £350	35 000	100 hectares @ £255	25 500	100 hectares @ £290	29 000	100 hectares @ £350	35 000
Common costs	100 hectares @ £250	25 000	100 hectares @ £250	25 000	100 hectares @ £250	25 000	100 hectares @ £300	30 000
	Profit	£10 000	Profit	£500	Profit	£4 000	Profit	£5 000

These examples are, of course, over-simplified but are intended merely to illustrate the principles involved before passing on to deal with detailed examples. The distinction between these three faults is emphasized because the remedies may be quite different. In practice, a farm may have more than one type of fault and need a combination of remedies.

Fault 1. *Low Gross Margins*
(Improve the present system)

Improve crop yields (fertility and drainage problems, diseases, etc.).
Improve livestock yields (disease, poor stock, poor housing, etc.).
Economize on livestock costs (especially feeding-stuffs, utilization of grass and fodder).

Fault 2. *Low Intensity*
(Plan a more intensive system)

Change to more intensive livestock systems. Add pigs or poultry. Grow more high-value crops.
Contract for new enterprises.

Fault 3. *High Common Costs*
(Economize on labour, machinery, overheads)

Streamline buildings and layout of fields to economize on labour and machinery.
Specialize to ensure full use of expensive equipment.
Keep a check on overhead expenses.

Fig. 13.4 Diagnosis of faults with gross margins – outline scheme

an intensive system; but if the farmer has enough land his *total* profit will be adequate. This can be illustrated by a simple example.

	Large—Extensive 500 ha		Intermediate 200 ha		Small—Intensive 50 ha	
	Hectares	GM	Hectares	GM	Hectares	GM
		£		£		£
Cereals	400 @ £320	128 000	140 @ £350	49 000	30 @ £370	11 100
Roots (or vegetables)			40 @ £600	24 000	20 @ £800	16 000
Cattle	100 @ £150	15 000	20 @ £200	2 000		
Total GM	500 @ £286	143 000	200 @ £375	75 000	50 @ £542	27 100
Common costs	500 @ £200	100 000	200 @ £250	50 000	50 @ £300	15 000
Profit	500 @ £86	£43 000	200 @ £125	£25 000	50 @ £242	£12 100

In this case, the large farm has a gross margin of only £286 a hectare. But with 500 hectares, and a simple system, he can keep common costs down to £200, leaving a profit of £43 000. The small farm by comparison has an intensive system with a gross margin of £542 a hectare, leaving him a profit of £12 100. Indeed, if any given farmer is to secure a reasonable living from a small area, he must have a high output per hectare. If the farm is too poor to produce such an output, the holding is not viable. The medium or large farm could also have an intensive system, provided the land is productive and the farmer has the capital and ability required to conduct a business on this scale. It is worth noting that the total gross margin is a better measure of size of business than hectares. The 500 hectare farm with a total gross margin of £143 000 thus has a business five and a quarter times as large as the 50 hectare farm (£27 100).

Farm B
To illustrate *Gross margin analysis*, we shall take farm B. This is a mixed arable and dairy farm of 190 hectares. The profit is £2123 or £11 per hectare. Other farms of similar type are showing profits of £120 per hectare. Unlike farm A, however, the gross output per hectare (£806) is above average (£756).

(1) The first step is to prepare a modified trading account. This is shown in Fig. 13.5. As an allowance of £2000 has been made for the farmer's manual work, the management and investment income falls to £123.

Variable costs	£	£	Outputs	£	£
Seed	3 760		Dairy cows		38 315
Fertilizer	5 849		Young stock		5 251
Sprays	2 889		Pigs		46 600
Other crop costs	337				90 166
		12 835			
Feeding-stuffs	55 420		Wheat	13 421	
Vet and medicines	1 647		Barley	17 179	
Other livestock costs	2 732		Beans	7 376	
		59 799	Sugar-beet	25 162	
Forage costs		2 747			63 138
		75 381			153 304
Common costs					
Wages	28 624				
Farmer's manual	2 000				
	30 624				
Machinery and power	26 764				
Overheads	10 412				
Rent	10 000				
		77 800			
		153 181			
Management and investment income		123			
		£153 304			£153 304

Fig. 13.5 Modified trading account for Farm B

(2) The second step is to calculate the gross margin from each enterprise. It will be noted that in the trading account, the costs have been segregated into two groups—'Variable costs' and 'Common or fixed costs'. There are three types of livestock—dairy cows, young stock, pigs and four crops—wheat, barley, beans and sugar-beet. To calculate the gross margins, the variable costs must be charged to these enterprises. This is not unduly difficult—it means, for example, charging fertilizer to the crops to which they were applied and feeding-stuffs to the stock that consumed them. Home grown crops fed to livestock (e.g. barley fed to pigs) are credited to crop output and also charged to the livestock consuming them. The dairy herd could be treated as a single unit but in this case it was considered more interesting to separate the young stock. This meant crediting the young stock with the value (£300 per head) of 16 heifers transferred and charging the value to the dairy cows.

Hectares	Crop	Output	Seed	Fertilizer	Sprays	Other costs	Total VC	Gross margin
		£	£	£	£	£	£	£
30	Wheat	13 421	958	890	789	—	2 637	10 784
53	Barley	17 179	1 643	1 408	263	—	3 314	13 865
15	Beans	7 376	491	16	272	30	809	6 567
30	Sugar-beet	25 162	668	3 535	1 565	307	6 075	19 087
128	Total	63 138	3 760	5 849	2 889	337	12 835	50 303

Fig. 13.6 Allocation of crop variable costs

Average numbers	Stock	Output	Feeding-stuffs	Vet & medicines	Other costs	Total VC	Gross margins
		£	£	£	£	£	£
70	Dairy cows	38 315	18 621	473	2 026	21 120	17 195
60	Young stock	5 251	1 721	157	143	2 021	3 230
—	Pigs	46 600	35 078	1 017	563	36 658	9 942
	Total	90 166	55 420	1 647	2 732	59 799	30 367

Fig. 13.7 Allocation of livestock variable costs

Crop	Output	Seed	Fertilizer	Sprays	Other costs	Total VC	Gross margin
	£	£	£	£	£	£	£
Wheat	447 (499)	32 (30)	30 (41)	26 (36)	— —	88 (107)	359 (392)
Barley	324 (366)	31 (25)	27 (32)	5 (19)	— (1)	63 (77)	261 (289)
Beans	492 (593)	33 (39)	1 (1)	18 (26)	2 (1)	54 (67)	438 (526)
Sugar-beet	838 (783)	22 (23)	118 (100)	52 (54)	10 (72)	202 (249)	636 (534)

Fig. 13.8 Crop variable costs per hectare (Local averages in brackets)

Stock	Output	Feeding-stuffs	Vet & medicines	Other costs	Total VC	Gross margin
	£	£	£	£	£	£
Dairy cows	547 (601)	266 (247)	7 (8)	29 (41)	302 (296)	245 (305)
Young stock	88 (104)	29 (33)	3 (2)	2 (5)	34 (40)	54 (64)
Pigs	*100 (100)	76 (66)	2 (1)	1 (2)	79 (69)	21 (31)

* Per £100 output of pigs.

Fig. 13.9 Livestock variable costs per head (local averages in brackets)

The crop output and costs per hectare are given in Fig. 13.8 together with averages for the same type of farm. The gross margins per hectare for wheat, barley and beans are all below average. This is mainly due to low yields.

	Tonnes per Hectare	
	This farm	Local average
Wheat	4·9	5·5
Barley	3·8	4·3
Beans	3·5	4·2
Sugar-beet	36·3	33·9

It is not due to low prices or excessive use of inputs. On the contrary, expenditure on fertilizer and sprays is below average. This may indeed help to account for the low yields. Sugar-beet is the exception with a Gross Margin (£636) well above average.

Turning to livestock (Fig. 13.9) the gross margin per cow is below average—due partly to a low output per cow (£547—average £601). The milk yield per cow is 4500 *l.*; which is somewhat below the average of about 5000 l. In spite of this, food consumption per cow (£266) is above average (£247).

The stocking rate of the grazing livestock to be expected can be calculated from averages

70 cows @ 0·6 ha per head	42	
60 young stock = 20 units		
(*see* Chapter 18) @ 0·8 ha	16	
	58	hectares

In fact the stock are using 62 hectares. The forage hectares are thus quite well stocked.

So far, the GM per head makes no allowance for the cost of maintaining pasture and other forage crops. This can now be taken into account

	GM
Dairy cows	17 195
Young stock	3 230
Total grazing stock	20 425
Less Forage costs	2 747
Total GM (after allowing for forage)	£17 678
Per hectare (62 hectares)	£285

The Gross Margin from grazing livestock is thus £285 which can be compared with $\dfrac{50\,303}{128} = £393$ per hectare from the cash crops. Cash crops are thus giving a higher return than the dairy herd.

The pig enterprise appears to be unsatisfactory. We could compare the results *per sow* or *per fat pig* with the average of other herds but as some herds sell small porkers, and others large fat pigs, it may be difficult to make fair comparisons of costs and returns. A simple solution is to calculate costs and gross margins per £100 of pigs produced. In this case, the costs per £100 output are £79 compared with an average of £69. This is entirely due to high food costs (£76, average £66). Another obvious fault is that the number of fat pigs sold per sow (13) should be about 16.

Turning to the fixed or common costs, these can be compared per hectare to farms of similar type.

Cost per hectare	This farm	Local average
	£	£
Labour	161	109
Machinery and power	141	118
Overheads	55	34
Rent	52	62
	£409	£323

Common costs are thus £86 above average. Most of this is due to labour and machinery. The farmer employs six men; three field workers, one cowman, one pigman and an assistant stockman. With more convenient piggeries and an efficient milking parlour, one cowman should easily be able to deal with the 70 cows and one pigman with the 64 sows. Methods of assessing crop work requirements will be dealt with later but with a good field lay-out and choice of crops, it should be possible to reduce the staff by two men, especially if the farmer himself works at the busy seasons.

Conclusions

The following conclusions can be drawn from this analysis.

(1) The land is used for two enterprises—dairy cows and cash crops. At the moment, the return is better for cash crops. If the balance tips more strongly towards one or the other, the farmer might consider specializing in one of them.

(2) Cash crops are reasonably satisfactory, but it should be possible to improve cereal yields—even if this means more expenditure on fertilizers and sprays.

(3) Food costs are too high and milk yields are too low. Low-yielding cows should be weeded out. The rationing system requires attention.

Efforts should be made to obtain more of the return from pasture and forage crops.

(4) A proper set of records for the pig herd on the lines set out later in this chapter would be well worthwhile. A better system of food rationing is required. Unproductive sows should be eliminated.

(5) The labour force is too large. Too much is being spent on machinery.

If it were possible to raise the standards of efficiency to a reasonable level, the effect would be as follows

	£
GM wheat £359 to £392 = 33 × 30 ha	990
GM barley £261 to £289 = 28 × 53 ha	1 484
GM per cow £245 to £305 = 60 × 70 cows	4 200
GM per £100 pigs £21 to £31 = 10 × 466	4 660
Two men less	9 500
Estimated increase in profit	£20 834
Existing profit	123
	£20 957

The profit would be £110 per hectare. The average arable and mixed livestock farm from which these averages are derived had a profit of £120 per hectare in the year concerned. The ten most profitable averaged £167 per hectare.

The farmer has not, of course, solved his problems at this stage—the analysis has, however, pinpointed the chief weaknesses. It is obvious from the table above that high labour costs are by far the most important, followed in order by the pig and dairy herds. The improvement of cereal yields would be worthwhile, but it is of far less importance than livestock feeding. The correction of these faults will take time and may require technical advice. In the meantime, the farmer has an objective and a clear list of priorities.

Enterprise management studies

So far, we have been dealing with the farm as a whole and, although gross margins give an insight into the profitability of individual crops and types of livestock, it is often worth going beyond this point to measure the efficiency of one enterprise in some detail. This applies particularly to a major enterprise on which the farmer's income largely depends. Some types of livestock indeed lend themselves to such treatment. This is particularly true of pigs, broilers and laying hens. If such units are large, they have their own specialist labour, equipment and buildings and it is comparatively easy to cost them and show a realistic profit. Such livestock are usually kept under conditions where the farmer can control temperature, heating, lighting and food supplies. It is thus possible to devise very precise efficiency standards.

Some enterprises—such as broilers—have largely left the general farm and are managed on factory lines. With strong competition, managers must keep a very careful check on performance. Quite a small variation in efficiency—as little as 0·1 in the food conversion rate—can be of vital importance in the level of profit obtained.

Costing records can also be prepared for dairy herds (e.g. the scheme operated by the Milk Marketing Board) and for beef cattle. With grass-eating livestock however, the standards are not so precise and costs can vary quite legitimately according to system. For this reason, they need care in interpretation.

Crop costings are on the whole rather less useful as an aid to management. Nonetheless, a farmer with a large fruit or vegetable enterprise with its own staff, packing sheds, etc. on a general farm might well find a departmental account worthwhile.

One example of an enterprise account will be given in this chapter—a pig herd. It is particularly suitable for such analysis and (unlike broilers) it is still a farm enterprise.

Efficiency in pig production

Farm E

A farmer has a herd of 100 sows and sells the progeny as bacon pigs. As a substantial amount of capital is invested in this enterprise it is well worth keeping a check on results. The trading account for the pig herd is given overleaf. It takes the familiar form—opening valuation and expenses on the left, sales and closing valuation on the right. It is convenient to split this account into two stages in order to obtain the gross output of pigs as a separate item to set against the main items of cost.

Having prepared the account in this form, the second stage can be used to calculate costs of labour, foods and other items per £100 of output,* e.g.

$$\text{Cost of foods per £100 output} = \frac{\text{Cost of foods}}{\text{Gross output}} \times 100$$

---

* Costs per £100 output is a convenient unit. 'Costs per pig' would be feasible if the farmer always sold pigs of the same size. In practice, a farmer selling bacon pigs might be tempted to sell a few weaners or porkers if the market were favourable and he will certainly sell cull sows and boars. 'Per £100 output' has the advantage that it can be applied to any pig herd.

Trading Account for pig herd
Stage 1

Purchases	£	£	Sales	£	£
3 boars		577	3 boars		240
34 sows and gilts		2 550	27 sows and gilts		1 781
		3 127	1 507 bacon pigs		90 420
			3 casualties		71
					92 512
Opening valuation					
5 boars	600				
103 sows and gilts	7 210		*Closing valuation*		
228 suckling pigs	2 307		4 boars	550	
667 feeding stock	18 342		107 sows	7 490	
		28 459	292 suckling pigs	3 345	
1 876 pigs born alive			614 feeding stock	19 705	
					31 090
Livestock output			*Deaths*		
Carried down		92 016	316 before 8 weeks		
			39 after 8 weeks		
			4 boars and sows		
2 916		£123 602	2 916		£123 602

Stage 2

	£		£
Feeding stuffs		*Livestock output*	
(655 tonnes)	70 625	Brought down	92 016
Labour	9 941		
Share of overheads,			
machines, electricity,			
repairs, water, etc.	8 600		
	89 166		
Profit	2 850		
	£92 016		£92 016

The results are as follows and compared with averages

	This farm	Average farm
Costs per £100 output	£	£
Food	76·8	71·8
Labour	10·8	8·9
Other costs	9·3	10·6
	96·9	91·3
Profit	3·1	8·7
	£100·0	£100·0

This herd shows a profit of £3·1 per £100 output—less than half the average obtained by other herds (£8·7).

The costs in this herd are, however, above average. This may mean *either* that the costs are excessive *or* that the output is below average. This can be ascertained by calculating a series of efficiency factors. For this purpose, it is necessary to split the herd into two sections

Breeding herd—sows, boars, gilts, unweaned pigs
Feeding herd—fattening pigs after weaning

Breeding herd

The purpose of a breeding herd is to produce weaned pigs at minimum cost. Most of the costs are for feeding sows and a large part of this is the upkeep of the sow itself. Indeed a sow (and litters) producing 18 weaners a year does not use much more food than one producing 14 weaners. For this reason, the more weaners produced per sow, the lower the cost per weaner.

The number of weaners depends on two factors: the number of pigs weaned per litter and the number of litters per year. The number weaned per litter depends in turn on the number born per litter and the number that die before weaning. The number of litters per year should be two or more. Early weaning (e.g. at three to six weeks) can help to increase this.

Fattening herd

The success of the fattening herd depends on turning out the maximum value of pigs for the lowest cost of food. This in turn depends on

(a) the food conversion rate, i.e. kg food per 1 kg liveweight gain;
(b) the cost of food per tonne;
(c) the price received for pigs sold.

Results for this farm are as follows

Breeding herd	This farm	Average all herds
Litters per sow	1·77	2·0
Pigs born per litter	10·6	10·6
Pigs weaned per litter	8·8	8·8
Pigs weaned per sow per year	15·6	17·6
Food cost per weaner	£9·9	£9·06
Weight at weaning	18 kg	18 kg
Cost of food per tonne	£108	£109

Feeding herd		Bacon herds
Weight of bacon pigs sold (kg)	68	68
Mortality	2·5%	2·5%
Cost of meal per tonne	£106	£106
Food conversion rate	3·8	3·4
Price per kg deadweight (bacon)	76p	76p

The faults in this herd are now obvious. In the breeding herd, the food cost per weaner is high—due to too few pigs per sow (15·6 compared with an average of 17·6) and this in turn is due to too few litters per sow (1·77 compared with 2·0). This is probably due to a fault in management in failing to have the sows served at the proper time. The farmer already uses six weeks weaning which increases the number of litters per sow. Other factors such as litter size, cost of food and size of weaners are satisfactory.

In the feeding herd, the fault lies in the food conversion rate (3·8 compared to an average 3·4). It will now be necessary to investigate the cause which is likely to be one of the following

(a) poor insulation and uncomfortable housing;

(b) a slow-growing strain of pigs (check growth rate of litters from individual sows);

(c) some sub-acute infection (mortality, however, is not high).

If the litters per sow per year were increased from 1·77 to 2·0 and the conversion rate reduced from 3·8 to 3·4, the profit would be increased from £2850 to £9900. Many 'above average' pig herds would show a profit of £14 000 to £16 000 from a herd of this size in the same year.*

There is another point worth attention. The labour cost per £100 output is nearly £2 above average. One pigman should be able to tend about 70 sows. A unit of 100 sows may be too large for one man but hardly justifies two men. If buildings can be provided, the farmer might consider expanding the unit to employ two men or, if one man is likely to leave, contracting it if one man cannot manage.

With a system of records, a farmer can delegate a fair amount of responsibility to a good pigman knowing he can still keep a tight control on levels of efficiency. With a large unit, it would be wise to check the more important factors at least once every six months.

* The profits from pigs have fluctuated widely in recent years. The 'above average' farmer can, however, usually show a modest profit even when the average farmer sustains a loss. The author is indebted to Mr R F Ridgeon for the data on pig herds.

Questions

1. Calculate efficiency factors for Manor Farm for the first three years of operation. Comment on the performance and make suggestions on how it might be improved in future years.

2.
Modified Trading Account

Inputs	£	Outputs	£
Seeds	3 249	34 ha winter wheat 153T	15 304
Fertilizers	4 140	11 ha winter barley 44T	4 410
Sprays	2 792	22 ha spring barley 85T	8 589
Feeding-stuffs	526	12 ha beans 30T	3 595
Labour	6 200	12 ha oil seed rape 28T	5 568
Depreciation	8 490	3 ha potatoes 88T	4 400
Repairs	2 025	8 ha beef cattle	1 160
Fuel	2 984	102 ha	
Other overheads	4 200		
Rent	8 160		
	42 766		
Farm income	260		
	£43 026		£43 026

You are an agricultural adviser. This farmer has asked your advice on improving his farming system. At your request the accountant has prepared a modified trading account. The farmer has given you an estimate of the crops to which the seed fertilizer and sprays were applied, as follows

Seeds—wheat £1004, w. barley £260, s. barley £520, beans £365, rape £190, potatoes £910.
Fertilizers—wheat £1400, w. barley £420, s. barley £790, rape £760, potatoes £510, beans £180, cattle £80.
Sprays—wheat £1170, w. barley £325, s. barley £450, beans £145, rape £445, potatoes £257.
Cattle—10 store cattle fattened.

Calculate yields, gross margins and costs per hectare and any other factors you consider to be relevant. The following are local averages.

	GM per hectare	Seeds	Fertilizers	Sprays	Tonnes per hectare
Winter wheat	£435	£30	£50	£55	5·7
Winter barley	£382	£25	£44	£39	4·9
Spring barley	£329	£26	£35	£20	4·1
Winter beans	£278	£33	£15	£22	2·9
Oil seed rape	£311	£19	£80	£30	2·3
Potatoes	£1030	£240	£170	£90	30
Cattle	£150	—	£30	—	—

Labour	£71 per ha
Machinery and power	£150 per ha
Rent	£65 per ha
Overheads	£41 per ha
Farm income	£70 per ha

You are about to visit the farm. In the meantime, write a preliminary report on the present organization of the farm and prepare a list of questions you will ask to confirm your opinions. Make a list of improvements that you will suggest to the farmer.

14 Introduction to budgeting

The aim of this chapter is to plan for the future. As can be seen from the previous chapter, there are two distinct ways in which a farm can be improved. In the first place, it may be possible to farm better without changing the existing farm plan. The farmer may grow heavier crop yields, feed a better dairy ration or breed a pig with a better bacon carcase. Improvements of this kind can have a marked effect on profit and should never be neglected. There are occasions however when the farm plan itself must be altered. The farmer may be producing beef cattle when dairy cows would give a better return. He may be growing oats when it would pay to grow barley and buy any oats required. Quite apart from remedying faults there are many other occasions when a budget may be useful. A farmer might be offered a contract to produce some new crop (e.g. peas for quick freezing) and wonder whether he should accept it. A new machine (e.g. a self propelled spraying machine) might come on the market and the farmer wonder whether he should buy one. Eggs might fall in price and the farmer wonder whether he should change to pig production. Quite apart from its effect on profits, a change in the farm plan may entail heavy capital expenditure. Thus before embarking on it, the farmer may need an estimate of the amount so that he can decide whether the results are worth the cost and if so where the funds required are to be found.

Even when the farmer has evolved what he regards as a good system, he should not expect it to maintain him for the rest of his farming career. Changes in methods and prices are continually occurring and the farmer must always be prepared to take advantage of them. It is thus obvious that a farm plan well suited to conditions at one time may be quite out of date ten years later. This does not mean that the farmer should neglect the rules of good husbandry. But within the bounds of good farming there is still a wide choice of methods and the onus is on the farmer to find the one that gives him the best return.

At first sight, it may seem difficult to forecast changes in receipts and expenses that will occur if the farm programme is altered. Fortunately, a method has recently been devised that greatly simplifies this task. This depends on dividing all costs into two groups—*fixed costs* and *variable costs*.

Variable costs

In this category we include items such as seed, fertilizers, sprays, feeding stuffs, veterinary expenses, casual labour, transport (e.g. for cattle or sugar-beet) and stores (detergents, twine, etc.). These are all costs that vary directly with the area of crops grown and the numbers of livestock. If one hectare of wheat needs 300 kg fertilizer, two hectares need 600 kg and 10 hectares need 3000 kg. If 300 kg of meal fattens five pigs then 600 kg should fatten ten pigs. Once the farmer has decided on his system of management, these expenses are inevitable and are fairly easy to estimate beforehand.

Fixed or common costs

This category includes regular labour, machinery costs, rent and other overhead expenses such as insurance and telephone. These costs are usually incurred for the farm as a whole and not for any special enterprise. They are thus 'fixed' costs in the sense that they do not vary directly according to the crops and livestock kept. They are also 'fixed' in the sense that once incurred, they tend to run on whether proper use is made of them or not. Once the farmer has bought a combine harvester, it continues to depreciate at nearly the same rate whether he uses it to cut 100 or 200 hectares of corn. Once the farmer has employed a cowman, he must pay his wage every week whether he tends 50 or 100 cows. The same consideration applies to the rent and the other overhead expenses.

There is another point. Many fixed items can be bought only in large units. Regular workers can be hired only one at a time. If there is work for one and a half men the farmer may have no alternative but to employ two men. In such a case, the farmer could budget for an increase in crops or livestock (up to a full-time occupation for two men) without any extra wage costs. But if the programme were further expanded, the wage bill would jump (from say £10 000 to £15 000) when a third worker was recruited. The same consideration applies to tractors and large implements, like a combine harvester or a baler.

This distinction between fixed and variable costs is a very important one and is fundamental to all budgeting. At first sight it may seem rather theoretical but it has a very practical use. A variable cost item such as fertilizer can be measured out and used in the exact quantities required and if there is any left over it can be put back into store. Fixed costs (e.g. regular wages) are a steady stream and tend to run on whether they are used or not.

It will be seen, therefore, that if the farm plan is changed, the variable costs will change in a way that can be budgeted. The fixed or overhead costs on the other hand may hardly change at all—especially if the alteration to the farm programme is not a very extensive one. For example, if the farmer grows an extra five hectares of barley the extra receipts might be £2000 and the variable costs for seed, fertilizer, etc., £500. How about the fixed costs? The barley might need an extra 50 man hours and 40 tractor hours. Should these be charged in the budget? If the farm staff can find the time to cultivate and harvest the extra barley the answer is no, because the farmer has incurred no extra cost.* The net gain from growing five extra hectares of barley is thus £2000 less £500 = £1500 or £300 per hectare. This difference is called the *gross margin* and is defined as: Output less Variable Costs = Gross Margin.

This gross margin is not of course pure profit. Taking the farm as a whole, about two-thirds of the gross margin is likely to be swallowed up by fixed costs. None the less, the gross margin represents the contribution made by a farm enterprise to these overhead costs. It also shows the gain or loss that can be expected if the enterprise is increased or reduced in size. The gross margin allows only for variable costs and there are occasions (especially if a large change is made to the farm plan) when the fixed costs do alter. But these are best considered for the farm as a whole and will be dealt with at a later stage.

Calculations of gross margins

1. *Cash Crops*   Cash crops are comparatively simple.

Wheat (10 hectares)

		£
Output: 5 tonnes		6000
Less variable costs		
Seed	£400	
Fertilizer	600	
Sprays, etc.	600	
		1600
Gross margin		£4400

Gross margin per hectare £440

---

*If overtime or an extra bonus were paid to grow this barley, this would of course be a variable cost and would be charged in the budget.

Potatoes (10 *hectares*)

		£
Output: 300 tonnes		17 000
Less variable costs		
Seed	£2600	
Fertilizer	2000	
Sprays, etc.	2400	
Casual labour (lifting)	2000	
		9000
Gross margin		£8000

Gross margin per hectare £800

If the farmer had enough regular staff to lift the potatoes without hiring casual labour the gross margin would have been £1000 per hectare.

It is usual to treat grain crops (and indeed any other crop with a recognizable market value) as a cash crop. If barley, for example, is fed to pigs its market value should be inserted as the output when calculating the gross margin for barley and as a food cost when calculating the gross margin for pigs. By giving the barley a gross margin on its own, the farmer can compare barley as a crop with other cash crops on the farm. By charging the pigs with the full market value, he can judge whether it is profitable to market his barley through pigs instead of selling it as grain.

2. Livestock

Poultry flock (1000 *laying birds*)

		£
Eggs sold		9000
Culls		250
Total sales		9250
Less replacements		2200
Poultry output		7050
Less variable costs		
Foods	£6100	
Medicines, etc.	350	
		6450
Gross margin		£600

The gross margin is thus £600 for 1000 birds or 60p per bird. The gross margin for pigs is calculated in a similar way. As neither of these enterprises occupies much space, the return per hectare is irrelevant. A better test is the gross margin as a percentage of output. In this case

$$\frac{600 \times 100}{7050} = 8.5 \text{ per cent}$$

Dairy cows, beef cattle and sheep differ from these enterprises in using substantial areas of pasture and fodder crops, such as kale, silage or hay.* These crops usually have no recognized market value and it is convenient to regard them as part of the livestock enterprise. For this reason, their variable costs for seed, fertilizers, etc., are included in the livestock account.

Beef herd (40 *cattle*)
18 month's beef from purchased calves

		£
Sales 40 fat cattle @ £450		18 000
Purchased calves 43 @ £110		4 730
Output		13 270
Variable costs		
Feeding stuffs	6500	
Other costs	870	
		7 370
Gross margin (before charging forage costs)		5 900
Forage costs (fertilizer, seed, etc.)		1 600
Gross margin (after charging forage costs)		4 300

The gross margin is thus £4300 or £107 per head. If the cattle require 16 hectares of forage crops, the GM per hectare is £269. This return can be compared with other cattle enterprises that might have been kept on the land, e.g. beef cows selling suckled calves at about £150 per hectare or fattening strong store cattle at, £120 say, per hectare. The GM per hectare of forage crops is not of course the only criterion in choosing an enterprise. A farmer short of labour whose main concern is cash crops might prefer a beef enterprise that provided a reasonable return from permanent pasture with very little supervision.

The GM (before deducting forage costs) is sometimes useful. It provides a form of comparison if more than one class of stock share grazing and forage costs are not easily allocated. It may also be useful in budgeting for changes of grazing stock if the forage costs are not likely to change.

---

*If hay is grown deliberately for sale, it should be treated as a cash crop. Otherwise, it should be treated as a fodder crop even if an occasional tonne of surplus hay is sold.

Budgeting

Having dealt with gross margins, it is now possible to prepare farm budgets. The purpose of a budget is to estimate the effect of some change in the farm programme (such as a change in cropping) or a change in the circumstances of the farm (such as a change in prices). If the change is an extensive one, a complete budget for the farm as a whole will be required. If the change is a simple one, a partial budget will suffice. The latter will be considered first. If a farmer is planning a change, he really has two questions to answer. First, is the change likely to increase the farm profit? Second, if the change is worth while, how much capital will be required to carry it out? These two problems should be considered quite separately and care should be taken not to include 'once and for all' capital costs in the profit budget. The example that follows will make this distinction clear.

Partial budgeting

There are many problems that can be set out in the form of a partial budget. On the whole, two situations are likely to be encountered.

(1) INTRODUCTION OR EXPANSION OF A SUPPLEMENTARY ENTERPRISE. Some enterprises such as pigs or poultry can be introduced without displacing any other. In this case, the form of the budget is as follows

Losses	*Gains*
Increase in fixed costs	Gross margin from the new
Difference (if any) is the	enterprise.
estimated *increase in profit*.	

As an example, let us assume that a farmer intends to keep a herd of 20 sows, selling porkers at 48 kg dead weight. The sows should produce 360 weaners of which seven are retained as gilts; seven fattening and one breeding pig die during the year. Housing includes a new fattening house and accommodation for the sows and boar. The farmer's son will look after the pigs. The gross margin is as follows

	£
Sales—346 porkers at £40	13 840
6 cull sows at £60	360
	14 200
Less purchases—boar £240, sold for £40 after two years, cost per year	100
Pig output	14 100

Less variable costs

Food: 20 sows at 1·3 T = 26 T at £120		£ 3 120	
Boar 1 tonne		120	
Creep food: 390 young pigs at 13 kg = 5 T @ £190		950	
Feeders: 360 at 150 kg* = 54 T @ £128		6 912	
		11 102	
Other costs		600	11 702
Gross margin			£2 398

The estimated gross margin is thus £2398—approximately £120 per sow or £6·93 per porker produced. For all practical purposes, this is the gain per sow or per fat pig that the farmer can expect whatever the number kept—assuming that he can provide the housing and attention required. Having decided on the number to be kept, a budget can be prepared as follows

Losses	£	Gains	£
Increase in fixed costs		Gross margin of new enterprise	2398
Fattening house			
(90 pigs at £45)	4050		
Farrowing pens			
(6 at £400)	2400		
Boar pen	400		
Sow huts, trolley,			
weighing machine, etc.	1000		
	7850		
Charge 10 per cent a			
year for repairs and			
replacement	785		
Increase in profit	1613		
	£2398		£2398

It thus appears that if the estimates are reasonable, an increase in profit of about £1600 a year can be expected. Having prepared such a budget, the farmer can use it to estimate the risks that he might face if he introduced the pig herd. If pig prices fell by five per cent without a fall in meal prices, the profit would be reduced by $14\,100 \times 5/100 = £705$. If home-grown barley reduced the cost of the ration by 10 per cent profits would be raised by £1110 a year.

It should be noted that this budget shows the position say in two years' time *after* the pig herd has been established. The cost of erecting

*Assume that pigs are weaned at 17 kg and sold at 67 kg live weight: 50 kg gain at a conversion rate of 3·0 is 150 kg.

the buildings or of buying the gilts is not included because these are 'once and for all' capital items. On the other hand, replacements for breeding-stock and equipment have been provided and for this reason the estimated profit can be maintained indefinitely provided that conditions remain as expected.

Capital budget

A capital budget is intended to show the amount of money that must be spent before the new enterprise is self-supporting. In this case, the farmer would probably buy the gilts two or three at a time spread over the first six months. This will make better use of the farrowing pens and will need less capital than if the gilts were all purchased at the same time. If the gilts farrow a month after purchase, the first sales will occur about six or seven months after the herd has been started and after this point the herd should be self-supporting. The costs for the first six months will thus be as follows

	£
	£
Housing and equipment	7 850
Stock: 20 gilts at £90, 1 boar at £240	2 040
Working capital; food, etc., for half year	5 851
Total capital	£15 741

In fact, the allowance for food and other costs is slightly generous because the numbers of pigs are being built up during the first six months. On the other hand, a small margin of safety is desirable in case the first litters prove disappointing and the farmer has to wait longer for his first receipts than he expects.

It will be seen in this case that the investment is £15 741 or £787 per sow—a much larger sum than many farmers would expect. The return on this capital is:

$$\frac{1613 \times 100}{15\,741} = 10 \cdot 2 \text{ per cent.}$$

This return is not very high and the farmer in this case might consider whether some better system (e.g. by using home-mixed meals) could be devised before starting this new enterprise.

It will be noticed that the return from this enterprise depends on the fact that the farmer has a son with the time to tend 20 sows. If a pigman were recruited, it would be necessary to keep 70 or 80 sows to pay this addition to fixed costs. In this case, the farmer might conclude that he should choose a part-time unit of 20 sows or a full-time unit of 80 sows—any number between would be less economic.

(2) SUBSTITUTION OF ONE ENTERPRISE BY ANOTHER. When dealing with cash crops or with cattle or sheep that require land for fodder crops then the expansion of one enterprise usually means the sacrifice of another. The form of budget is as follows

Losses	Gains
Gross margin from enterprise displaced.	Gross margin from the new enterprise.
Increase in fixed costs. Balance (if any) = increase in profit.	Decrease in fixed costs.

If the farmer already has the labour and equipment to deal with the change, there will be no change in fixed costs and the budget is a simple one. For example, a farmer intends to grow ten hectares of barley at the expense of oats. He has grown both crops before and estimates their gross margins

Losses	£	Gains	£
Gross margin from oats, 10 hectares @ £250	2500	Gross margin from barley, 10 hectares @ £310	3100
Increase in profit	600		
	£3100		£3100

In this case, the same equipment will do for either crop.

However, if the farmer must buy extra equipment, this is an addition to fixed costs. Assume that a farmer intends to grow ten hectares of potatoes (for the first time) at the expense of barley. He must buy a potato harvester and hire casual labour to lift the potatoes. The regular staff can deal with the planting and riddling.

Losses	£	Gains	£
Gross margin from barley, 10 hectares @ £310	3100	Gross output from potatoes, 30 tonnes @ £50	1500
Increase in fixed costs, Harvester (£8000) charge 15% for repairs and depreciation	1200	Less variable costs: seed, fertilizer, casual labour, etc.	800
	4300	Gross margin per hectare	£700
Increase in profit	2700	Total GM 10 hectares at £700	7000
	£7000		£7000

In this case, the estimates for the gross margin for potatoes have been given in full because they are based on yields obtained on neighbouring farms. The margin from barley, however, is based on his own records from previous years. It appears, therefore, that if the estimates are correct and the farm staff can deal with the work on the potatoes, a change from barley to potatoes would increase profits by £2700 or £270 per hectare.

A break-even budget

A break-even budget is a form of budget used when the farmer is uncertain about one item in the budget and wishes to assess the risks involved. Suppose that the farmer in the previous example is rather uncertain about the receipts that he can expect from potatoes, which appear to be more profitable but are also more risky than barley. The risk can be assessed by setting out a break-even budget. This entails a calculation of the return necessary to balance both sides of the budget. At this point there would be neither a profit nor a loss from changing from one crop to the other. In our example, losses on the left-hand side amount to £4300. Thus if the potatoes had a gross margin of £4300 (or £430 per hectare) the account would balance and both crops would be equally profitable.

But if the gross margin is £430 per hectare and the variable costs are £800, the corresponding output must be £1230 per hectare. This figure of £1230 per hectare is the 'break-even' point. If the output of potatoes is more than £1230, a change to potatoes would be profitable. If the yield is 30 tonnes, then any price above £41 a tonne will show a profit. If the price is £50 a tonne, then any yield above 25 tonnes would pay. With this information, the farmer can decide whether the odds in favour of making a profit are sufficiently attractive to justify the risk.

Capital requirements

When one enterprise replaces another the capital saved from the enterprise given up may partly finance the new one. This is especially true of crop changes. The change from oats to barley shown above is unlikely to entail extra capital because the requirements for both crops are nearly the same. A change from barley to potatoes would require some extra capital as follows

	£
Seed, fertilizer, etc., for potatoes 10 hectares at £800	8 000
Less seed, fertilizer, etc., for barley 10 hectares at £100	1 000
Extra working capital (for variable costs)	7 000
Extra fixed capital (harvester)	8 000
	£15 000

The extra capital is thus £1500 per hectare. This is a large sum but the extra revenue (£270) gives a return of 18 per cent on the sum invested—an adequate reward for the trouble and risk entailed. This is a change to a more intensive crop. A change to a less intensive one might entail a withdrawal of capital.

A change from one type of livestock to another can be calculated on similar lines to those shown for the pig herd, the working capital for the enterprise being set against the amount withdrawn from the old one. The cost of buildings and equipment for the new enterprise may be a heavy item, however, whereas equipment from the old enterprise may have very little salvage value to set against it.

15 Introduction to farm planning

In this chapter we shall consider methods of planning the whole farm. Gross margins have already been described (Chapter 14) and used to prepare partial budgets for minor changes in the farm programme. Now they will be used to prepare complete budgets for major changes. Before dealing with the details, however, it is necessary to look first at the way in which a farm is organized and financed. It will be seen that gross margins and fixed costs can give a new insight into the way that a farm functions. Not only can they assist the farmer to frame a budget when he has decided on a plan but they can help him to choose the plans most likely to be profitable.

Basically, the farm organization can be divided into three parts as shown in Fig. 15.1. First, there is the farm land occupied either by cash crops or by fodder crops (pasture, kale, silage, etc.) supporting cattle or sheep. As the farmer has only a limited number of hectares, these enterprises have to compete for use of the land and the more hectares given to one the less there is for the others. So far as land is concerned, therefore, these are *competitive* enterprises.

Second, there are enterprises, such as pigs and poultry, which usually occupy very little land. If the farmer has the capital and can provide the labour and buildings, pigs or poultry can be added to almost any farm organization without displacing one of the other enterprises. So far as land is concerned, therefore, these are not competitive but *supplementary* enterprises.

Third, there is the farmer and his men who supply the labour and equipment to tend the crops and livestock.

Having stated this proposition in concrete terms it can now be stated in financial terms (Fig. 15.2). Each enterprise—whether cash crop, cattle, sheep, pigs or poultry—has its own output and its own specific (or variable) costs. After paying these costs, each enterprise then contributes its gross margin to the central pool. From this central pool are deducted the fixed costs for regular labour, machinery, rent and other overheads. As already explained, these fixed costs are considered separately because they pay for services provided for the farm as a

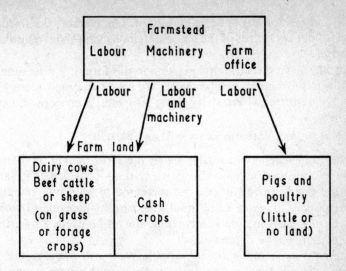

Fig. 15.1 The farm plan in real terms. Each type of enterprise is provided with labour, machinery and other services

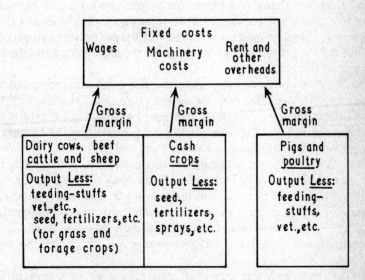

Fig. 15.2 The farm plan in cash terms. Each enterprise should contribute a gross margin to pay for the fixed costs

whole and not for any specific enterprise. On average, the fixed costs absorb about two-thirds of the gross margin, leaving about a third as the net profit.

Having shown the farm organization in this form it is now simpler to see how improvements can be made. We have two propositions. So far as each enterprise (wheat, dairy cows, pigs, etc.) is concerned, its gross margin is

Output *less* Variable Costs = Gross Margin.

Other things being equal, the higher the gross margin the better. A higher output will increase the gross margin—provided that variable costs are not increased or are not increased to the same extent. If a farmer obtains an extra £2 of grain a hectare by applying £1 worth of fertilizer the gross margin is increased. But, if he needs £3 worth, the gross margin will be depressed.

Alternatively a reduction in variable costs will increase the gross margin—provided that output is not reduced to the same extent. If, by better rationing, a farmer can obtain a litre of milk with $0 \cdot 31$ kg of meal in place of $0 \cdot 35$ kg the gross margin will be increased. These are all methods of increasing gross margins with improved techniques and better farming.

There is, however, an equally effective way of raising the total gross margin that is sometimes overlooked. A farmer can increase or introduce enterprises that give a high gross margin and reduce or eliminate those that give a low gross margin. In some cases, the choice is a fairly simple one. If barley has a gross margin of £300 per hectare and oats has one of £260 then (other things being equal) the more barley and the less oats grown the better.

There are of course limitations to the size of an enterprise and the farmer cannot specialize entirely on the crops and livestock with the largest gross margins. Potatoes may give twice as high a return per hectare as cereals but the area of potatoes is limited by the amount of labour that can be obtained to harvest them and by the risk of eelworm disease. Wheat may pay better than spring barley but be limited by the area that can be sown by December. Dairy cows may pay better than sheep but be limited by the size of the cow-house. The usual restrictions are labour, buildings, capital, and the requirements of good husbandry. In spite of these, however, the farmer usually has a wide choice of alternatives and should use budgets to discover which are the most profitable.

Having dealt with the individual enterprises, we now turn to the second proposition. As already stated

Total Gross Margin *less* Fixed Costs = Net Profit.

It follows, therefore, that the profit will be increased if fixed costs can be reduced. It must be stated, however, that direct reduction of fixed costs is often difficult to accomplish. The largest single item is labour and while there is often scope for saving man hours through mechanization or work study, the saving of enough labour to spare one man for the whole year may not be easy. Unfortunately, anything less will not reduce the labour bill. So far as machinery costs are concerned, every care should be taken to avoid extravagance because a large part of this item is for depreciation of equipment which has been bought in the past. The purchases may not have been justified at the time but they have been made. Depreciation will, therefore, continue until the equipment is discarded. So far as rent is concerned, once a price is agreed for a farm, it must be paid. Many of the minor overhead expenses, such as insurance, are inevitable and no large savings may be possible.

In practice, a much more fruitful course is to examine fixed costs not by themselves but in conjunction with the total gross margins. When this is done, profitability can often be improved by accomplishing one or other of the following.

(1) An increase in the gross margin without an increase (or with a smaller increase) in fixed costs. Labour and machinery make up most of the fixed costs and having paid for them the farmer is entitled to use them fully. It is thus often possible, with careful planning, to intensify production with the existing staff. A farmer buys a sugar-beet harvester to save labour and, instead of trying to reduce the labour staff, he uses the man hours saved in October and November to grow more sugar-beet or potatoes or drill more winter wheat. Care must of course be taken when intensifying production not to create a seasonal peak that will overtax the labour force. Methods of avoiding this will be shown later.

(2) A reduction in fixed costs without a reduction (or with a smaller reduction) in gross margins. This may be more difficult to accomplish but is sometimes possible. A cow-house for 100 cows employing two men might be converted into a yard and parlour requiring only one man. A farmer faced with the loss of an irreplaceable worker might manage to simplify the cropping so that the reduction in gross margin was less than the wage of the man lost.

To summarize, the questions to be asked in replanning a farm are usually as follows

(a) are the gross margins from each enterprise high enough? This is a measure of good farming;

(b) which enterprises produce the highest gross margins and can they be profitably expanded? This is a measure of wise choice of enterprises;

(c) can fixed costs be reduced? If not, can the programme be rearranged to give a better return from labour and machinery employed? This is a measure of good organization.

The example that follows illustrates an increase in gross margins without an increase in fixed costs. (The increase in gross margins is partly due to greater efficiency and partly to a rearrangement of the cropping programme.)

Example 1

The farmer has a dairy and crop farm of 100 hectares. The dairy herd of 40 cows give 5000 l. a year. Cash crops include wheat, oats, barley and potatoes. The cropping is as follows

Wheat	20 ha	Potatoes	5 ha
Barley	30 ha	Fodder crops and pasture	40 ha
Oats	5 ha		

The farmer employs a cowman and tractor driver. The farm profit of £1475 is disappointing. The trading account (Fig. 15.3) is shown in a form suitable for calculating gross margins with outputs on the right and expenses split into fixed and variable costs on the left.

Trading Account*

Variable costs	£	Outputs	£
Feeding stuffs	11 850	Milk	22 000
Seed	2 879	Culls	2 280
Fertilizers	5 243	Calves	1 600
Sprays	1 969		25 880
Other costs	4 064		
	26 005	Wheat	10 600
Fixed costs		Barley	11 700
Labour	10 200	Oats	1 800
Machinery	10 500	Potatoes	8 000
Rent	7 000		
Overheads	2 800		
	56 505		
Net profit	1 475		
	£57 980		£57 980

Fig. 15.3

* To simplify the account, sales have been adjusted for valuation changes to give outputs. Grain fed to the dairy herd has been added to the crop outputs and also to the feeding costs—as if sold at market value by cash crops to the dairy herd.

Now suppose that variable costs have been deducted from these outputs (the wheat crop for example being charged with its seed and fertilizers and the dairy herd with feeding stuffs and fodder crop costs). A budget for the present farming system now appears (Fig. 15.4) with gross margins on the right and fixed costs on the left.

Budget—present system

Fixed costs	£	Gross margins	£
Labour	10 200	Wheat	8 100
Machinery	10 500	Barley	8 670
Rent	7 000	Oats	1 260
Overheads	2 800	Potatoes	4 000
	30 500	Dairy herd	9 945
Net profit	1 475		
	£31 975		£31 975

Fig. 15.4

The gross margin per hectare can now be calculated and set alongside averages for the area concerned.

	Hectares	GM per hectare	Local standards
Wheat	20	£405	£400
Barley (spring)	30	289	300
Oats	5	252	260
Potatoes	5	800	780
Dairy herd	40	249	400

The fixed costs per hectare can also be compared with averages for dairy and arable farms in the area.

	Cost per hectare	Local average
Labour	£102	£110
Machinery	105	95
Rent	70	55
Overheads	28	35
	£305	£295

It will be seen that the gross margins total £31 975 and of this £30 500 or 95 per cent is absorbed by fixed costs. Does this mean that fixed costs are too high? A comparison with local averages shows however that they are fairly normal. The rent is above average but this has been agreed and must be accepted. While machinery costs are slightly above average, much of this is depreciation on past purchases and cannot easily be changed. As fixed costs are reasonable, the fault must lie elsewhere. The gross margins of the cash crops seem quite reasonable. While potatoes are the most profitable crop, the farmer doubts whether he can get enough casual labour to harvest more. One possibility is to grow more wheat or some winter barley which has £40 more GM per hectare than spring barley. The difficulty here is that autumn sown cereals clash with potato harvesting.

The greatest weakness however is the dairy herd. The return per hectare devoted to the cows (£249) should be about £400. An extra £150 per hectare on 40 hectares would increase the profit by £6000. How could this be done? The farmer seeks the advice of the ADAS officer, who examines the farm records and makes the following points.

(1) On reasonably good land, it should be possible to support 40 cows and their followers on 30 hectares.

(2) The pasture could be improved.

(3) Purchased concentrates are being used wastefully. Food consumption is about 25 per cent more than seems necessary.

The correction of these points need not concern us here, but there is little doubt that the efficiency of the herd could be raised at least to average levels. The 40 hectares could carry another 10 cows and the cowman could manage them. There is, however, a shortage of building space. Alternatively the present dairy herd could be supported on 30 hectares. The 10 hectares saved could be put into winter barley and the oats into wheat.

Budget—proposed plan

Fixed costs	£	Gross margins	£
As before	30 500	Wheat 25 ha @ £405	10 125
Net profit	7 595	Spring barley 30 ha @ £289	8 670
		Winter barley 10 ha @ £330	3 300
		Potatoes 5 ha @ £800	4 000
		Dairy herd 30 ha @ £400	12 000
	£38 095		£38 095

Fig. 15.5

The estimated profit (Fig. 15.5) is now £7595 or five times the original. Of the increased profit of £6120, 54 per cent comes from keeping the cows on a smaller area of improved pasture and putting 10 hectares to spare into winter barley, 34 per cent comes from improved rationing of the cows and 12 per cent from changing oats to wheat.

The effect of the improved plan is also shown diagrammatically in Fig. 15.6. It will be noted that while the fixed or common costs remain unchanged, the gross margins have increased. The whole of this increase is thus extra profit.

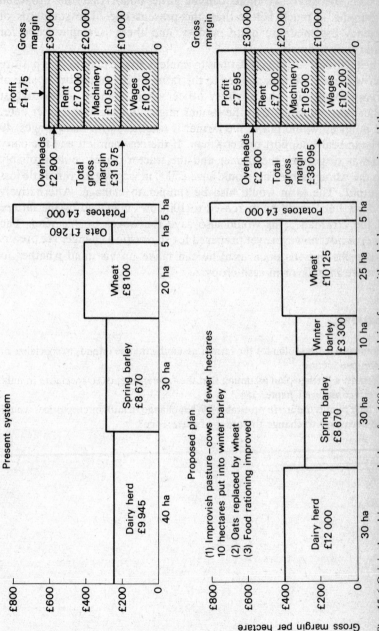

Fig. 15.6 Original and improved plans for 100 hectare dairy farm with a higher gross margin and the same common costs. Profit increases from £1475 to £7595

Present system

Gross margin per hectare

- Dairy herd £9 945 — 40 ha
- Spring barley £8 670 — 30 ha
- Wheat £8 100 — 20 ha
- Oats £1 260 — 5 ha
- Potatoes £4 000 — 5 ha

Overheads £2 800
Total gross margin £31 975

Profit £1 475
Rent £7 000
Machinery £10 500
Wages £10 200

Gross margin
£30 000
£20 000
£10 000
0

Proposed plan

(1) Improvish pasture – cows on fewer hectares 10 hectares put into winter barley
(2) Oats replaced by wheat
(3) Food rationing improved

Gross margin per hectare

- Dairy herd £12 000 — 30 ha
- Spring barley £8 670 — 30 ha
- Winter barley £3 300 — 10 ha
- Wheat £10 125 — 25 ha
- Potatoes £4 000 — 5 ha

Overheads £2 800
Total gross margin £38 095

Profit £7 595
Rent £7 000
Machinery £10 500
Wages £10 200

Gross margin
£30 000
£20 000
£10 000
0

137

Although the exact profit calculated in such a budget should not be accepted too literally, there can be little doubt that the proposed programme is much better than the present one. The standards of efficiency assumed are quite modest, and there is ample scope for further improvement.

The technical recommendations to implement the plan such as pasture improvement, can be explained to the farmer who should be capable of carrying them out. The advisory officer could then go on to suggest further improvements that the farmer might undertake at a later date. One point he would put to the farmer is whether, with rising wages, 40 cows can really support one cowman. If the cowman left and the dairy herd was dispersed, the farmer and the tractor driver could probably crop the whole farm. This would save £5000 in wages with very little loss in output. The farm would also be simpler to manage. Alternatively the dairy herd could be increased to 100 cows managed by the farmer and the cowman. This would also save the wages of one man. The farmer is not, however, yet prepared for so drastic a change. He prefers to keep his options open until he can make up his mind whether to specialize in milk or in cash crops.

Questions

1. Prepare a further plan for the farmer assuming that he intends to specialize in crop production.
2. Prepare a further plan assuming that the farmer intends to specialize in milk production (*see* Chapter 18).
3. Which plan is the more profitable? What change in milk or crop prices would be necessary to change the order of preference?

16 Farm mechanization

One of the major expenses in running a farm is the upkeep of machinery. A recent survey (Fig. 16.1) showed that in England and Wales, machinery costs were £44 per hectare or 14 per cent of the total. On cropping farms the cost was £76 per hectare or 20 per cent of total costs. As can be seen from Fig. 16.1 the largest item was *depreciation*.

Cost per hectare	All farms	General cropping farms
	£	£
Repairs	12·51	20·23
Fuel and oil	8·00	12·32
Contract work	6·05	8·96
Depreciation	17·11	34·36
Total machinery	£ 43·67	£ 75·87
Total inputs	£310·96	£369·70
Machinery (%)	14·0%	20·5%

Fig. 16.1 Machinery costs (Farm Incomes in England and Wales, 1976–77, MAFF)

This item was calculated from the original cost of buying the machinery or *historic cost*. If it were based on the much higher cost of replacing the machinery now, the cost (according to the report) 'might be three times higher'.

For such an important item we thus require tests to judge past performance and standards to prepare plans for the future. One simple test is to compare the machinery costs on any particular farm with averages, such as those given above. This is of some value if we can obtain costs for the right type of farm in the right year to make a fair comparison.

Another test is to calculate *the machinery cost per standard tractor hour*. Data on the average number of tractor hours required per hectare of crops or per head of livestock are available and from this we can estimate the expected number of tractor hours on any particular farm. These are called the standard tractor hours (STH). If the machinery costs on a farm are divided by the STH for that farm we obtain the machinery cost per STH. A reasonable standard is £4 per STH on an arable farm and £5 on a dairy farm. For past records, this test can be quite useful.

For planning the future, however, past records are of limited value and in a period of inflation are soon out of date. In any case, we may be planning for a new type of machine on a novel system of production for which no past records are available.

We thus require a method for estimating depreciation, repairs, fuel and oil.

Depreciation

If a farmer buys a machine for £1000 and sells it ten years later for £100 for scrap, he has lost £900 over this period. This loss will not of course be known until the machine is finally sold, but it is prudent during these ten years to make allowance for the fact that the value of the machine is steadily falling. This is *depreciation*. As explained in Chapter 10 this can be calculated in two ways. We can say that if the machine loses £900 in value in 10 years, the average depreciation is £90 a year. This is *straight line* depreciation. The alternative is to deduct a percentage each year, e.g. using an allowance of 20 per cent.

	£
Purchase price	1000
Depreciation, 1st year, 20% of £1000	200
Value after one year	800
Depreciation, 2nd year, 20% of £800	160
Value after two years	640

This is the *diminishing value* method. When a machine is purchased, its value falls more steeply in the early years and this method reflects more accurately the way that second-hand prices behave. If this 20 per cent depreciation calculation above is continued over 10 years, the value will have dropped to £107 or approximately 10 per cent of the new price.

The actual depreciation will depend on the life of the machine. Some last for 15 or even 20 years, others after heavy use or damage are scrapped after five or six years. To make estimates, however, reasonable assumptions must be made. The following procedure is therefore recommended.

(1) Assume that most machines last ten years and are then sold for scrap for 10 per cent of the new price. This fits fairly closely to 20 per cent depreciation on the diminishing value basis.

(2) Assume that machines that have many moving parts or seem likely to become obsolete and replaced by better models, last eight years and are then sold for 10 per cent of the new price. This fits very closely to 25 per cent depreciation on the diminishing value basis.

The following is a suggested list:

20 per cent depreciation *10 year life*	25 per cent depreciation *8 year life*
Tractor	Combine harvester
Corn drill	Sugar-beet harvester
Balers	Potato harvester
Plough	Precision drill
Cultivator	Potato planter
Harrow	Sprayers
Roll	FYM spreaders
Mower	Fertilizer distributor
Tedder	Forage harvester
Trailer	Hedge cutters
Fork lift	

The life of a machine depends on its treatment and on the amount of use it receives. As an alternative to a set number of years, the life of a tractor can be stated as about 10 000 h. As the average tractor is used for about 1000 h this is consistent with a life of ten years. But if the tractor is used for 2000 h per year, its life might be only five years. In budgeting for a newly invented machine that might soon be superseded by a better one, it would be prudent to allow a life of only five or six years. On the other hand, an expensive machine bought for a small farm could be given a life of 12 or 14 years as a special case.

Unlike tractors that are worked constantly throughout the year, most machines on the farm are used only at certain seasons. For this reason they are often discarded not because they are worn out, but because they are superseded by a better machine. A combine harvester, for example, is seldom used for more than 20 days or 200 h a year. After ten years it has been used for only 2000 h and is not really worn out. The farmer, however, is offered an improved model and decides to change after ten years or sooner. So far as he is concerned, the old model is obsolete.

It should be added that discarded machinery is not necessarily scrapped. Farmers with small holdings who could not justify the purchase of an expensive new machine often buy an old one which can deal quite satisfactorily with their few hectares. But although some machines may continue to function until they are 15 or 20 years old, the assumption of a scrap value of 10 per cent after eight or ten years is a good working hypothesis for farms where machines are given reasonably full employment.

Repairs

Repairs vary greatly with the care given to a machine and the conditions under which it works. They also increase continuously in a period of inflation. It has been observed however that the cost of repairs tends to keep pace with the price of new machines. Thus if the price of a new machine increases by 50 per cent it is reasonable to assume that repairs will also increase by 50 per cent. This means that repair costs remain a fairly constant percentage of the price of the new machine. Thus if we know this percentage and the hours of use, we can estimate the cost of repairs. If, for example, cultivator repairs are 0·10 per cent per hour then the repair cost of one used for 100 h will be 10 per cent of the new price. If the cultivator cost £800, repairs should be 10 per cent of £800 or £80. The ratios derived from a survey of arable farmers in the East of England are given in Fig. 16.2.*

Ploughs	0·07	Seed drills	0·04
Cultivators	0·10	Combine harvesters	0·03
Harrows	0·07	Balers	0·03
Disc harrows	0·05	Sugar-beet harvesters	0·04
Rolls	0·03	Potato planters	0·03
Sprayers	0·04	Potato harvesters	0·03
Fertilizer distributors	0·04	Tractors	0·008
Combine drills	0·03		

Fig. 16.2 Cost of repairs and spares per hour as percentage of new price of machine

Fuel

When fully loaded an engine uses about 3 *l*. of diesel fuel per 10 kW (1 gallon per 20 hp). On the farm, tractors and other engines usually work well below capacity. For this reason, fuel consumption can be taken as 2 *l*. per 10 kW.

Cost of machine operation

We are now in a position to estimate the cost of operating a machine. Suppose we take a large combine harvester with a 130 kW engine,

* Sturrock, Cathie and Payne, *Economies of Scale in Farm Mechanisation*, OP 22, Department of Land Economy, Cambridge.

normally harvesting 12 tonnes of grain per hour. Allowing for delays, changing fields, etc., we can allow 1·36 hectares per hour. In one season the machine should harvest 270 hectares in 200 h. Fuel consumption is 130/10 × 2 = 26 *l*. per hour. The machine costs £40 000.

	Per annum £	Per hectare £
Fuel, 200 h @ 26 *l*. = 5200 *l*. @ 15p	780 ⎫	
Oil, grease, 10% of fuel	78 ⎭	3·17
Depreciation, £40 000 *less* 10% = £36 000 over		
8 years, per year	4500	16·67
Repairs $\frac{0·03}{100}$ × 200 h × £40 000	2400	8·89
Labour 200 hours @ £3	600	2·22
	£8358	£30·95

The cost is thus £8358 per annum or £30·95 per hectare. The cost of other areas of cereals from 50 to 270 hectares are shown in Fig. 16.3. An eight year life is assumed for 250 hectares and nine to 12 years for 200 down to 50 hectares.

Hectares	50	100	125	150	200	250	270
Hours	37	74	92	110	147	184	200
Life (years)	12	11	10½	10	9	8	8
	£	£	£	£	£	£	£
Fuel, oil	159	317	395	472	631	789	858
Repairs	444	888	1104	1320	1764	2208	2400
Depreciation	3000	3273	3429	3600	4000	4500	4500
Labour	111	222	276	330	441	552	600
Total cost	£3714	£4700	£5204	£5722	£6836	£8049	£8358
Per hectare	£74·3	£47·0	£41·6	£38·1	£34·2	£32·2	£31·0

Fig. 16.3 Cost of operating a large combine harvester

The costs omit carting, drying and storing grain which are not relevant to the question of choosing a combine.

The cost of £31 per hectare for 270 hectares is the minimum. With a smaller area to harvest the cost per hectare rises, at first gradually, then more steeply, up to £74·3 per 50 hectares. The reason is that while fuel, repairs and labour all vary with the area harvested, depreciation does not and this raises the cost per hectare to a high level when the area is small. This is the typical cost curve for all field machinery. In fact, the cost per hectare would fall below £31 if the machine could harvest more than 270 hectares (for example by harvesting early peas or oil seed rape). Cereals, however, must be harvested within about 200 h—if harvested too soon, the grain will be unripe and if too late, some grain will be shed.

Figure 16.4 shows the costs for a medium combine costing £22 000 that harvests up to six tonnes per hour. If we assume an effective rate of 0·625 hectares per hour, the combine will harvest 125 hectares in 200 h. As before, costs per hectare fall as the area harvested increases. When the machine reaches its capacity of 125 hectares in 200 h, the cost is at the minimum of £38·9.

Hectares	50	100	125	125	150	200	250
Hours	80	160	200	200	240	320	400
Life (years)	11	9	8	11	10	9	8
	£	£	£	£	£	£	£
Fuel, oil	185	370	462	462	554	739	924
Repairs	528	1056	1320	1320	1584	2112	2640
Depreciation	1800	2200	2475	3600*	3960*	4400*	4950*
Labour	240	480	600	600	720	960	1200
Total cost	£2753	£4106	£4857	£5982	£6818	£8211	£9714
Per hectare	£55·1	£41·1	£38·9	£47·9	£45·5	£41·1	£38·9

*Two machines.

Fig. 16.4 Cost of operating a medium combine harvester

With more than 125 hectares, two machines are required. At this point the cost rises sharply to £47·9, then falls gradually to £38·9 for 250 hectares, which is the capacity of the two machines together.

It is now possible to compare the range of costs in the two tables. As we might expect, the smaller machine has lower costs per hectare up to 125 hectares. Above 125 hectares, the large machine has the advantage and has lower costs than two smaller machines.

This point is also shown in Fig. 16.5. The cost curve for the large machine starts on the left, well above the smaller machine. It then falls steeply and dips below the line for the smaller machines at 125 hectares. To complete the picture a line has been added for a third alternative—a contractor who offers to combine the cereals for a flat rate of £50 per hectare. Choosing the lowest line in each case, the farmer with less than 60 hectares should hire the contractor. A farmer with 60 to 125 hectares should buy the medium machine and a farmer with more than 125 hectares should buy the large machine.

Cost, however, is not the only criterion. If a large machine breaks down the harvest is halted completely. With two smaller machines, one could continue if the other one stops. Two machines, however, require two drivers and the farmer may not have two men to spare. This may be the more important consideration. A farmer short of capital or with a more profitable use for any funds he can spare, might use a contractor even if a machine of his own would cost rather less.

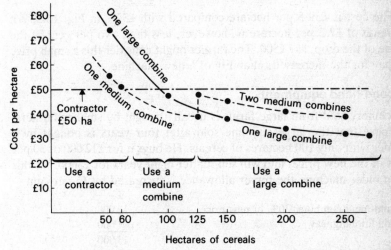

Fig. 16.5 Cost of cereal harvesting per hectare using (*a*) large combine harvester; (*b*) medium-sized combine harvester; (*c*) contractor

This comparison of a large and a medium-sized combine refers mainly to large farms. A similar comparison could be made for smaller farms to show the point at which a small combine might be replaced by a medium-sized one.

Early replacement of equipment

On many large farms, equipment is bought new, worked hard and then sold after three or four years. The farmer will argue that a new machine is less liable to breakdown and incorporates improvements that could be useful. Suppose that a farmer with say 250 hectares of cereals sells his combine after four years for 30 per cent of the new price. Because repairs are covered by guarantee in the first year and are below average in the second, we have assumed that repairs are 70 per cent of normal.

The cost can be estimated as follows.

	£
Purchase of large combine	40 000
Sold after 4 years for 30%	12 000
Depreciation	28 000
Depreciation per year (4 years)	7 000
Repairs 70% of £2208	1 546
Fuel and labour	1 341
Total cost	£ 9 887
Cost per ha (250 ha)	£39·5

The cost is £39·5 per hectare compared with £32·2 in Fig. 16.3. An increase of £7·3 per hectare is, however, less than two per cent of the value of the crop, say £500. The farmer might consider this a small price to pay for the increased reliability of a new machine.

Second-hand equipment

Machinery sold from large farms is usually bought by smaller farmers. Suppose that the large combine sold after four years is bought by a farmer with only 100 hectares of cereals. He buys it for £12 000 or 30 per cent of the new price, and will sell it after eight years for £3000. As this is an older machine the repair allowance is increased by 15 per cent.

	£
Second-hand combine, 30% of new price	12 000
Reconditioning, say	1 000
	13 000
Sold after eight years for	3 000
Depreciation	£10 000
Depreciation per year	1 250
Fuel	317
Repairs (115% of £888)	1 021
Labour	222
Total cost	£2 810
Per hectare	£28·1

The total cost of £28·1 per hectare is fairly reasonable. By comparison, a new small combine at £15 000 harvesting 0·5 hectares per hour could cost

	£
Fuel (50 kW, 10 l. @ 15p × 200 h)	300
Oil, etc.	30
Repairs $\frac{0·03}{100}$ × 200 h × £15 000	900
Depreciation £15 000 $less$ 10%, £13 500 over 8 years	1688
Total cost	£2918
Cost per hectare	£29·2

The costs of the two machines are thus fairly similar.

The disadvantage of the second-hand machine is that it may be less reliable and the farmer should make sure that it is in good condition before he buys it. The advantage is that the large machine will harvest the cereals in about 74 h instead of 200 h. This saving could be put to good use. Autumn cultivations could start earlier and the farmer might grow more wheat, winter barley or sugar-beet with high gross margins instead of spring barley. The farmer might harvest some cereals for a neighbour on contract. These considerations are, in fact, more important than small differences of £2 or £3 per hectare.

This example illustrates a general principle. Tractors and implements are becoming steadily larger and require an increasing area of crops to justify them. If all farmers had to buy their implements new, the small farmer would be at a serious disadvantage. In fact, although their numbers are falling, there are still many arable farmers with less than 100 hectares that compete quite successfully with larger farms. One reason is that in the United Kingdom there are many men with large farms that can afford to buy large new equipment and in consequence there is a well-stocked, second-hand market of equipment they sell in good condition for a reasonable price. Indeed there is an export market for agricultural machinery to countries such as Denmark where there are fewer large farmers to buy large, expensive machines.

Cost of cultivations
It is now possible to calculate the cost of individual cultivations. For example, a tractor pulling a cultivator

	£
Tractor, cost	12 000
Depreciation, £12 000 *less* 10% = £10 800 over 10 years, per year	1 080
Repairs $12\,000 \times \dfrac{0 \cdot 008}{100} \times 1000$ h per year	960
Fuel 70 kW, i.e. 14 *l.* × 1000 h @ 15p	2 100
Oil, etc. (10% of fuel cost)	210
Annual cost	£4 350
Per hour (1000 h)	£4·35

	£
Cultivator, cost	1 600
Depreciation £1600 *less* 10% = £1440 over 10 years, per year	144
Repairs $1600 \times \dfrac{0 \cdot 10}{100} \times 120$ h	192
Annual cost	336
per hour (120 h)	£2·80

Cost per hour		£
	Tractor	£4·35
	Cultivator	£2·80
	Labour	£3·00
		£10·15

Speed 6 km/h, width 4 m.
In one hour does 6000 m × 4 = 24 000 sq m = 2·4 ha.
In 20 ha field, 65% of 2·4 = 1·56 ha per hour.
Cost £10·15 ÷ 1·56 = £6·51 per hectare.
Work per day 1·56 ha × 7 h = 11 ha.

Field size

Having dealt with the cost of maintaining machinery we must now deal with its use in field operations. One characteristic of crop production is that the work is seasonal and operations must be carried out at the right time when soil and weather conditions are suitable. The farmer is thus often working under pressure and field operations must be completed as quickly as possible—provided that the quality of the work does not suffer.

If a tractor is moving at 6 km/h pulling a cultivator 3 m wide, then in one hour it will cover 6000 × 3 = 18 000 sq m or 1·8 hectares. This is known as the *Spot working rate*. In practice the tractor does not move steadily forward all day in a straight line. Time is lost turning at the end of the field, cultivating headlands and changing fields. In addition a contingency allowance (in this case 20 per cent) has been added for minor adjustments and for the personal needs of the tractor driver. As can be seen from Fig. 16.6, these items take up 63 per cent of the time in a small two hectare field, leaving only 37 per cent of effective time actually cultivating. The effective time increases to 65 per cent in a 20 hectare field, to 71 per cent in a 40 hectare field and 74 per cent in an 80 hectare field.

(Implement 3 m wide moving at 6 km/h)

Field size (ha)	2	4	10	20	40	80
Effective work	37	47	59	65	71	74
Turns	20	19	14	12	8	7
Headlands	4	3	3	2	2	1
Changing fields	22	14	7	4	2	1
Contingencies	17	17	17	17	17	17
	100	100	100	100	100	100
Hectares per day	4·64	5·96	7·42	8·27	8·94	9·39

Fig. 16.6 Effect of field size on time spent on effective work

The amount of work accomplished increases in proportion. Leaving out the extremes, it increases by 50 per cent from a four hectare to a 40 hectare field. This estimate in fact understates the advantages of large fields because they also allow the farmer to use larger tractors and implements that move at a higher speed.

Speed of work is a factor that is sometimes overlooked. ADAS surveys indicate that tractors are often driven well below capacity. Allowance must of course be made for adverse weather and soil conditions in slowing up operations, but in reasonable conditions most cultivations could be carried out at 6 to 10 km/h. In practice, it is often only 4 km/h. Some jobs such as rolling or cultivating between rows must be done slowly but apart from that, speed is often a matter of habit. Poor seat design and excessive noise often tempt the tractor driver to reduce speed but modern designs are helping to overcome these problems.

When all these factors—width of implement, speed of operation and size of field—are put together, the effect on the amount of work accomplished can be substantial. (*See* Fig. 16.7.)

Width (m)	Speed (km/h)	Field size (ha)	Tractor (kW)	Hectares per day
3	4	10	45	4
5	6	20	70	13
8	10	40	110	34
10	10	80	160	46

Fig. 16.7 Effect of width, speed and field size on work accomplished

It is hardly surprising that arable farmers have been steadily increasing the size of fields. A field of 20 hectares is sometimes quoted as being the optimum size but, as can be seen, an increase to 40 hectares with the appropriate implements can more than double the rate of work. A field of 40 hectares does however imply a farm of at least 200 hectares.

The last example, based on a 160 kW tractor is inserted only for interest. While feasible in the USA or Australia, fields of 80 hectares are seldom practical or desirable in the UK. The wholesale removal of hedges would produce a bleak landscape and antagonize public opinion. In creating fields of up to 40 hectares, however, the removal of hedges can be compensated by planting trees in strategic positions. The length of hedge removed would depend on the shape of the farm. Let us take a simple example of a 400 hectare farm at present in 40 fields of 10 hectares. If these are enlarged to 10 fields of 40 hectares, the length of hedge removed internally could amount to 12 to 15 km occupying about three hectares. The recovery of land covered by hedges is sometimes quoted as one of the chief benefits of removing hedges. It is a benefit

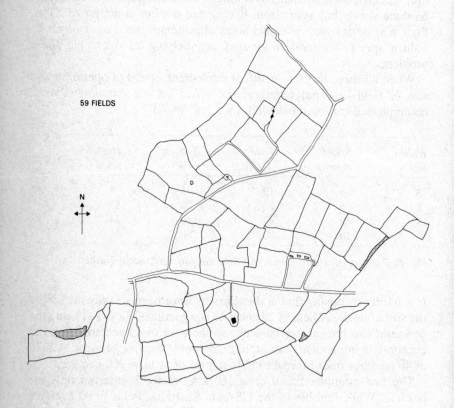

59 FIELDS

N

Fig. 16.8 Arable farm on heavy soil. 59 fields were amalgamated into 25, increasing their average size from 10 to over 20 hectares. One field is over 40 hectares. Many boundaries are limited by roads and watercourses. This is an area of large farms. As there are few trees the landscape is rather bare. This

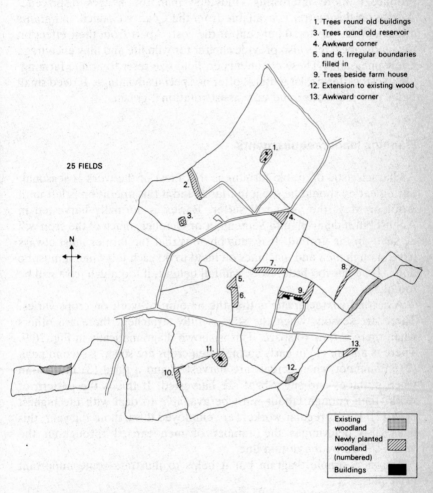

1. Trees round old buildings
3. Trees round old reservoir
4. Awkward corner
5. and 6. Irregular boundaries filled in
9. Trees beside farm house
12. Extension to existing wood
13. Awkward corner

25 FIELDS

N

Existing woodland

Newly planted woodland (numbered)

Buildings

farmer is planting 13 spinneys to fill in awkward corners and screen buildings. This shows how improved field lay-out can be combined with an improvement to the landscape. (With acknowledgement to Mr F. J. Roe, Woolley Leys Farm, Huntingdon).

that should be discounted. To avoid criticism of spoiling the landscape, it would be advisable in such a case to plant at least three hectares in well-placed belts of trees. In practice, if the trees were placed in awkward corners or were used to shelter ponds and buildings, the loss in arable land would be negligible. When the trees grow, they should produce a more interesting landscape than the hedges displaced.* Advice on this matter is available from the County Council and grants are available—up to 50 per cent of the cost. Apart from their effect on the landscape, trees also provide shelter for wild life and may encourage a few pheasants. These comments on field size refer to arable farming. On livestock farms, large fields offer no special advantage. Indeed small fields provide shelter and may assist rotational grazing.

Planning labour requirements

A characteristic of arable farming is that most of the work is seasonal. Spring barley should be sown in March and if this operation is left until April or May, the yield will suffer. Barley is normally harvested in August but if delayed until September or October, much of the crop will be shed on the ground. It is thus obvious that the farmer must always have enough men and machines on hand to do each job when it must be done. If he has too little, work will fall behind, if too much, cost will be too high.

A second characteristic is that the amount of work on crops varies. There are seasons when the staff is fully stretched, there are others when there is time to spare. This is shown diagramatically in Fig. 16.9. There is a peak (1) in early spring when crops are sown, a second peak (2) in summer when cereals are harvested and a third (3) in autumn when potatoes and sugar-beet are harvested. If this is the pattern of work, then enough labour must be available to deal with the highest peak (2). But as regular workers are employed throughout the year, this peak also determines the number of men carried throughout the year—shown by the dotted line.

This is a simple diagram but it helps to illustrate some important principles.

(1) Farmers buy machines to save labour. Saving labour is, however, of no financial benefit to the farmer unless he can either:
  (a) save a regular worker for the whole year;
  (b) eliminate casual labour or overtime;

* Sturrock and Cathie, *Farm Modernisation and the Countryside*, Department of Land Economy, Cambridge, 1980.

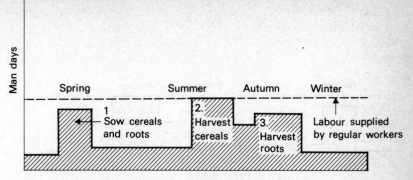

Fig. 16.9 Seasonal labour peaks—large proportion of cereals

(*c*) use the time saved to increase output.

Unless one of these alternatives is accomplished, there is no cash saving to set against the additional cost of the machine.

(2) The scope for saving labour thus depends on the seasonal pattern of labour requirements. On the farm illustrated in Fig. 16.9, a machine that saved labour during peaks (1) or (3), or in the gaps between, might make work easier but would do nothing to reduce the labour staff. On the other hand, a machine (e.g. a large combine harvester) that reduced peak (2) might enable the farmer to reduce the labour staff by one man. If so, the saving due to the machine would be not a few man hours during harvest but the wages of a man for a whole year. Farmers are usually reluctant to dismiss men. In course of time, however, one leaves or retires and this provides an opportunity to replace him with further mechanization. Figure 16.9 shows a farm with a high proportion of cereal crops. On another farm with more potatoes or sugar-beet, period (3) (particularly October) would become the highest peak. (Fig. 16.10.)

(3) Sometimes casual labour can be employed to take care of a peak, e.g. picking fruit or lifting potatoes. Casual workers can generally only be used for a limited number of unskilled jobs and they are not always available.

(4) In Figs 16.9 and 16.10 there is a substantial amount of 'spare' time between peaks not required for cropwork. This time need not be wasted and the farmer can fill in with repairs, ditching, draining, etc., and other work not closely tied to any one season. Nevertheless, this spare time could usually be reduced without any ill effects on the farm.

(5) If possible, the best way to use this 'spare' time is to introduce an enterprise that fills some of the gaps without adding to the highest peak. The farm illustrated has a high proportion of wheat and barley. The introduction of winter rape, sown in autumn (period (3)) and harvested

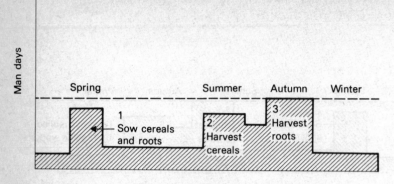

Fig. 16.10 Seasonal labour peaks—large proportion of roots

just ahead of peak (2) in summer would fit very well. So also would sugar-beet sown just after spring cereals (1) and harvested in autumn (3).

Having stated our requirements in financial terms, it now remains to show how labour and machine requirements can be estimated in practice. In Appendix 1 a suggested list of cultivating and harvesting machinery is given for smaller farms (around 80 hectares), medium farms (200 hectares) and very large farms (800 hectares). Details are also given of the minimum tractor required and the price (at the time of writing). From the width and speed, it is a simple matter to estimate the *spot rate*, e.g. a harrow 5 m wide moving at 10 km per hour will cover 50 000 sq m or five hectares in an hour. As already indicated one cannot then assume that $5 \times 8 = 40$ hectares would be covered in a day. Allowances made were as follows.

(1) For adjustments, turning, cultivating headlands and changing fields—reduced to 60 per cent on a medium-sized farm (fields 10 to 20 hectares), 65 per cent on a very large farm (fields over 20 hectares) and 57 per cent on a smaller farm (fields 5–10 hectares). These figures were reduced by a further 10 per cent for seed drills, planters and fertilizer distributors and 20 per cent for sprayers that must stop from time to time for reloading.

(2) One hour a day for getting to the field and two hours when materials such as seed or fertilizer have to be loaded and taken.

The harrow with a spot rate of 5 ha/h can thus be expected to cover $5 \times \frac{7}{8} \times 60\% = 2.63$ ha/h or $1 \div 2.63 = 0.38$ man hours per hectare on a medium-sized farm.

To estimate peak labour requirements, we need to define the critical periods. These have been chosen carefully to include in each, the operations likely to compete for labour.

(1) Early spring (March–April). Seed bed preparation, sowing cereals and sugar-beet, planting potatoes.

(2) Late spring (May, June, half July). Spraying, tractor hoeing, harvesting hay and silage.

(3) Early summer (half July, half August). Harvesting winter barley, winter rape and 1/3 spring barley.

(4) Late summer (half August, half September). Harvesting winter wheat, 2/3 spring barley, sowing winter rape.

(5) Early autumn (half September, October). Harvesting main crop potatoes and half sugar-beet, sowing winter wheat and barley.

(6) Late autumn (Nov., half December). Harvesting half sugarbeet.

(7) Winter (half December, January, February). Odd jobs including some ploughing and early sowing of cereals. As provision has been made for most of this field work elsewhere, this period can usually be ignored. (Data for barley and potatoes are included to give the total man hours for these crops.)

This list includes only the major operations likely to cause a bottleneck in the period concerned. There are many other jobs that can be done on days unsuitable for field work.

It is now possible to compile an estimate of the man hours required for each crop in each of these periods. A list for medium-sized farms is given in Fig. 16.11. The number of man hours a man can expect to work in the field is also given in each period, allowing for unsuitable weather, holidays, illness and other contingencies. No allowance is made for overtime which can be regarded as a reserve for particularly bad weather and other difficulties.

Man hours/ hectare	Early spring	Late spring	Early summer	Late summer	Early autumn	Late autumn	Winter	Total
Winter wheat	2·0	0·9	—	2·4	3·3	0·5		9·1
Winter barley	2·0	0·5	2·4	—	3·3	0·5		8·7
Spring barley	4·4	0·5	0·8	1·6	0·5	1·1	(0·5)	9·4
Sugar-beet	7·2	13·0	—	0·5	10·5	10·7		41·9
Potatoes	11·6	5·2	0·9	—	28·4	10·1	(42·5)	98·7
Winter rape	1·5	—	2·4	4·5	0·5	—		8·9
Leys	1·1	11·0	—	—	—	—		12·1
1 man supplies	180	275	115	110	150	105	—	—

Fig. 16.11 Seasonal labour requirements (medium-sized farms). Straw baling (4 to 5 man hours per ha) not included.

It is now possible to calculate the number of men required for a farm, e.g. a 200 hectare arable farm (Fig. 16.12).

Crop	Hectares	Early spring	Late spring	Early summer	Late summer	Early autumn	Late autumn
Winter wheat	80	160	72	—	192	264	40
Winter barley	40	80	20	96	—	132	20
Spring barley	40	176	20	32	64	20	44
Winter rape	20	30	—	48	90	10	—
Leys	20	22	220	—	—	—	—
Total	200	468	332	176	346	426	104
3 men supply		540	825	345	*330*	450	315
4 men supply		720	1100	460	440	600	420

Fig. 16.12 Labour requirements for 200 hectare arable farm

It appears that four men could do all the field work required. Three men would be sufficient except for late summer. Thus if the farmer himself worked at that time, three men should be sufficient. A much more intensive system including 40 hectares of sugar-beet is given in Fig. 16.13.

Crop	Hectares	Early spring	Late spring	Early summer	Late summer	Early autumn	Late autumn
Winter wheat	75	150	68	—	180	247	38
Winter barley	50	100	25	120	—	165	25
Spring barley	35	154	18	28	56	18	38
Sugar-beet	40	288	520	—	20	420	428
Total	200	692	631	148	256	850	529
5 men supply		900	1375	575	550	*750*	525
6 men supply		1080	1650	690	660	900	630

Fig. 16.13 Labour requirements for intensive arable farm

It is evident that six men are required. In fact five men would be sufficient except in the autumn. This is a case where the purchase of a larger sugar-beet harvester might smooth out this bottleneck and enable the farmer to manage with five men.

It is perhaps worth emphasis that the labour estimates in this chapter are fairly tight—as estimates should be. They assume a fairly brisk rate of work in the field but provision has been made for contingencies.

A similar set of estimates for smaller and very large farms is given in Figs 16.14 and 16.15.

Crop	Early spring	Late spring	Early summer	Late summer	Early autumn	Late autumn	Winter	Total
Winter wheat	3·5	1·5	—	4·0	4·1	0·7		13·8
Winter barley	3·5	0·8	4·0	—	4·1	0·7		13·1
Spring barley	6·1	0·8	1·3	2·7	0·8	1·6	(0·8)	13·3
Sugar-beet	7·7	14·2	—	0·6	11·3	12·0		45·8
Potatoes	11·8	6·2	1·5	—	24·5	10·7	(45·8)	100·5
Winter rape	2·4	—	4·0	6·2	2·1	—		14·7
Leys	1·3	11·0	—	—	—	—		12·3

Fig. 16.14 Labour estimates for smaller farms (about 80 hectares)

Crop	Early spring	Late spring	Early summer	Late summer	Early autumn	Late autumn	Winter	Total
Winter wheat	1·5	0·8	—	1·5	1·6	0·4		5·8
Winter barley	1·5	0·4	1·5	—	1·6	0·4		5·4
Spring barley	2·5	0·4	0·5	1·0	0·3	0·6	(0·3)	5·6
Sugar-beet	4·3	9·9	—	0·2	5·7	6·0		26·1
Potatoes	5·5	3·0	0·8	—	25·9	9·6	(36·3)	81·1
Winter rape	0·8	—	1·5	2·5	0·8	—		5·6
Leys	0·7	8·0	—	—	—	—		8·7

Fig. 16.15 Labour estimates for very large farms (about 800 hectares)

The estimates for very large farms are added for interest but should be used with caution. They assume the large machinery shown in Appendix 1 and fields of more than 20 hectares. They also assume a well laid-out farm. In practice, the majority of farms of over 600 hectares are irregular in shape and often not all within one ring fence. If the fields are not large and the machinery resembles that of a medium sized farm, the standards of performance will be those of a medium-sized farm.

The estimates for the smaller farm assume the smaller machines given in Appendix 1. If the farmer buys large machines second hand, his estimates will be closer to those for the medium-sized farm.

Labour profiles

In the previous section, we have been dealing with labour requirements for the farm as a whole. The problem of finding sufficient labour may, however, apply to only one season. To give an example, let us take the farm shown in Fig. 16.13. Six men are employed but one is retiring. Can the farmer manage with five men? Apparently he can, except in the autumn, when so much labour is required to harvest the sugar-beet. One solution would be to reduce the sugar-beet. The farmer is reluctant to do so because it would reduce his income. He therefore considers further mechanization. Where solving a particular problem of this kind, it is advisable not to rely on averages but to set out the labour requirements of the farm concerned on a graph. The man hours available in each period are measured along the horizontal axes—in this case 150 and 105 man hours respectively for early and late autumn. The labour required for each job is inserted as a block—the length being the time that the machine takes and the height the number of men required. The area then represents the number of man hours. The graph is, in practice, more informative than numbers in a table. The operations can be set out in order with the appropriate gang size. If the total number of men is to be reduced, the farmer can manipulate the operations to see whether they can be rearranged or mechanized to use less labour. In this case one medium-sized harvester working continuously can hardly complete the harvest by Christmas, i.e. well beyond the autumn periods prescribed (Fig. 16.16). There is thus some risk of losing part of the crop. Other operations can be completed quite comfortably in the time available. Can one man be spared? One solution would be a larger tractor with larger plough and cultivator. This would probably save enough labour for the purpose. It might be better, however, to deal with the overworked sugar-beet harvester. If this were replaced by a larger machine with twice the throughput, the harvest could be completed quite easily. Indeed, there would be no difficulty in growing 10 hectares more sugar-beet in place of spring barley (Fig. 16.17). This would employ the large new machine more fully and help to pay for it.

A budget for this change would be somewhat as follows. An SB harvester costing £8000 is replaced by another costing £22 000.

Losses	£	Gains	£
Machine costing £22 000 *less*		Wage of 1 man	5000
10% ÷ 8 years, per year	2475	Extra gross margin:	
Less £8000 machine, *less*		10 ha SB @ £550 in place	
10% ÷ 8 years, per year	900	of spring barley @ £270	2800
Extra depreciation	1575		
Extra repairs + fuel, say	1000		
	2575		
Extra profit	5225		
	£7800		£7800

The larger machine thus appears to be well justified. This example will help to emphasize the point that the benefit of mechanization is not

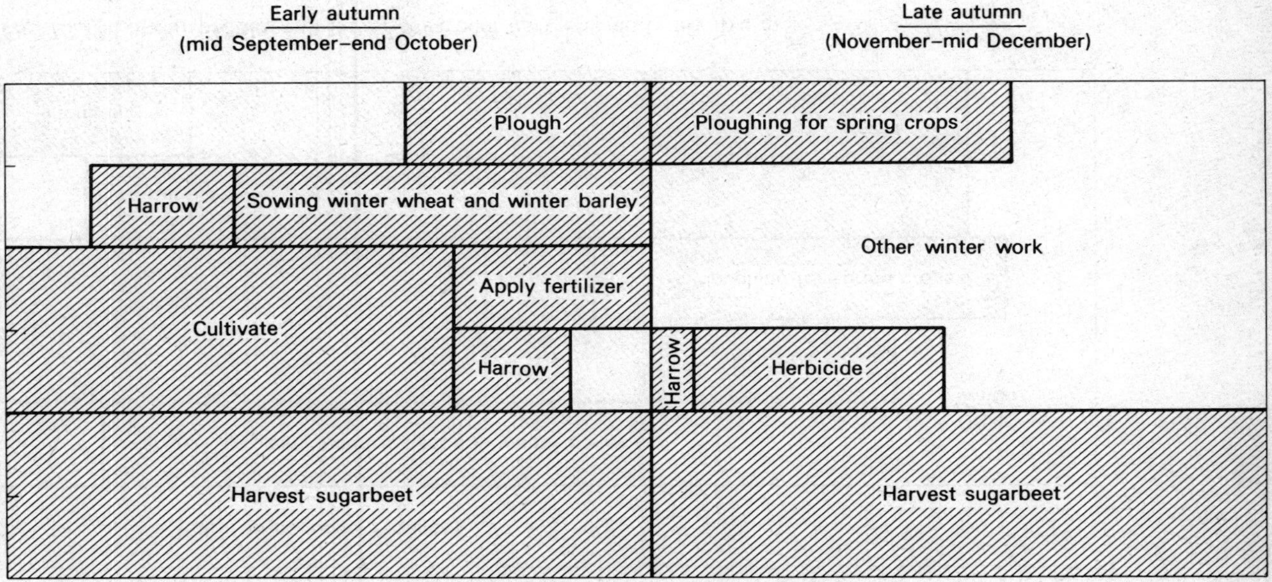

Fig. 16.16 Labour profile with medium sugarbeet harvester (cultivations are shown as solid blocks, but in practice would be interspersed as each field was cultivated)

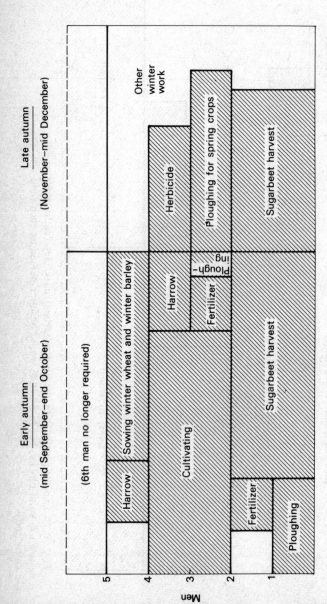

Fig. 16.17 Labour profile with larger sugarbeet harvester and only five men

necessarily a reduction in the cost of field operations. Indeed, in this case, the cost of harvesting per hectare might be slightly greater if the new machine requires heavy maintenance. The advantage is that it permits the farmer both to save labour and intensify production. The only disadvantage is that capital is required to purchase the new machine. If the farmer is short of cash, he should therefore arrange for an overdraft and prepare a cash flow statement to show how long it would take to repay the loan (*see* Chapter 19).

Interest on capital employed

One item has not so far been included in the costs—interest on capital used to purchase machinery. Suppose a farmer buys a tractor for £10 000. He is short of cash and arranges an overdraft at 12 per cent, intending to repay it in eight months when the cereal harvest is sold. The cost would be

$$£10\,000 \times 0.12 \times \frac{8}{12} = £800.$$

This sum could be included in the partial budget making depreciation and interest £1700 in the first year and an average of £900 for depreciation alone in the remaining nine years. The interest charged is a real cost and the increased profit in the partial budget would agree with the increase.

Some advisory officers take the view that as capital is a scarce commodity, interest should always be charged to discourage farmers from spending capital unless they obtain a reasonable return on the sum invested. A convenient method is as follows.

Suppose that a tractor is bought for £10 000 and sold for £1000 after 10 years. The advisory officer considers that a reasonable return on money invested on the farm is 15 per cent or more. In other words, farmers should not be encouraged to invest in projects yielding less than 15 per cent. The cost of borrowing and repaying a loan can be obtained from a mortgage repayment table. Consulting the table (in Appendix 2) we find that the cost of borrowing £1000 and repaying it in 10 years at 15 per cent is £200. The cost for £9000 is therefore £1800 per year. £1800 is therefore charged in the budget in place of £900 for depreciation alone. If after charging £1800, the budget still shows a profit, the project can be recommended on the grounds that the return on capital exceeds 15 per cent. The extra £900 for interest is of course a nominal not a real cost. An economist might justify it as representing the opportunity cost of capital, i.e. the return that could be expected by investing it in the next best alternative use which we expect to yield at least 15 per cent.

A farmer drawing up a plan for his own use would be well advised to charge interest only if he has to borrow money to buy the machinery. The answer will then give him an estimate of the real change in farm income he can expect.

Effect of high rainfall

In areas of high rainfall less time is available for cultivations and harvesting. Manhours supplied by a man (Fig. 16.11), could thus be reduced by 10 or even 20 per cent—particularly on heavy soil. This is one of the reasons why arable crops are less popular in such conditions.

Questions

1. Calculate the cost of drilling cereals per hectare.

	Tractor	Seed drill
Cost	£10 000	£3000
Life	10 years	10 years
Size	45 kW	4 m
Annual use	1000 h	150 ha
Repairs (per hour, % of new price)	0·008	0·04

The drill moves at 10 km per hour, works 6 h a day of which 50 per cent is actually drilling. Fuel 15p per litre. Oil, etc. 10 per cent of fuel price.

2. (a) A farmer has 50 hectares of sugar-beet. Would you advise the purchase of one large SP machine or two smaller tractor drawn machines?

(b) A farmer has 18 hectares of potatoes. Would you advise the purchase of an elevator harvester requiring 10 casuals at £12 a day, or a larger machine requiring only two. (See Appendix 1 for details of machines.)

3. A farmer has the following cropping:

Wheat	50 ha	Potatoes	25 ha
Spring barley	100 ha	Leys	25 ha

He employs six men costing £30 000 a year.

(a) Prepare a labour profile and decide whether six men are necessary. (As the farmer holds himself in reserve for emergencies, do not include more than 50 hours from him in any period.)

(b) He is likely to lose two or three men in the near future. He wonders whether a feasible programme is possible with fewer men.

Plan 1—Replace potatoes with winter rape.

Replace 50 hectares spring barley with winter barley.

Plan 2—Replace potatoes with sugar-beet.

Replace 50 hectares spring barley with winter barley.

(c) Estimate the effect on farm income of these changes. (Use gross margins from Appendix 1; leys are £150 per hectare.) Assume that the change from potato to sugar-beet machines will increase costs by £1000 a year. Other fixed costs will not be affected.

(*d*) Prepare a plan of your own with a greater increase in farm income than those given above.

4. Prepare a cropping programme for a large farm with 800 hectares of arable land using large farm labour standards.

5. Prepare a cropping programme for a farm with 80 hectares of arable land using small farm standards. The farmer and his son work full time.

6. You have just been appointed manager of a farm with 600 hectares of arable land. The largest tractors used for ploughing and cultivating are 90 and 55 kW and are two years old. You would like to replace them with one tractor of 135 kW. The managing director doubts whether this change would reduce costs appreciably and it would certainly increase the bank overdraft. Prepare a memorandum for the next board meeting. (Make any assumptions that seem reasonable.)

7. The farmer in Q.5 has two more young sons who will soon be leaving school. How would you change the plan to employ them? Will the revised plan produce enough extra revenue to support them both or would you advise one of them to seek employment elsewhere? (Extra revenue = extra GM plus saving in wages, if any. For such an approximate estimate, overheads can be taken as unchanged.)

17 Farm planning by computer

As we have already seen, there are two ways of improving the profitability of farming.

(1) We can farm the present system more efficiently by improving yields, using inputs more economically, etc.

(2) We can change to a more profitable system by choosing crops and livestock that give a better return for our resources.

It is with the second of these that we are now concerned. In the examples given so far, the choice of better enterprises has been largely a matter of intuition and trial and error. It is the purpose of this chapter to show that the choice of enterprises is a matter of logic that can be solved mathematically with the aid of a computer.

A computer can be regarded as a very industrious and rather pedantic clerk that can carry out thousands of calculations in a few seconds. It has been said that a computer lacks discretion and can give absurd answers. That is unfair, because the machine sticks rigidly to the rules and if it gives a wrong answer it is because the operator has failed to instruct it properly. Thus if the computer print-out suggests that we keep 1000 cows on a smallholding this is an indication that we have forgotten to limit the numbers according to the buildings available to house them, the capital available to buy them or the labour available to milk them. Apart from instructions, it will be obvious that the results are only as accurate and reliable as the data fed in.

But if reasonable data are used and sensible instructions are given, we can obtain farm plans that are practical and quite acceptable to a farmer. One can go further. If the computer is asked to produce the optimum answer to a problem, the result will be the best one obtainable *under the conditions stated* and no amount of budgeting by hand will produce a better answer. There is a further advantage. If we wish to estimate the effect of a change, e.g. the introduction of a new machine or higher prices, the computer will give a far more precise and sophisticated answer than could be obtained by hand calculations. It is for this reason that a study of the processes by which the computer can

program can give an insight into the way that economic forces help to determine the shape of improved farm plans.

Linear program for an arable farm

The technique employed is called *linear programming* and the principles employed can be illustrated by taking a very simple example. Suppose that a farmer has 100 hectares of arable land and can grow only two crops—wheat and sugarbeet. The inputs and outputs per hectare are as follows

Per hectare	GM	Man hours in autumn
Wheat	£400	3·33
Sugar-beet	£800	10·00

Total labour available—400 man hours (in autumn).

This information is entered on a graph (Fig. 17.1) with hectares of wheat on the horizontal and sugar-beet on the vertical axis.

(1) The line AB indicates how the 100 hectares could be allocated to the two crops, e.g. 100 hectares wheat or 100 hectares sugar-beet or 60 hectares wheat with 40 hectares sugar-beet, etc.—these all lie along AB.

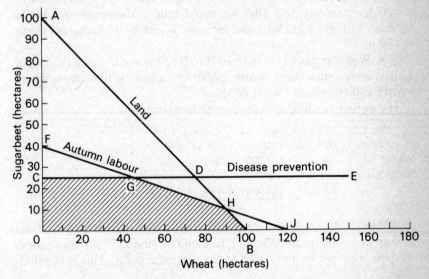

Fig. 17.1 Simple programming exercise for 100 hectares cropped with wheat and sugarbeet. All feasible solutions lie in shaded area and optimum point is H. (3 constraints—25 per cent maximum sugarbeet, autumn labour peak and land)

165

(2) The horizontal line CDE shows the top limit of sugar-beet which is 25 hectares to avoid eelworm disease.

(3) 400 man hours are available in autumn. This is enough to grow 40 hectares sugarbeet (F) or 120 hectares wheat (J). The line FGHJ thus indicates all the combinations of the two crops that can be grown with 400 man hours.

It is thus obvious that from the original area of OAB, slices have been cut off by FJ and CE leaving only the hatched area. Any plan that falls within this area obeys the rules and is feasible. We now require the one that produces the maximum gross margin. This is likely to lie along the *perimeter* CGHB because any point further in would include less wheat or sugar-beet than a point on the boundary.

We can now test along the line CGHB to find the optimum point.

Plan 1. Point C. 25 hectares sugar-beet × £800 = £20 000.

Plan 2. Point G. This is better than C because we have added 45 hectares wheat × £400 = $18 000, making a total of £38 000. We are now using 70 hectares of land.

Plan 3. Point H. In moving from G to H, we have lost some sugar-beet and gained some wheat. Will this pay? The plan is limited along GH by autumn labour. The effect of subtracting one hectare of sugar-beet worth £800 would be to release 10 man hours. This could be used to grow three hectares wheat worth 3 × £400 = £1200, a net gain of £400. As 30 hectares are still idle, we could reduce the sugar-beet by 15 hectares (a loss of £12 000) and increase wheat by 45 hectares (worth £18 000).

Plan 4. Would it pay to move from H to B? This would entail the loss of 10 hectares of sugar-beet (worth £8000) and a gain of 10 hectares wheat (worth £4000)—a net loss of £4000.

The optimum solution is thus point H where

	Hectares	GM	Autumn labour used
Wheat	90	£36 000	300
Sugar-beet	10	8 000	100
	100	£44 000	400

No other solution will produce a higher total GM. In this case land and labour were fully used. When more than two resources are used, some of them may not be fully used at the optimum point. This is unavoidable.

With only two crops to choose from, it was easy to solve the problem on a graph. When there are several resources and enterprises, the arithmetic of adjusting one to the other becomes extremely complex. There is a technique called *program planning** for dealing by arithmetic with fairly simple examples but if a number of solutions are required, the calculations can become very time consuming. The obvious answer is to use a computer which, in a few seconds, can do calculations that would take weeks to complete by hand.

Preparation of a matrix

The technique of linear programming is based on matrix algebra and can produce solutions to problems of maximizing (or minimizing) some stated objective. In this case, the objective is to maximize farm income. As we can usually take fixed or common costs for granted, the objective becomes the maximization of total gross margin. Most computers have a ready made program for linear programming and farm data can be fed into this to give a solution.

As an example, let us take the data given at the end of Chapter 16.† Standards of seasonal labour requirements were given and used to calculate the number of men required for any given cropping program. In other words, if we have decided on the cropping program how many men are required to operate it? In this case, we are considering the converse problems; given (say) 200 hectares arable land, and a staff of five men, what is the most profitable cropping program that they can operate?

The crops that can be grown are the following

	Gross margin		Gross margin
Winter wheat	£350 per ha	Potatoes	£650 per ha
Winter barley	£300 per ha	Winter rape	£290 per ha
Spring barley	£270 per ha	Leys	£150 per ha
Sugar-beet	£550 per ha		

As already stated, there are six critical labour periods during the year, and a reasonable allowance of man hours of field work per man is as follows

I Early spring	180 hours	IV Late summer	110 hours
II Late spring	275 hours	V Early autumn	150 hours
III Early summer	115 hours	VI Late autumn	105 hours

We shall assume that each man costs £5000 and that other fixed costs

---

* Examples were given in Chapter 16 of the 6th edition of this book.
† The author is indebted to Mr M. C. Murphy for computing this example.

(machinery, rent, overheads) amount to £30 000. Total fixed costs with five men are therefore £55 000. As the farm income is the surplus after paying these fixed costs, the problem is to choose the crops that will give the largest total gross margin without overloading the five men.

There are certain restrictions on the crops that can be grown—to avoid eelworm infestation, neither sugar-beet nor potatoes can exceed 50 hectares and the farmer is unwilling to grow more than 50 hectares of oil seed rape, which is a new crop. As rape is a host for sugar-beet eelworm, the British Sugar Corporation object to it on any farm growing sugar-beet. The cereal crops are harvested in this order— winter barley, spring barley, then winter wheat. The present combine harvester cannot deal with more than 130 hectares of any one of these. The sugar-beet harvester can harvest 33 hectares. Perhaps up to half the sugar-beet is lifted too late to allow the sowing of winter cereals. This land must be sown with the only spring cereal, i.e. spring barley. These limitations must now be translated into instructions.

The simplest way to deal with the last point is as follows. If two hectares of sugar-beet are followed by one hectare of spring barley, we can add their gross margins and labour requirements, divide by three and call this one hectare of sugar-beet/barley. As the farmer cannot grow both sugar-beet and rape, we can run one program with sugar-beet and no rape and a second with rape and no sugar-beet and compare the two results.

All the information about the crops is now written into a two-way table or *matrix*. The standard form is given in Fig. 17.2. The activities (in this case the crops that can be grown) are listed X_1 to X_6. Sugar-beet is included this time but no rape. The second line is the net revenue—in this case the gross margins of the crops per hectare.

On the left-hand side, the activities are repeated with the maxima already mentioned in Column B. The sign ⩾ means 'equal to or less than'. Thus winter wheat can have 130 hectares or less. The 50 hectare limit for sugar-beet/barley includes 33 hectares sugar-beet (2/3) and 17 hectares spring barley (1/3). Spring barley is allowed 120 hectares (instead of 130 hectares) to make some allowance for barley with the sugar-beet.

The lower part of the first column lists the man hours of labour available in the six periods already described.

The remaining columns give a list of the production and requirements of each activity. Thus reading the X_1 winter wheat column downwards, one hectare wheat provides a gross margin of +£350. It requires one hectare of land (line 1) and takes one hectare from the limit of 130 hectres (line 2). It also requires 2·0 man hours (line 8) in labour period I (in early spring), 0·9 hours in labour period II (late spring), etc.

				Activities			
	B Column	X_1 Winter wheat	X_2 Winter barley	X_3 Spring barley	X_4 Sugar-beet and spring barley	X_5 Potatoes	X_6 Leys
Net revenue		+350	+300	+270	+457	+650	+150
(1) Land (hectares)	200 ≥	1	1	1	1	1	1
(2) Max winter wheat (hectares)	130 ≥	1	0	0	0	0	0
(3) Max winter barley (hectares)	130 ≥	0	1	0	0	0	0
(4) Max spring barley (hectares)	120 ≥	0	0	1	0	0	0
(5) Max sugar-beet with spring barley (hectares)	50 ≥	0	0	0	1	0	0
(6) Potatoes (hectares)	50 ≥	0	0	0	0	1	0
(7) Leys (hectares)	200 ≥	0	0	0	0	0	1
Labour (5 men)							
(8) Max labour I (hours)	900 ≥	2·0	2·0	4·4	6·3	11·6	1·1
(9) Max labour II (hours)	1375 ≥	0·9	0·5	0·5	8·8	5·2	11·0
(10) Max labour III (hours)	575 ≥	—	2·4	0·8	0·3	0·9	—
(11) Max labour IV (hours)	550 ≥	2·4	—	1·6	0·9	—	—
(12) Max labour V (hours)	750 ≥	3·3	3·3	0·5	7·2	28·4	—
(13) Max labour VI (hours)	525 ≥	0·5	0·5	1·1	7·5	10·1	—

Fig. 17.2 Linear programming matrix; 200 hectare arable farm, medium-sized combine, medium-sized sugarbeet harvester. Sugarbeet included but no rape

Interpretation of results

These data are then fed into the computer and the answer printed out as follows

Solution
objective   72382·3876   ← Total GM in £
              Activities

Variable	Amount	
X_1	130·0000	← Hectares of wheat
X_2	—	

169

X_3	27·3134	←Hectares of spring barley
X_4	42·6866	←Hectares of sugar-beet/barley
X_5	—	
X_6	—	

Of 43 hectares X_4, 1/3 or 14 hectares is spring barley +27 = 41 hectares. The solution is thus (ignoring decimals)

130 hectares winter wheat (the maximum)
41 hectares spring barley
29 hectares sugar-beet

The total gross margin is £72 382. This is the optimum and no other combination of crops will produce a higher figure.

The print out gives additional information.

Optimal
ranges

Variable	From	To
X_1	348·1492	Infinity
X_2	−Infinity	348·1493
X_3	187·2821 X_2	273·1796
X_4	361·2545 X_5	461·4285
X_5	−Infinity	1048·7013
X_6	−Infinity	256·0448

This shows how much the gross margins would have to change before the solution would alter. X_3 (spring barley) has a GM of £270 per hectare. The present solution of 27 hectares holds good if the GM remains between £187·2821 and £273·1796. If the GM dropped below £187, some would be replaced by X_2, winter barley. Similarly if the return from sugar-beet/barley dropped below £361·2545, some of it would be replaced by potatoes. The area of X_1, winter wheat, holds good from £348·1492 to 'infinity'. Infinity means that the 130 hectares is the maximum and a price rise naturally could not increase the area.

The three crops X_2, X_5, and X_6 are marked 'from–infinity'. This means that they did not appear in the program. The figures in the second column indicate the GM necessary to bring them into the program. A GM of £1048 per hectare would, for example, be necessary to bring in potatoes (present GM £650).

Each of these responses to price change assumes that no other change occurs. This information is nevertheless useful and helps to show how stable the solution is. If a price change falling outside these limits seems likely, it would be best to run the program again with the alternative price to discover the extent to which the program would change.

Another useful piece of information is the amount of 'slack'.

Constraints

Slack	Slack Amount	Effective Dual Value	
LP 1	250·8955	LP 5	27·9104
LP 2	868·7015	LD 1	256·0448
LP 3	540·3433		
LP 4	155·8806		
LP 6	109·8060		
Max 2	130·0000		
Max 3	92·6866		
Max 4	7·3134		
Max 5	50·0000		
Max 6	200·0000		

We can see that of the six labour periods (LP), five are not fully used and the man hours unused are listed. Of the crop limits only one (Max 1, winter wheat) is not listed because it is fully used.

The next two columns give us information about the resources that are fully used. LP 5, labour in early autumn, is fully stretched. This is not surprising because at that time lifting sugar-beet conflicts with sowing winter wheat. It is thus obvious that if this is the only place where the shoe pinches, then if this constraint could be eased, a more profitable program should be feasible. The 'value' of £27·9104 is, in fact, the marginal value of labour, i.e. the extra income that could be obtained if we had an extra hour of labour in early autumn.* The marginal value of an extra hectare added to the farm appears to be £256·0448. This is only of academic interest, because no more land is available.

It would thus be worth considering the introduction of a larger sugar-beet harvester or, possibly, hiring an extra man. One point is evident—there is no bottleneck during the cereal harvest (LP 3 and LP 4). A larger combine harvester alone would thus be of no assistance to *this* program.

Alternative programs

Having considered this program (Plan 1) in detail, alterations can be made to the assumptions to discover whether a better solution can be found. This is done by *overwriting* the existing matrix. Suppose we try the following (Fig. 17.3).

---

* Strictly speaking, it is the penalty from losing one hour, but the statement in the text is near enough for our purpose.

Plan 2. The introduction of a larger combine harvester with reduced labour requirements in periods III and IV.
Plan 3. The introduction of a larger sugar-beet harvester with reduced labour requirements in periods V and VI.
Plan 4. The introduction of both machines.

Extra depreciation on either of these machines is £2000 per year.

Men	Plan 1 5	Plan 2 5	Plan 3 5	Plan 4 5
Winter wheat	130	177	125	125
Winter barley	—	—	—	—
Spring barley	41	8	25	25
Sugar-beet	29	15	50	50
Potatoes	—	—	—	—
Leys	—	—	—	—
Total GM	£72 382	£72 469	£78 115	£78 115
Fixed costs	55 000	57 000	57 000	59 000
Farm income	£17 382	£15 469	£21 115	£19 115
Combine harvester	Medium	Large	Medium	Large
SB harvester	Medium	Medium	Large	Large

Fig. 17.3 Effect of introducing larger machines (5 men) (hectares rounded to whole numbers)

As predicted, the introduction of the combine harvester does not pay (Plan 2). More winter wheat is grown but the extra income does not pay for the new machine. The larger sugar-beet harvester (Plan 3) reduces the autumn labour bottleneck and allows the farmer to grow more sugar-beet without sacrificing much winter wheat. The increased output more than pays for the new machine and increases the profit by £3733. The addition of a larger combine (Plan 4) adds nothing to output but its costs lower the farm income.

We can now consider some further permutations. Suppose that the farmer was likely to lose one man or possibly two (Fig. 17.4).

Plan 5. Same as Plan 1 but only four men.
Plan 6. Larger sugar-beet harvester and four men.
Plan 7. Oil seed rape instead of sugarbeet. Medium combine harvester and three men.
Plan 8. Oil seed rape. Large combine harvester and three men.

The loss of one man (Plan 5) reduces output by just over £4000 (compared with Plan 1) but as the saving in wages is £5000, the farm income is increased to £18 196. The larger sugar-beet harvester (Plan 6)

Men	Plan 1 Sugar-beet 5	Plan 5 Sugar-beet 4	Plan 6 Sugar-beet 4	Plan 7 Rape 3	Plan 8 Rape 3
Winter wheat	130	130	107	71	125
Winter barley	—	—	—	54	—
Spring barley	41	56	59	61	56
Sugar-beet	29	14	34	—	—
Rape	—	—	—	14	19
Potatoes	—	—	—	—	—
Leys	—	—	—	—	—
Total GM	£72 382	£68 196	£72 157	£61 568	£64 386
Fixed costs	55 000	50 000	52 000	45 000	47 000
Farm income	£17 382	£18 196	£20 157	£16 568	£17 386
Combine harvester	Medium	Medium	Medium	Medium	Large
SB harvester	Medium	Medium	Large	—	—

Fig. 17.4 Alternatives with four or three men

increases this to £20 157. Plan 7 introduces oil seed rape in place of sugar-beet. A comparison of several plans showed that with rape the best plan was three men (farm income £16 568). An examination of the details showed labour bottlenecks in early spring, late summer, and early autumn. This suggested that a large combine harvester might be helpful. Plan 8 shows that this was so. The larger machine allows more winter wheat in place of winter barley and more rape in place of spring barley (farm income £17 386).

To summarize, the best plans are

(1) with five men, Plan 3, sugar-beet with large sugar-beet harvester, farm income £21 115;

(2) with four men, Plan 6, sugar-beet with large sugar-beet harvester, farm income £20 157;

(3) With three men, Plan 8, rape with large combine, farm income £17 386.

There was no advantage in having six or seven men—the extra output failed to pay for their wages.

Labour supply and cropping programs
The effect of the labour force on the crops grown is illustrated in Fig. 17.5. This assumes a medium-sized combine and sugar-beet harvester

and a labour force varying from two to eight men. With only two men, 40 hectares are left uncultivated and 42 hectares go into leys. With four men, or more, much of the barley is replaced by sugar-beet and winter wheat reaches the maximum permitted. As potatoes have the highest GM per hectare, one might expect them to feature more prominently. The large amount of labour they require in early autumn rules them out, however, until there are six men or more.

As the number of men increases, so also does the total gross margin. The amount added by each extra man declines, however, from £16 994 for the third to £2043 for the eighth

3rd man	£16 994	6th man	£2 744
4th man	6 879	7th man	2 043
5th man	4 186	8th man	2 043

As the wage is £5000, it pays to have the fourth man (£6879) but not the fifth (£4186). This point is illustrated in Fig. 17.5. Total gross margin flattens out, whereas costs increase steadily, leaving a smaller margin of profit when more than four men are employed.

Programming livestock

In the matrix (Fig. 17.1) the only enterprises were crops for sale. Livestock enterprises can, however, also be included. Let us assume that a farmer grows barley and fattens pigs. We can show these as two independent activities

	Barley 1 hectare	Fat pig 1
Net revenue	£300	£25

This means that one hectare barley has a net revenue of £300 (i.e. GM—£400 for barley sold less £100 variable costs) and £25 per fat pig (sold for £50 less feed £25).

Suppose that the farmer feeds the barley to the pigs. Sales disappear from the barley column, leaving £100 variable costs. £25 food cost disappears from the pig column, leaving £50 sales. To link the two enterprises, we add a new line 'barley grain'.

	Unit	Barley 1 ha	Fat pig 1
Net revenue	£ =	−100	50
Barley grain	t ≥	−4	0·25

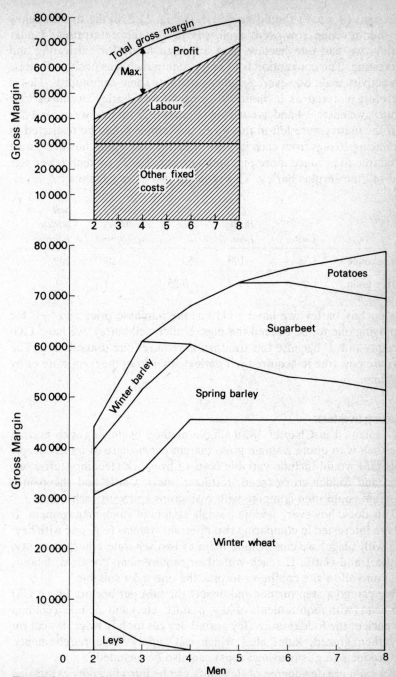

Fig. 17.5 As men increase from 2 to 8, more potatoes and sugarbeet are grown. The increase in output falls off, however, and profits decline with more than four men.

The signs (+ or −) should be noted. In Fig. 17.2 all the figures below the net revenue row were *requirements* for the enterprises. Under barley, we had one hectare land and man hours for cultivating and harvesting. The convention is to enter requirements as positive figures. An activity may, however, *produce* or *supply* some commodity. This is therefore entered as a *minus*. As one hectare barley produces four tonnes, we enter −4 and as each pig requires 0·25 tonnes, we enter 0·25.

If the matrix were left in this form, the farmer would be restricted to producing 16 pigs from each hectare of barley. He might, however, wish to be free to produce more pigs and buy extra barley or keep fewer pigs and sell the surplus barley. This requires two extra columns.

	Unit	Barley 1 ha	Fat pig 1	Buy barley 1 tonne	Sell barley 1 tonne
Net revenue	£ =	−100	50	−110	100
Barley grain	t ⩾	−4	0·25	−1	1

Under 'buy barley' we have −£110 as the purchase price and '−1' for supplying one tonne to feed the pigs. Under 'sell barley' we have £100 receipts and '1' because this transaction requires one tonne to sell. The pigs are now free to acquire their barley either from the farm store or by purchase.

Grazing livestock
As explained in Chapter 18, a simple method of dealing with grazing livestock is to quote a single gross margin per hectare of fodder crops. This GM would include variable costs of livestock (feeding-stuffs, vet, etc.) and fodder crops (seed, fertilizer, etc.). Cattle and sheep in a program could then compete with cash crops and with each other.

This does, however, assume a single system of stock management. If we are interested in comparing two different systems (e.g. one with hay, one with silage) we can include them as two separate enterprises, say, Cattle I and Cattle II (each with their requirements for field, labour, etc.) and allow the computer to pick the one most suitable.

We can go a step further and dissect the GM per hectare into a GM per head (with requirements of hay, pasture, etc.) and include a column for each of the fodder crops (ley grazed, ley cut for hay twice, ley cut for hay then grazed, kale, etc.) which can supply these requirements. By-products (e.g. sugar-beet tops) can also be included.

An even greater degree of flexibility can be introduced by expressing the yield of fodder crops in units of metabolizable energy, starch equivalent, or whatever standards are adopted. The computer can then supply the nutritional needs of the livestock from the fodder crops and purchases that pay best. The technical details of such programs can, however, be quite complex and a reader wishing to pursue the subject should obtain advice from a specialist.

One point that has not been mentioned is the labour requirement for livestock production. We can of course include a livestock enterprise with the man hours required in a matrix alongside cash crops. Care must be taken however to ensure that the result is realistic. If crops and livestock are included together, we are assuming that labour is freely interchangeable. On a small family farm, this may be true. If, for example, the program prescribed 12 sows, this might be acceptable because the farmer could break off from field work to feed the pigs. But on a large farm such a unit would be a nuisance. It would certainly be unrealistic to believe that a few hours saved from the fieldwork could be utilized by purchasing 12 sows to keep the tractor man fully occupied.

Stockmen are becoming increasingly specialized and the tendency is to have a livestock unit large enough to justify at least one skilled stockman or none at all. A simple method of dealing with the point is as follows. Suppose that a large arable farmer has 60 dairy cows. He considers that 120 cows is an economic unit for one man. One program could be run with a fixed unit of 120 cows and compared with a second program with no cows.

Crop rotations

When linear programming was first used, much attention was given to the incorporation of rotational restrictions. This can be done in various ways. If it were considered necessary to have a break from cereals once in four years and to avoid wheat following wheat, this could be done by prescribing a maximum of 25 per cent of wheat and 75 per cent in cereals. If a succession of three wheat crops were allowed but a fall in gross margins was expected in the second and third due to lower yields, or more fertilizer was required to maintain the yield, this could be handled by introducing three separate wheat crops.

	Units	B Column	Sign	Wheat 1	Wheat 2	Wheat 3
Net revenue	£	0	=	350	300	250
Maximum wheat 1	ha	50	≥	1	0	0
Maximum wheat 2	ha	50	≥	0	1	0
Maximum wheat 3	ha	50	≥	0	0	1

If wheat came into the program, the computer would choose Wheat 1 first because it had the highest GM, then Wheat 2 and Wheat 3 in that order if more than 50 hectares came into the program.

An alternative might be to permit two wheat crops in succession only after potatoes or a three year ley, as follows

	Units	B Column	Sign	Wheat 1 ha	Potatoes 1 ha	3 year Ley 1 ha
Net revenue	£	0	=	350	650	−60
Land	ha	200	≥	1	1	1
Maximum wheat	ha	0	≥	1	−2	−0·67

One hectare potatoes 'gives permission' for two hectares of wheat. As three hectares of ley give permission for two hectares of wheat, one hectare ley gives permission for 0·67 hectares wheat.

It must be added that rotational restrictions are being steadily discarded. Indeed, some farmers are able to grow cereals more or less continuously and still obtain satisfactory yields. There are still definite restrictions on growing sugar-beet or potatoes more often than once in about four years but this is one of the few still being observed.

One disadvantage of rotational restrictions is that they are apt to predetermine the answer. If we were growing wheat, barley, potatoes, and clover and restricted wheat to 25 per cent, cereals to 75 per cent, and potatoes to 12½ per cent, the cropping would be practically fixed and programming would be a waste of time.

The general advice is therefore to start with as few restrictions as possible. If the answer is not feasible, it can be corrected on the next run. On the other hand, the answer may be quite unexpected and give a valuable insight into some possibility that had been overlooked.

Capital
The lack of capital can be a great handicap to a farmer wishing to make improvements. For this reason, capital restrictions are sometimes used to keep the plan within the farmer's resources. This can be a useful exercise and can help to show where scarce resources could most profitably be employed. There are two reservations. The first is that although the capital *owned* by the farmer is fixed, the amount he can use in the business is fairly elastic if he can use credit. There is also the consideration discussed in Chapter 19, that the amount required for a given enterprise can be substantially altered by the *timing* of operations. It is therefore possible that capital restrictions in a program could

obscure promising opportunities. For this reason there might be an advantage in starting with little or no capital restriction. If a useful opportunity is revealed, the plan might be used as a means of raising capital. If a substantial sum were borrowed, it would be advisable to prepare a detailed cash flow analysis to show how the loan can be repaid.

Least cost rations

Linear programming can be used to formulate least cost rations. The feeding stuffs available can be listed together with their analyses and prices. A minimum cost ration can then be formulated to satisfy the requirements of stock for minimum protein, metabolizable energy, maximum fibre, etc. This is likely to be of more use to a feeding-stuffs merchant than an individual farmer.

Other techniques

Although linear programming is the most popular form of farm planning on the computer, there are other techniques that are sometimes employed for research rather than advisory work. Three of these that have some practical applications will be mentioned.

1. The Monte Carlo Method. Although linear programming produces a single optimum solution to each problem, there are other solutions with different programs that may give answers almost as good as the optimum. Some of these might be worth consideration because they might be better suited to the needs of individuals or local considerations not taken into account is designing the program.

The Monte Carlo Method can produce a series of such sub-optimal plans. The matrix is similar to that already described with a list of enterprises and their requirements. Upper and lower limits are, however, set on the size of each enterprise. The computer selects enterprises and their size at random and prepares a series of perhaps 3000 plans. Out of these, it selects the 20 or so best ones. These will show quite a variation in their programs but their farm incomes will be only slightly below the optimum.

2. Parametric Programming. In this case one or two items in the matrix are allowed to vary. If used on the program of a typical farm, it could be used to show the effect on production of, say, wheat if prices were changed over a wide range. One could find the point at which wheat appears in the program and the extent to which the area expands in response to price increases. The response of real farmers of the type concerned would of course be much more sluggish. Nonetheless the investigation would help to show the direction and extent to which their farming pattern might eventually change.

3. Dynamic Linear Programming. This technique can be used to trace changes in a program over a period. One could, for example, start an enterprise with a given amount of capital and trace its growth as the surplus capital generated in one period was reinvested in successive periods.

Programming for policy decisions

There are several ways in which programming could be used as an aid in formulating government policy. These include the following.

(1) If it is intended to use price changes to encourage farmers to increase production of a commodity, models of 'typical' farms could be programmed to find whether the price change appeared to be great enough to induce changes in production and the size of the change if it occurred. There are two difficulties. The first is that in a programmed model the changes would occur not smoothly but in distinct steps. These could, however, be smoothed out by using the mean of a number of farm models. The second difficulty as mentioned under Parametric Programming is that while some alert farmers react quickly to price changes (much as the model does) others are slow to move. It does, however, indicate the direction in which change will eventually take place.

(2) The advisory services can use the same technique. If farm models suggest that it would pay to increase production in response to a price change, then this course can be confidently recommended to farmers.

The methods described above would be useful in less developed countries.

(3) Another use for programming is in deciding on the optimum size of holding, in cases such as schemes of land settlement when the government has control over the size. The following is an example where the technique was used to produce changes in the size of existing holdings.

Optimum size of family farms

Before 1939, many County Councils in England and Wales (and the Department of Agriculture in Scotland) purchased farms and divided them into small holdings. They were intended as a 'farming ladder' to enable farm workers and others with limited amounts of capital to become farmers. Some were small market garden holdings, others were miniatures of the large farms around them. It is with the latter that we are now concerned. In the early 1960s, it became apparent that many of these holdings were too small to provide a reasonable living for a family in a more affluent society.

There was another reason. In 1935, a man with a pair of horses was fully occupied cultivating 20 hectares, and on that area he could make a modest living above the level of a farm worker. By 1965, he had a tractor and could have cultivated 40 hectares or more. He also needed 40 hectares to provide what he regarded as a reasonable living. The author was asked to conduct a survey of arable smallholdings in Norfolk.*

They varied in size from 12 to 28 hectares and more than half the 45 holders investigated had incomes below £1000, then judged to be the minimum tolerable level to provide a living for a family and some margin to finance improved methods. The problem was to estimate the size of holding that could be operated by family labour and the income it would provide. A model was set up including the crops and livestock already carried and the methods already in use. The level of husbandry compared favourably with that of larger farms in the area.

In the programming example given earlier in this chapter, the area of land was kept constant and the labour staff was varied. In this case, the parameters were reversed. The family was the fixed asset and the size of holding was varied. Figure 17.6 gives the optimum cropping for a two man family on holdings of 20 (the present average size), 48, and 80 hectares.

Cropping (ha)

Wheat	6	13	—
Barley	7	19	58
Sugar-beet	3	7	4
Potatoes	2	4	7
Leys	2	—	3
Pasture	2	5	8
Size of holding (ha)	20	48	80
Gross margin per ha	£103	£100	£85
Gross margin per man	£1025	£2423	£3383
Family income	£1010	£2751	£3464

Fig. 17.6 Effect on cropping and income of increasing the size of smallholdings

* F. G. Sturrock: *The Optimum Size of Family Farms*, O.P. 9 1965, Agricultural Economics Unit, Cambridge.

All these holdings were within the capacity of two men who were indeed under-employed on 20 hectares. In moving from 20 to 48 hectares, the gross margin per man has doubled but per hectare has hardly changed. At 80 hectares, the gross margin has trebled. The GM per hectare is slightly less because the proportion of cereal crops has increased.

In Fig. 17.7 the estimated incomes are given for three family sizes.* The optimum for a one-man holding appears to be 40 hectares, with a family income of £1843. Above that level, income declines because the

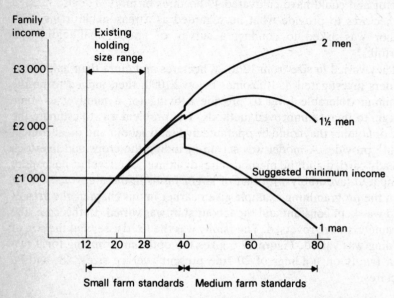

Fig. 17.7 Optimum size—40 hectares for a one-man smallholding, 60 hectares for 1½ men and 80 hectares for a two-man smallholding

holder is unable to cultivate all the land with the methods and equipment available. For 1½ men, 60 hectares is the optimum with an income of £2525. For two men, 80 hectares is the optimum with an income of £3464—nearly 3½ times the existing average income.

What verdict could one draw from this information? The smallholding authority might come to these conclusions.

(1) These farms already have tenants. The only scope for change is that when a holding falls vacant, it can be amalgamated with a neighbour. This would double the holding size to about 40 hectares and double the family income to a reasonable level.

* Since 1965, inflation has reduced the value of money. The incomes quoted would have to be multiplied by more than 4 to give the same purchasing power in 1982.

(2) A few holdings might be increased to 60 hectares to provide for large families.

(3) A holding of 80 hectares would provide an excellent income but must be ruled out on social grounds. If three or four holdings were amalgamated, very few vacancies would occur for new tenants and the authority would be failing to provide the 'farming ladder' that it was created to provide. Men with enough capital for 80 hectares or more could be told to look to the open market.

18 Planning a livestock farm

It is sometimes said that gross margins are less useful on a livestock farm. On an arable farm, there is a choice of crops and gross margins are obviously useful in deciding which to include in the rotation. On a livestock farm the choice may be far more limited. On a mountain sheep farm there may be no real alternative to sheep. On a dairy farm, a unit large enough to employ full-time cowmen may force the farmer into specialization, leaving little room for anything else. But if the choice is limited, what part can gross margins play?

The answer is that gross margins are just as useful but there is a change in emphasis. On an arable farm the problem is mainly *what* to produce. On a livestock farm what to produce may be obvious and the problem is *how* to produce it. In other words, the emphasis is not on choosing between gross margins but on increasing the gross margin itself. Our main concern is thus with the internal organization of the enterprise chosen. On a grassland farm with a high rainfall and good dairy buildings, dairy cows may obviously be the most profitable enterprise. But within a dairying enterprise there is a wide choice of methods of feeding, housing and management, and each of these affects the size of the gross margin. Indeed, the different dairy systems are alternative enterprises within which we must make a choice.

As already stated, the gross margin from livestock is

Output *less*
(*a*) variable cost of livestock, e.g. purchased feeding-stuffs, veterinary charges, medicines, etc;
(*b*) Variable costs of fodder crops, e.g. seeds, fertilizers, sprays, etc.

There are thus two kinds of variable costs—animal costs that vary with the number of animals, and crop costs that vary with the hectares of fodder crops. In practice it is worth keeping these separate because stock numbers can be altered without changing the fodder crops and vice versa.

For example, the gross margin of a herd of 60 dairy cows and followers might be as follows

	£	£
Output (milk, calves, cull cows, *less* replacements)		38 000
Less animal variable costs		
Concentrates	14 000	
Vet, AI, dairy stores, etc.	2 000	
		16 000
Gross margin (without forage costs)		22 000

Gross margin per cow $\dfrac{22\,000}{60}$ = £367

The next point to calculate is the return per hectare of fodder crops. Suppose the cows utilize

Grazing	24 hectares
Hay and silage	16 hectares
Kale	4 hectares
Cereals	4 hectares
	48 hectares

The convention is to include only fodder crops such as pasture, hay, silage, kale and roots. Cereal crops are usually cash crops in their own right and there is nothing to be gained by including their profit with the dairy herd. The dairy cows must therefore 'buy' the cereals they use at market price. The farmer indeed has the choice of feeding home-grown cereals or selling them and buying dairy meal. The implications of the choice are much clearer if the cereals are treated as a separate enterprise.

Assuming that the variable costs (seed, fertilizer, etc.) for the pasture, hay, silage and kale are £3000, the calculation of gross margin is completed as follows

	£
GM (without forage costs)	22 000
Variable costs of forage crops	3 000
GM (including forage costs)	19 000
Area utilized 44 hectares	

GM per hectare $\dfrac{19\,000}{44}$ = £432

This means that if we regard the cows, young stock and fodder crops as a single unit, the gross margin is £432 per 'hectare of cows'.

The gross margin per cow depends on the output per cow and the deductions for animal variable costs, especially for concentrates. The gross margin *per forage hectare* depends on the gross margin per cow, the stocking rate and (to a minor extent) on the forage costs. An estimate of the relative importance of these items can be gained by showing the effect on gross margin per hectare of improving each of them by 10 per cent

	Increased GM per hectare £
10% higher stocking rate	44
10% higher output per cow	86
10% less concentrates	32
10% less fodder costs	6
10% less other variable costs	5

It is thus apparent that output per cow, and stocking rate followed by the cost of concentrates, are by far the most important items; the others are of negligible importance. Similar conclusions can be drawn from a study of beef cattle and sheep. Concentrates may be less important and stocking rate more so, but by and large the same factors operate.

It will be observed that half the dairy output is absorbed by variable costs. An increase of 20 per cent in variable costs would thus reduce gross margins by 20 per cent. This is quite different from cash crops. Cereals, for example, with an output of £500 per hectare might have variable costs of only £125. An extra 20 per cent spent on variable costs would reduce the gross margin by only seven per cent. With cash crops, therefore, output of yield per acre is all important. A high-yielding crop usually has a high gross margin and a low-yielding one, a low gross margin. With livestock, yield per head is only one of several factors affecting gross margins. The gross margin from a high-yielding dairy herd, for example, can be quite low owing to extravagant use of feeding-stuffs, and a moderate-yielding one can have a high gross margin because feeding costs are cut to a minimum.

It is thus worth listing the most important factors determining the gross margin per hectare from dairy cows, beef cattle and sheep

Output per head
Stocking rate
Efficiency in use of feeding-stuffs
Availability of by-products.

Output per head
Other things being equal, the greater the output per head the better. High milk yields from cows and rapid growth of fattening animals are important for two reasons. First, food required for *maintenance* is an overhead that has to be paid for by production. For this reason a bullock that gains 50 kg in 50 instead of 70 days saves the cost of 20 days'

maintenance. Second, livestock on hand occupies land and buildings and ties down capital. The more rapid the turnover, therefore, the greater the return per unit of land, buildings and capital.

The relative importance of stocking rate and output can be illustrated with sheep. The table below shows the gross margin per hectare with varying lambing rates (output) from 120 to 160 lambs per 100 ewes. The stocking rate varies from 7 to 13 ewes per hectare.

Gross margin per hectare*

Ewes per hectare	Lambs reared per 100 ewes		
	120	135	160
7	113	134	174
9	126	155	206
11	139	174	237
13	159	200	274

* John Nix: *Farm Management Pocket Book.*

As can be seen, an increase in ewes per hectare from seven to 13 and in lambing rate from 120 per cent to 160 per cent trebles the GM per hectare from £113 to £274 per hectare. The relative importance of these two factors in raising GM per hectare can, however, be assessed by noting that with seven ewes per hectare the GM per hectare can be raised from £134 to £174 per hectare by increasing the lambing rate from 135 per cent to 160 per cent. Almost exactly the same result could be obtained (with 135 per cent lambs) by improving the pasture and increasing the stocking rate from seven to 11 ewes per hectare. This is a simpler task than that of increasing the lamb crop and serves to emphasize the importance of improving grassland and fodder crops.

Joint enterprise

If one type of stock is kept, the calculation of gross margin per hectare is a simple matter. If two types of stock, e.g. cattle and sheep, share the same pasture or fodder crops, this introduces difficulties. One way is to attempt to allocate pasture and the fodder costs between them. If they use separate pasture, this may be a simple matter. But if the pasture is shared, a small error in estimation can tilt the balance quite unfairly between the two enterprises. A better way is to admit that we are dealing with a joint enterprise and present the results as such. Suppose that a farmer has 40 single suckling cows and 200 ewes sharing 50 hectares. The procedure is to calculate the gross margin in two stages, deducting livestock variable costs from the cows and ewes separately and fodder variable costs from both together.

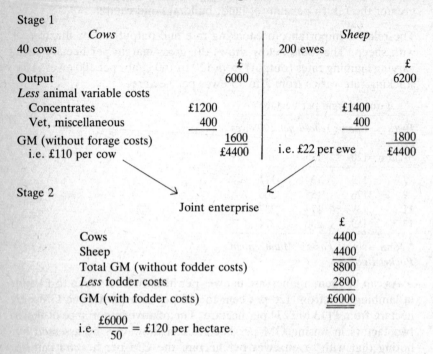

Stage 1

	Cows		Sheep	
	40 cows		200 ewes	
		£		£
Output		6000		6200
Less animal variable costs				
Concentrates	£1200		£1400	
Vet, miscellaneous	400		400	
GM (without forage costs)		1600		1800
i.e. £110 per cow		£4400	i.e. £22 per ewe	£4400

Stage 2

Joint enterprise

	£
Cows	4400
Sheep	4400
Total GM (without fodder costs)	8800
Less fodder costs	2800
GM (with fodder costs)	£6000

i.e. $\dfrac{£6000}{50}$ = £120 per hectare.

At Stage 1 the gross margin (without fodder costs) is £110 per cow and £22 per ewe. This means a loss of £110 for every cow removed from the enterprise and (provided the fodder crops can carry it) a gain of £110 for every cow added. For sheep, the corresponding figure is £22 a head. The joint enterprise has a gross margin of £120 per hectare for the area devoted to pasture and fodder crops such as silage, hay, kale, mangolds, etc. This figure of £120 per hectare can then be compared with cash crops or dairy cows or any other alternative enterprise. Having set the information out in this form it is easy to see how the changes would affect GM. Suppose we substitute cows for sheep. If 10 cows displace 45 ewes, the effect would be

	£
Gain: 10 cows at £110	1100
Loss: 45 ewes at £22	990
Net gain	£110

As the fodder costs are unchanged, the gain would be £110. It will be seen that cows (£110 each) have a gross margin (without fodder costs)

five times as great as sheep (£22). Thus, if one cow displaces five ewes, the margin would remain unchanged. But if a cow displaces fewer than five ewes, then the gain from the cows will more than offset the loss from the sheep. In such a situation, it would pay to change over entirely to beef cows.

The effect of changing the livestock density can also be calculated quite easily. Suppose that by spending £600 more on fertilizer the farmer could carry five more cows and 15 more ewes on the same area of fodder crops as before

	GM
	£
45 cows at £110	4950
215 ewes at £22	4730
GM (without fodder costs)	£9680
Fodder costs (£2800 + 600)	3400
Gross margin	£6280

i.e. $\dfrac{6280}{50}$ = £125·6 per hectare.

The new gross margin of £125½ per hectare is £5½ more than before.

The food conversion rate depends on a variety of factors. It depends on the environment: cattle and sheep in cold and wet conditions use far more food for maintenance, leaving less for production. Food conversion also depends on the age of the animal: the amount of food consumed per 1 kg liveweight gain falls steadily as the animal grows older. For this reason, it may pay to fatten a young animal on a concentrated and expensive diet and to stop before the conversion rate rises too high. This is the basis of systems such as barley beef.

Individual animals also vary greatly in their ability to convert food into liveweight gain. As it is partly an inherited characteristic, the ability to select stock likely to fatten quickly and efficiently is an important element in success.

Availability of by-products

In calculating gross margin per hectare it is customary to count only the hectares of pasture and fodder crops. It is not usual to include cash crops from which they derive sugar-beet tops, residues of vegetable crops, or aftermath from grass seeds. (These hectares have already been counted in calculating the gross margins per hectare from cash crops and should not be counted again.) A sheep flock on an arable farm with a large supply of such by-products may thus obtain a substantial 'bonus' of fodder at no cost in money or hectares. As the sheep are 'charged' with only the hectares of fodder they use exclusively, these few hectares can appear to have a very high gross margin of £200 a hectare or more.

One word of warning should be added. The high gross margin per hectare applies only within the limit of the by-products available. If existing stock are using all the by-products and the farmer introduced more cattle or sheep, they would require a full complement of grazing and fodder crops to sustain them. The extra stock might thus produce a much lower gross margin per hectare than the original livestock.

Another point of importance is competition between dairy cows on the one hand and beef cattle and sheep on the other. As already mentioned, beef cattle and sheep commonly show a gross margin per hectare of £150 compared with £400 from dairy cows. On what grounds, therefore, can one justify cattle or sheep when dairy cows could be kept? The answer is that dairy cows require specialized buildings and specialized labour. Therefore, unless the buildings are already available or the enterprise is large enough to justify their erection and the employment of full-time cowmen, the extra fixed costs of introducing dairy cows would offset the higher gross margin per hectare. There is also the consideration that dairy cows require more care and longer hours than beef cattle.

The point about size of enterprise can be illustrated by a simple example. Suppose that a farmer has 20 hectares devoted to beef cattle managed part time by the field staff or himself.

		Total GM
		£
(a) 20 hectares beef cattle at £150		3000

If the farmer changed this to 25 dairy cows, employing a cowman and altering the buildings to suit, the result might be

		£
(b) 20 hectares dairy cows at £400		8000
less cowman	5500	
alterations	1500	
		7000
GM less extra common costs		£1000

The dairy cows thus contribute a net addition of £1000, which is substantially less than the £3000 from beef cattle. The difficulty is that the cowman is necessary but underemployed. On the other hand, if 40 hectares were available

	£
(a) 40 hectares beef cattle at £150	6000

If the 40 hectares were devoted to 50 cows, one cowman could easily deal with them.

		£
(b) 40 hectares dairy cows at £400		16 000
less cowman	5 500	
alterations	3 000	
		8 500
GM less extra common costs		£7 500

With 40 hectares or more, dairy cows show a substantial advantage over beef cattle. It is obvious, therefore, that unless it is large enough, a dairy herd is not worthwhile on a mixed farm, and small areas of pasture and leys are more efficiently utilized by beef cattle and sheep.

The position would be rather different on a small upland family farm. If there is family labour to spare, a small dairy herd would give a better return for their small area than beef cattle.

Dairy herd management

As already indicated the gross margin from livestock can be changed by the system of management. This point can be demonstrated in milk production. There are three levels of cow management. There are traditional dairy farmers, who make up the bulk of milk producers, and there are progressive farmers who concentrate on raising output with high milk yields per cow, or reduce costs by using improved pasture and cheap bulky foods. The gross margins that might be expected from these groups are shown in Fig. 18.1. After charging forage costs the gross margin per cow is £270 for the average herd and £305 for the high-yield herd. Per hectare, the figures are £491 and £555 respectively. For poor yielding herds, the return is only £427. The young dairy stock give a gross margin of £170 per head for the whole rearing period or £200 per hectare. Young stock, as might be expected, have returns per hectare close to those for rearing beef cattle.

It now remains to give the return for a dairy herd as a whole and to show how this can be influenced by the system of management.

(1) Average traditional dairy herd. Followers equal the cows in numbers, i.e. enough heifers are reared to replace 33 per cent of the herd each year.

	GM	Hectares
1 cow	£330	0·55
1 young heifer	77	0·28
	407	0·83
less forage, 0·83 hectares at £90	75	
	332 ÷ 0·83 = £400 per hectare	

191

Dairy cows	Low yield	Average	High yield
Litres per cow	4000	5000	6000
Total hectares per cow	0·55	0·55	0·55
	£	£	£
Output—milk	440	550	660
calf	70	70	70
culls (25%)	60	60	60
	570	680	790
less replacements	80	90	100
Total output	490	590	690
Variable costs—concentrates	160	220	280
vet, AI, etc	40	40	40
GM (excluding forage costs)	290	330	370
Forage costs	55	60	65
GM (including forage costs)	235	270	305
GM per hectare	£427	£491	£555

Young dairy stock		Per 3 years*	Per heifer
		£	£
Per heifer calved: value into herd		450	150
less calf		70	23
Output		380	127
less variable costs: concentrates	£120		
miscellaneous	£30		
		150	50
GM (excluding forage costs)		230	77
Forage costs		60	20
GM (including forage costs)		170	57
Hectares used		0·85	0·28
GM per hectare		£200	

* These costs are for the full rearing period of nearly three years. Alternatively, it can be regarded as the annual costs of a 'rearing unit' of three young stock—calf, yearling and down-calving heifer, producing one heifer per year for the dairy herd. *One* young dairy animal thus costs one-third of the above per year.

Fig. 18.1 Gross margins from dairy cows

(2) Farmer retains all the young stock, selling the surplus as stores or dairy heifers.

	GM	Hectares
1 cow	£330	0·55
3 young stock	230	0·85
	560	1·40
less forage, 1·40 hectares at £90	126	
	£434 ÷ 1·4 = £310 per hectare	

A large proportion of young stock reduces the gross margin per hectare from £400 to £310.

(3) Poorly managed herd (yield 4000 l.) uses 0·10 kg concentrates per litre more than No. 1 (say 400 kg extra at £130 = £52). Cow and follower use 1·3 hectares.

	GM	Hectares
1 cow	£238	0·8
1 heifer	77	0·5
	315	1·3
less forage, 1·3 hectares at £60	78	
	£237 ÷ 1·3 = £182 per hectare	

(4) High yielding herd on productive pasture. Three young stock to every four cows, i.e. enough to replace 25 per cent of the herd each year.

	GM	Hectares
1 cow	£370	0·49
1 heifer	77	0·23
	447	0·72
less forage, 0·72 hectares at £130	94	
	£353 ÷ 0·7 = £504 per hectare	

As can be seen, better management raises the gross margin from £400 to £504 per hectare.

(5) A small farm. Standards as for No. 4 but the farmer rears no young stock. (GM per cow reduced by £20 to allow for extra cost of buying heifers.)

	GM	Hectares
1 cow	£350	0·49
less forage, 0·49 hectares at £130	64	
	£286 ÷ 0·49 = £584 per hectare	

The standards of management given above are by no means extreme. The yields from Nos 1 and 2 are 5000 l., from Nos 4 and 5 are 6000 l. and from No. 3 is 4000 l. Many herds are better managed and give higher yields than Nos 4 and 5. Many others are far worse than No. 3. Nevertheless the gross margin per hectare on the best (£584) is three times as great as the worst (£182).

This example thus emphasizes the point that within a single enterprise there are many alternatives and there is as much scope for planning on a specialist farm as there is in mixed farming.

Example

This example is a dairy farm of 80 hectares. The buildings are substantial but inconvenient. There are standings for 50 cows and ample space to rear young stock. Most of the farm is in grass but it could be ploughed. The farmer ploughs up about six hectares each year and puts it through a rotation of wheat, potatoes and kale, oats, long ley. The cowman employed also tends the young stock. The farmer does the field work and can replace the cowman on holiday. The cowman helps in the field when necessary. Casual workers lift the potatoes; a contractor bales the hay. Surplus young stock are sold as stores or heifers at varying ages.

The farmer is not satisfied with this modest profit. He asks the help of the local Agricultural Adviser who prepares a normalized budget of his present position as follows

Common costs	£	Gross margins	Hectares	£
Wages	5 500	Dairy cows	38	11 500
Machinery	8 000	Young cattle	28	3 920
Miscellaneous	3 900	Potatoes	2	1 220
	17 400	Wheat	6	1 920
		Oats	6	1 740
Farm income	2 900		80	£20 300
	£20 300			

How should the Agricultural Adviser deal with such a case?

(1) The first step is to set out the gross margins and compare them with local averages.

Gross margin per hectare	This farm £	Local average £
Dairy cows	303	490
Young stock	140	200
Potatoes	610	600
Wheat	320	300
Oats	290	280

The cash crops are reasonably satisfactory and can be left aside for the moment. The real weakness is in the dairy cows.

(2) A low GM per hectare from cows can be due to a low GM per cow or to too many hectares of fodder crops per cow. Taking first the GM per cow, the following estimate is made from the accounts.

	Per cow	£			£
Concentrates	250		Milk		560
Forage costs	60		Calf		70
Replacements	90		Cull cows		50
Vet, AI etc.	50				
Gross margin	230				
	£680				£680

The yield is 5090 *l.* per cow which is average. The costs seem reasonable, except for concentrates. At £130 per tonne, the quantity is 1·92 tonnes per cow or 0·38 kg per litre. The consumption should be about 0·33 kg per litre or 1·68 tonnes per cow. The cost should therefore be £218 per cow, instead of £250, a saving of £32 per cow. If corrected this would raise the GM per cow to £262. This is a fault but not the major one. The GM per hectare for young stock (£140) is below average (£200). With 60 head or 20 units, the GM per unit is £196 which is above average (£170).

(3) The utilization of forage crops is as follows

Hectares	Cows	Young stock	Total
Grazing	22	16	38
Hay	13	11	24
Kale	3	1	4
	38	28	66

This can now be compared with local averages.

Hectares	Total	Per unit	Average
50 Cows	38	0·76	0·57
60 Young stock = 20 units	28	1·40	0·85

The dairy herd is thus using far more land than seems necessary.

(4) As young stock have a much lower GM than adult stock, the farmer should carry no more than is necessary—12 units (36 head) should provide enough replacements for 50 cows.

Plan 1
   (*a*) Reduce the young stock to 12 units.
   (*b*) Improve the grassland to carry the stock on fewer hectares.
At average standards the dairy herd should require

50 cows at 0·57	29
12 units young stock at 0·85	10
	39 hectares

195

This will release 27 hectares for cash crops. Assuming that concentrate feeding can be improved, the GM per cow should be increased by £32 from £230 to £262.

Budget for Plan 1

Common costs	£	Gross margins	£
As before	17 400	Dairy cows 50 @ £262	13 100
Extra fuel, etc		Young stock 12 units	
17 hectares @ £15	255	@ £200	2 400
Extra fertilizer		Potatoes 2 hectares @ £610	1 220
on grass, etc.	2 000	Wheat 19 hectares @ £320	6 080
Farm income	9 145	Barley 20 hectares @ £300	6 000
	£28 800		£28 800

Barley has been substituted for oats as likely to give a somewhat higher GM per hectare. The estimated profit of £9145 is an improvement on the present one of £2900. It will be noted that crop and livestock yields are unaltered—although with close individual attention to 50 cows, the yield per cow should be increased.

The success of this plan depends, however, on the farmer's ability to improve the grassland so that the dairy herd can release 27 hectares for use as cash crops. This is a matter on which the farmer should take advice—although the stocking ratio assumed is no more than is obtained by other farmers in the area.

Plan 2

Suppose that the farmer concentrates on cash crops. 70 hectares can be ploughed and 10 hectares devoted to beef cows, rearing say early weaned calves for sale at 18 months. It is assumed that all the work can be done by the farmer and one man. As there is difficulty in recruiting labour to harvest more than two hectares of potatoes, sugarbeet (which could be harvested by one man if necessary) has been substituted.

Budget for Plan 2

Common costs	£	Gross margins		£
As before	17 400	Wheat	20 hectares @ 320	6 400
		Winter barley	10 hectares @ 300	3 000
		Spring barley	25 hectares @ 270	6 750
		Sugarbeet	15 hectares @ 550	8 250
Extra fuel, etc		Cattle	10 hectares @ 200	2 000
50 hectares @ £15	750			
Replacement of				
machinery	2 000			
	20 150			
Farm income	6 250			
	£26 400			£26 400

As can be seen, the estimated profit is £6250. This is less than Plan 1 but the farmer can sell off his dairy herd for at least £25 000. This could be used to finance some additional enterprise. As Plan 1 seems the most promising, the farmer wonders if he should intensify milk production. The alternative is explored in Question 1 below.

Questions

1. Having examined Plans 1 and 2, the farmer wonders whether he could specialize entirely on dairy cows. He estimates that for £25 000 he could adapt the buildings to save labour and take up to 100 cows. He can get a grant of £8000 and a 20-year mortgage at 12 per cent for the remainder. With no cash crops, the farmer and one cowman should be able to manage the farm. An overdraft at 12 per cent can be arranged to buy additional cows and heifers at £400 a head—this should be repaid within six years (treat as a six-year mortgage). Prepare Plan 3. (*See* Appendix 2 for Annual Mortgage Repayment.)

2. Prepare a table comparing gross margins and income of the present system and Plans 1, 2 and 3. Discuss the advantages and disadvantages of each. What course of action would you suggest to the farmer?

3. Suppose that the farmer waits a year and interest rates fall to eight per cent. Would this change you opinion of the feasibility of Plan 3?

4. Having examined all these plans, devise a better one of your own.

5. An arable farmer keeps sheep (GM £160 per hectare) on land that could grow cereals (GM £360 per hectare). He maintains that the sheep enhance the fertility of the soil. What increase in cereal yields would justify this proposition? How likely is this result to be obtained?

19 Starting a farm

The question is often asked: 'I would like to tender for a farm of (say) 100 hectares. I believe that I can raise £50 000; is this enough capital to take it as a tenant?' Capital requirements have been increasing for many years. Before 1939, a tenant could have established himself for £25 a hectare. Now he might require £800 and, if he bought the farm, he would need to add another £3000 or £4000 for land and buildings.

Average capital requirements are not, however, of much value in individual cases. The amount required varies greatly from farm to farm. Capital depends on the type of farm, and good arable land naturally requires far more per hectare than upland pasture. Capital also depends on the intensity of the system adopted and the speed with which the enterprises are built up. A farmer who starts with high-grade stock and a full range of new machinery can easily spend twice or three times as much per hectare as another who starts with poorer stock and second-hand equipment. It is certainly possible to start a little understocked and hope to build up numbers out of profits. Indeed a farmer short of capital would be well advised not to spend too lavishly at the beginning because he may modify his ideas after a few months and may need a margin to make a change.

There is, however, a lower limit to the amount of capital needed for any particular farm and below this level the farm business is likely to founder. Too much cheese-paring in the early stages can hamper growth and cause more loss in output than is saved in costs. There is a further point. When a farmer tenders for a tenancy he may have stiff competition, and if he must offer a very high rent to obtain the tenancy and also make enough profit to live on, he may need to farm intensively from the beginning. This in turn implies enough capital to build up the business fairly rapidly.

The aim of this chapter is to show a method of assessing capital requirements. When thinking of taking a farm, the intending farmer should make two separate plans

(1) He should prepare a budget to show how he would like to farm the holding when he is fully established. He should plan the crops and

livestock to explore the possibilities. He should estimate the profits and check this against economists' reports for the area and the opinion of the local Agricultural Adviser.

(2) Having decided on his goal, he should then make a plan to show how he is to reach it and how much capital this will require.

This entails the preparation of a *Capital profile* from the *cash flow* of receipts and payments over the first two or three years.

The question may be asked: is it not possible to estimate capital requirements by examining the balance sheets of existing farmers? The net capital in a balance sheet is certainly an estimate of the amount of capital a farmer could realize by selling up on the day concerned. This is not, however, necessarily the amount that would be required by a new occupier. The implements on an existing farm stand at a well-written-down value but a newcomer might have to buy much of his equipment new to obtain exactly what he requires. The inventory, moreover, might contain stocks of grain or other produce ready for sale that the new farmer need not take over because the existing occupier would probably sell them on the market before he left. Above all, however, the new farmer needs enough capital not only to buy the live and dead stock necessary but also enough to run the farm until the flow of receipts can pay for current expenses.

In practice, therefore, an incoming farmer needs enough capital for the following items.

On entry or soon after he will need money to pay for

(1) tenant right valuation, including cultivations and growing crops left by the previous occupier. In autumn an incoming tenant may also be glad enough to take over fodder crops and litter that he can use for his stock during the first winter;

(2) livestock, especially adult breeding stock. He need not necessarily *buy* a full quota of young stock at the beginning as he may breed his own replacements after entry;

(3) implements to get cultivations under way.

During the year he will also require

(4) working capital to pay for seeds, fertilizers, wages and other current expenditure until the flow of receipts exceeds payments;

(5) cash to pay living expenses for the same period as (4) above.

Example 1: Starting an arable farm

The construction of a capital profile can be illustrated by taking an example. Assume that Mr Brown is about to take over a 160 hectare arable farm at Michaelmas. He intends to run it on a five-course shift—two wheats, two barleys and a break crop consisting of leys, potatoes and a few fodder roots. He intends to buy 30 beef cows and keep them on 10 hectares of permanent pasture and 10 hectares of leys, etc. The tenant right (including cultivations for winter wheat and some fodder crops) is valued at £8000. Mr Brown estimates that he must spend £40 000 on tractors and implements on entry and a further £25 000 on a combine harvester before harvest. He intends to employ 3 men (wage £5000). Other costs are estimated as follows: fuel £4000, repairs £3000, miscellaneous £6000. Crop sales and variable costs per hectare are as follows

	Hectares	Output	Seed	Fertilizer	Sprays	Casual labour	Gross margin
		£	£	£	£	£	£
Wheat	60	500	35	55	40	—	370
Barley	60	360	25	55	20	—	260
Potatoes	20	1400	200	160	70	170	800
Leys, etc.	10	—	30	80	20	—	130*
Pasture	10	—	—	50	—	—	50*

*Fodder costs per hectare

It is assumed that the beef cows will calve in early spring and that 28 calves will be sold at eight months old around October. The cattle use £800 worth of purchased feeding-stuffs and cost £300 for veterinary and other expenses. During the second year, £2500 is allowed for replacement of breeding cows, and £4000 is also allowed in the second year for machinery replacement. This figure will increase in later years.

The next task is to list the payments and receipts and to date them. A monthly profile could be prepared but this is more detailed than is usually necessary because, quite apart from any deliberate granting of credit, there is usually a delay of a few weeks before accounts are sent and paid. It is thus sufficiently exact to divide the year into quarters and to assume that the farmer can use cash received during each quarter to pay expenses in that quarter. It is also assumed at this point that the farmer receives no credit and pays expenses in the quarter in which they are incurred.

Figure 19.1 shows a cash-flow profile over the first two years. During the first quarter (October to December) the farmer pays for tenant right, machinery and breeding cows. Seed and fertilizer for winter wheat was in the tenant right, and for spring-sown crops in the second quarter; crop sprays appear in the third and fourth. Purchased feeding-stuffs are placed in the two winter quarters. Most of the other expenses have been spread evenly over the year.

Expenditure in the first quarter (£66 400) is unusually high because it includes a number of non-recurrent items on entry. The second quarter is also heavy and includes rent and the bulk of the seeds and fertilizers. The third quarter is less, and the fourth shows an increase due to the purchase of the combine harvester and the second instalment of the rent.

By the end of the year £146 600 has been spent and no receipts have been obtained. Crop receipts appear from October onwards, in the fifth quarter. It has been assumed that half the cereals are sold before New Year and the remainder after. In practice, of course, the timing of sales depends on circumstances. If the farmer is short of cash, he will sell early, but if he expects prices to rise he will sell later in the season.

In the second-last line the surplus or deficit of receipts over expenses is shown in each quarter. In the last line is the cumulative deficit from the date of entry. At the end of the first year this reaches its maximum total of £146 600. In the fifth and sixth quarters this deficit falls to £110 300 and then climbs again to £139 500 at the end of the second year. The 'deficit' at any point is in fact the amount of money that the farmer has invested in the farm at that date—in other words, the capital. It will be seen that on an arable farm the capital invested rises to a peak at about Michaelmas and then declines as the crops are sold. This is because expenses are a more or less steady flow throughout the year, whereas receipts from cash crops appear from October onwards. An arable farmer thus tends to be short of cash in late summer, just before the crops are ready for sale. In other words, this is the point at which his capital requirements reach a peak. In the second year, the system has become established and the normal ebb and flow of capital investment can be clearly seen. Capital requirements again reach a peak in September of the second year, and this pattern is likely to repeat itself in future years. It will be noted that the peak at the end of the second year is somewhat less than at the end of the first. The reason is that a profit of £11 100 has been made during the second year. As only £4000 has been drawn for private purposes, the remaining £7 100 has been reinvested in the farm and this has reduced the deficit by that amount.*

It is evident that on a farm of this kind the critical date when capital requirements are at a maximum is around 30 September. Thus if the farmer has enough capital to pass this point, he has enough to continue indefinitely—provided that he continues to make a profit and can finance further expansion out of profits.

On an arable farm of the kind described it is indeed possible to estimate capital requirements without constructing a complete profile.

---

* This assumes that the valuation remains constant.

	1 Oct–Dec	2 Jan–Mar	3 Apr–Jun	4 Jul–Sep	Total for year 1	5 Oct–Dec	6 Jan–Mar	7 Apr–Jun	8 Jul–Sep	Total for year 2
On entry										
Tenant right	8 000	—	—	—	8 000	—	—	—	—	—
Machinery	40 000	—	—	25 000	65 000	—	—	—	—	—
Beef cows	10 000	—	—	—	10 000	—	—	—	—	—
	58 000	—	—	—	83 000	—	—	—	—	—
Current costs										
Cow replacement	—	—	—	—	—	2 500	—	—	—	2 500
Seed	—	5 800	—	—	5 800	2 100	5 800	—	—	7 900
Fertilizer	—	7 800	—	—	7 800	3 300	7 800	—	—	11 100
Sprays	—	—	4 200	1 000	5 200	—	—	4 200	1 000	5 200
Casual labour	—	—	—	—	—	3 400	—	—	—	3 400
Regular labour	3 750	3 750	3 750	3 750	15 000	3 750	3 750	3 750	3 750	15 000
Rent	—	6 000	—	6 000	12 000	—	6 000	—	6 000	12 000
Fuel	1 000	1 000	1 000	1 000	4 000	1 000	1 000	1 000	1 000	4 000
Repairs	750	750	750	750	3 000	750	750	750	750	3 000
Replacements	—	—	—	—	—	1 000	1 000	1 000	1 000	4 000

	1 Oct–Dec	2 Jan–Mar	3 Apr–Jun	4 Jul–Sep	Total for year 1	5 Oct–Dec	6 Jan–Mar	7 Apr–Jun	8 Jul–Sep	Total for year 2
Feeding-stuffs	400	400	—	—	800	400	400	—	—	800
Other costs	1 500	1 500	1 500	1 500	6 000	1 500	1 500	1 500	1 500	6 000
Living expenses	1 000	1 000	1 000	1 000	4 000	1 000	1 000	1 000	1 000	4 000
	66 400	28 000	12 200	40 000	146 600	20 700	29 000	13 200	16 000	78 900
Receipts										
Wheat	—	—	—	—	—	15 000	15 000	—	—	30 000
Barley	—	—	—	—	—	10 800	10 800	—	—	21 600
Potatoes	—	—	—	—	—	18 000	10 000	—	—	28 000
Calves	—	—	—	—	—	5 400	—	—	—	5 400
Cows	—	—	—	—	—	1 000	—	—	—	1 000
	—	—	—	—	—	50 200	35 800	—	—	86 000
Surplus or deficit	−66 400	−28 000	−12 000	−40 000	−146 600	+29 500	+6 800	−13 200	−16 000	+7 100
Cumulative deficit = capital	−66 400	−94 400	−106 600	−146 600	−146 600	−117 100	−110 300	−123 500	−139 500	−139 500

Fig. 19.1 Capital profile for first two years for a 160 hectare arable farm

The capital is the sum of the values of

(a) tenant right;
(b) livestock;
(c) implements;
(d) working capital, which is estimated as current costs *less* receipts generated in the course of the year and marketed before 30 September.

In this case

	£
Tenant right	8 000
Livestock	10 000
Machinery	65 000
One year's expenses	59 600
Personal expenses	4 000
	£146 600
Less receipts before 30 September	None
Capital required	£146 600

The total of £146 600 for 160 hectares is £916 a hectare. It should be emphasized, however, that this is an estimate for one plan carried out in the way described. With a different programme and different tactics in carrying it out, quite a different answer would be obtained. Indeed, if the farmer is short of capital, one of the main reasons for preparing a capital profile is to enable him to plan and replan in order to keep capital requirements within the total available. If capital requirements exceed the amount of money available he must decide how he is to deal with the situation. He has three alternatives

(1) he can rely on credit. We have assumed so far that all expenses are paid in the quarter in which they are incurred; Suppliers may, however, not press for payment for a few months.
(2) he may ask the bank for an overdraft;
(3) he may change the farm plan.

Suppose, for example, that Mr Brown has only £120 000. According to the profile, he will exceed this limit about July and will have a deficit until about November. He could therefore take this plan to his bank manager and ask for an overdraft not exceeding £30 000 for about four months. It will be noted, by the way, that he will need an overdraft at the same time in the next year. Provided he makes a substantial profit in the second year and does not spend it all, the overdraft will be smaller. But if he invests in some new enterprise it may well be greater.

Merchant credit for a few months is not hard to obtain at the cost of some loss of discounts. If reliance is placed on this source of credit, it is as well to note which bills can be postponed and for how long. The seed merchant might be willing to wait, but unless he can wait from March to November this would not solve the problem. The best one to postpone, if it could be arranged, would be the payment for the combine harvester.

In the long run the farmer should shape his farm plan to maximize his profit. But if he is short of capital, he may be compelled to modify his plans to some extent to keep within the limit of his resources.

How much can be accomplished by changing the farm plan? As will be shown, the tactics adopted can affect capital requirements quite substantially. This can happen for two reasons. In the first place, some crops and livestock give a much *quicker* return on money invested than others and will naturally be preferred by the farmer short of capital. In the second place, some crops and livestock are *complementary* to others in capital requirements. On an arable farm, for example, store cattle fattened in winter can be complementary to cash crops. Stores can be bought in autumn when crops are being sold and cash is plentiful and sold again in spring when cash is short. In this case the cattle do not need additional capital because they are using capital that would otherwise be idle.

It is thus worth considering farm enterprises in terms of the size and timing of the cash flow to which they give rise.

Cash crops

Most farm crops absorb capital over the year and give a cash return from September onwards. As already mentioned, such crops produce a shortage of capital in spring and summer and an ample supply in autumn and winter. Peas and some fruit and vegetables marketed in summer are thus complementary to crops marketed in autumn because they provide cash that helps to finance the late summer period.

Dairy cows

Dairy cows require a large fixed investment but give a quick return on money invested in feeding-stuffs. They also provide a flow of receipts throughout the year that may be very useful in providing working capital.

Cattle

Beef cows require a fixed investment and give a slow return, with a time lag of 12 to 24 months or more. Store cattle, on the other hand, need capital for only a few months and can be timed to be complementary to crops and other enterprises.

Sheep

Breeding ewes require a fixed investment and give a return after nearly 12 months. Late lambs marketed in autumn coincide with cash crops but early lambs can provide a useful flow of cash in late spring and summer.

Pigs

Sows resemble dairy cows in requiring a large fixed investment for buildings and working capital. They also provide a flow of cash throughout the year. If the farmer starts with gilts, he can expect a cash return from fat pigs in about seven to ten months. A fattening unit using weaners could give returns in three to five months. A new pig enterprise can therefore be timed to be complementary in its capital requirements to other enterprises.

Laying hens

Point-of-lay pullets give a return within a few weeks of purchase. Day-old chicks do so in about five months, and also need capital for rearing equipment. A new poultry enterprise can therefore be timed to be complementary to other enterprises.

Returning now to our example, it can be seen that all the enterprises chosen have a time lag of about 12 months and all produce a flow of receipts in the following autumn. None of them is therefore complementary to another. In other words, the total amount of capital required is more or less the sum of all the enterprises included. With care, it would have been possible to make one enterprise finance another. For example, if Mr Brown had purchased store cattle for winter fattening in place of beef cows, the sale of fat cattle in spring would have released capital for expenses and the grazing could have been let for the summer.

Example 2: Starting a dairy farm

Mr Green is about to take over a 78 hectare dairy farm. There were previously about 50 cows and some cash crops. Mr Green doubts whether 50 cows is really enough to justify the employment of a skilled cowman. If the dairy herd is increased there will be hardly enough hectares to justify a complement of field equipment. He therefore decides to specialize in milk production and the landowner is willing to adapt the buildings to accommodate more cows. The first point to decide is the size of the dairy herd.

Mr Green obtains the following information, assuming an average yield of 5000 l.

	Per cow	100 cows
Output	£550	£55 000
Concentrates 5000 l. cow @ 0·33 kg/l.	1·65 tonnes	
Concentrates @ £130	£215	£21 500
Forage variable costs (seed, fertilizers, etc.)	48	4 800
Other costs	28	2 800
Forage area (pasture plus forage costs)	0·57 hectares	57 hectares

Young stock consists of calves, yearling heifers and heifers about to calve. A 'unit' of three young stock will thus produce one adult heifer a year to join the dairy herd. About 20 per cent of the cows will be replaced annually. Allowing for an occasional unsatisfactory replacement, we can allow one replacement unit for every four cows.

	Per unit	25 units
Concentrates	£125	£3125
Forage variable costs	£ 57	£1425
Other costs	£ 20	£ 500
Forage area	0·85 hectares	21 hectares

The area required per cow is thus 0·57 + 0·85/4 = 0·78 hectares. With 78 hectares Mr Green can keep 100 cows and 25 replacement units. Costs on this basis have therefore been inserted above.

Mr Green has bought no young stock and will rear his own replacements. During the first year therefore he will have only about 25 heifer calves below one year. Requirements

	Per calf	*Per 25 calves*
Concentrates	£28	£700
Other costs	7	175

The forage includes pasture, hay, silage and some kale or other root crops. As the forage area for the young stock will be under-utilized, he decides to take a small crop of barley which will be combined by a contractor and sold.

Mr Green assumes that he can buy 100 cows for an average of £450. To allow for delays and young down calving heifers, he assumes 10 per cent less yield and input of concentrates for the cows in the first year. 20 per cent replacements are allowed for, although if he has chosen good young stock this figure may be somewhat high.

The capital profile is shown in Fig. 19.2. It is quite different in form from the previous example. On the arable farm, the farmer had to finance a whole year's costs before he had an appreciable amount of

	1 Oct–Dec	2 Jan–Mar	3 Apr–Jun	4 Jul–Sep	Total for year 1	5 Oct–Dec	6 Jan–Mar	7 Apr–Jun	8 Jul–Sep	Total for year 2
On entry										
Tenant right	2 000	—	—	—	2 000	—	—	—	—	—
Heifers	45 000	—	—	—	45 000	—	—	—	—	—
Machinery, etc.	25 000	—	—	—	25 000	—	—	—	—	—
	72 000				72 000					
Current costs										
Heifer replacement	—	—	4 000	5 000	9 000	—	—	4 000	5 000	9 000
Concentrates—cows	6 450	6 450	3 225	3 225	19 350	7 167	7 167	3 583	3 583	21 500
Young stock	175	175	175	175	700	781	781	781	782	3 125
Forage crops—cows	—	3 800	1 000	—	4 800	—	3 800	1 000	—	4 800
Young stock	—	925	500	—	1 425	—	925	500	—	1 425
Other costs—cows	700	700	700	700	2 800	700	700	700	700	2 800
Young stock	44	44	43	44	175	125	125	125	125	500
Wages	1 375	1 375	1 375	1 375	5 500	1 375	1 375	1 375	1 375	5 500

	1 Oct–Dec	2 Jan–Mar	3 Apr–Jun	4 Jul–Sep	Total for year 1	5 Oct–Dec	6 Jan–Mar	7 Apr–Jun	8 Jul–Sep	Total for year 2
Rent	—	2 500	—	2 500	5 000	—	2 500	—	2 500	5 000
Fuel and repairs @ £25	487	488	487	488	1 950	487	488	487	488	1 950
Combining barley	—	—	—	600	600	—	—	—	—	—
Overheads @ £30	585	585	585	585	2 340	585	585	585	585	2 340
Living expenses	1 000	1 000	1 000	1 000	4 000	1 000	1 000	1 000	1 000	4 000
	82 816	18 042	13 090	15 692	129 640	12 220	19 446	14 136	16 138	61 940
Receipts										
Milk	10 000	13 166	13 167	13 167	49 500	13 750	13 750	13 750	13 750	55 000
Calves	1 050	1 050	1 050	1 050	4 200	1 050	1 050	1 050	1 050	4 200
Cull cows	—	—	1 000	3 000	4 000	—	—	1 000	3 000	4 000
Barley	—	—	—	4 000	4 000	—	—	—	—	—
	11 050	14 216	15 217	21 217	61 700	14 800	14 800	15 800	17 800	63 200
Surplus deficit	−71 766	−3 826	+2 127	+5 525	−67 940	+2 580	−4 646	+1 664	+1 662	+1 260
Cumulative deficit = capital	−71 766	−75 592	−73 465	−67 940	−67 940	−65 360	−70 006	−68 342	−66 680	−65 420

Fig. 19.2 Capital profile and costs flow for first two years for 78 hectare dairy farm

receipts. On a dairy farm, milk provides a steady flow of receipts that help to finance current expenditure. There is in fact a cash surplus in three of the four quarters by the second year. (The deficit in the spring quarter is due to purchasing seeds, fertilizers, etc. for the forage crops and paying the half year's rent). Maximum capital requirements (£75 592, or £969 per hectare) occur in the second quarter. After that they decline somewhat (partly due to the sale of the barley) and then remain relatively constant.

It will be seen that unlike the arable farm where there is a surplus of over £7000 in the second year, the surplus in this case is only £1260. This does not mean that there is hardly any profit. The farmer has already drawn £4000 for personal expenditure which is part of the farm profit. There is a further point. During these two years, the farmer has been building up a herd of replacements worth at least £7000. The cost of doing so has been included and this represents an investment of part of the profit. Home bred heifers will begin to calve in the third year and this should reduce or eliminate the cost of buying adult replacements.

Capital requirements for such a farm would be estimated briefly as follows

	£
Tenant right	2 000
Livestock	45 000
Machinery and equipment	25 000
Working capital	
3 months expenses (including	
private drawings)	10 816
	82 816

This calculation differs in one respect from the estimate for the arable farm. In that example, working capital was calculated as one year's current costs less receipts during the year. A similar calculation here would be £57 640 costs less £61 700 receipts. This would suggest that no working capital is required. It is true that if the cows come into milk quite quickly, milk receipts soon begin to pay for current expenses. There is, however, a lag in the early stages between the purchase of down calving heifers and their first calving. There is also a delay between the despatch of milk and the first milk cheque. Prudence therefore suggests that enough capital should be available to finance expenses for the first three months. The total of £82 816 is slightly higher than the peak cash deficit £75 592 shown in the cash flow estimate which allows for milk receipts during the first quarter. A margin of safety to cover contingencies and unexpected difficulties is however advisable.

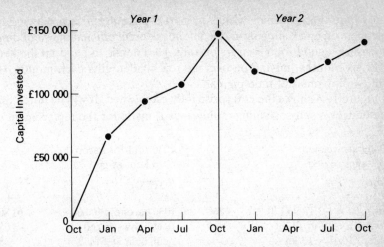

Fig. 19.3 Capital profile of the arable farm. Capital invested builds up to a peak each October, then falls off as the crops are sold. The farmer short of capital may need a bank overdraft to tide over the autumn peak.

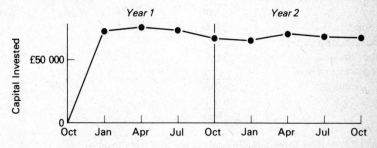

Fig. 19.4 Capital profile of the dairy farm. As milk receipts are spread over the year, there is usually no marked seasonal variation in investment.

Example 3: Starting a pig herd

So far we have been dealing with starting a farm. There is also the problem of estimating the amount of capital required to start a new enterprise on an existing farm. The process is essentially the same as that already described. The first step is to prepare a budget to show the profit expected from the enterprise. If the return seems sufficiently attractive, plans can then be made to show how the enterprise can be built up, how much it will cost and how these capital requirements fit in with those of the farm as a whole. The process can best be demonstrated by taking an example.*

* The author is indebted to Mr R F Ridgeon for preparing these budgets.

Assume that a farmer wishes to start a pig enterprise producing fat baconers on an existing farm. He intends to erect efficient new buildings to ensure a good food conversion rate. He intends to build up the herd over six months, buying on average ten maiden gilts each month. He will employ one full-time pigman.

Figure 19.5 shows the enterprise fully established. It will be noted that the budget is self-sustaining. Allowance is made for the replacement of

1080 pigs weaned	1030 sold for bacon
1050 pigs reared	20 kept as gilts

Costs	£	Receipts	£
Food		Sales	
Sows, 60 × 1·3 T @ £120	9 360	1030 baconers @ £60	61 800
Boars, 3 × 1 T @ £120	360	18 cull sows @ £60	1 080
Creep, 1080 × 13 kg @		2 cull boar @ £40	80
£190 per tonne	2 667		
Feeders, 1050 × 250 kg			
@ £125	32 812		
Gilts, 20 × 150 kg @ £120	360		
	45 559		
Labour	5 000		
Housing depreciation	3 150		
Other costs	3 000		
1 replacement boar	250		
Total costs	56 959		
Profit	6 001		
	£62 960		£62 960

Fig. 19.5 Budget for pig enterprise (when fully established)

sows by breeding gilts and of boars by purchase. Allowance is also made (in depreciation) for replacement of buildings. The valuation can thus be assumed to remain constant. The profit is estimated at £608 and, as this seems a reasonable return, the farmer then calculates the amount of capital required (Fig. 19.6). The fixed capital consists of the buildings (estimated at £29 000), the equipment (mill and mix, food trolleys, etc. £2500), and the gilts and boars (£6150), totalling £37 650. The next problem is to calculate the working capital required. This is shown in Fig. 19.7. It will be seen that as each batch of gilts farrow, their food requirements double until the young pigs are weaned. Provision is then made for food for the fattening pigs. This cost builds up until the first batch of pigs is ready to go, in the eleventh month after purchasing the first gilts. In the twelfth and succeeding months enough cash is being received from the sale of baconers to finance working capital for food and other costs. The peak requirement of working capital is £21 049.

The total fixed and working capital is thus £58 699, or £978 per sow. Of this total, nearly two-thirds is fixed equipment. The estimated profit of £6001 represents a return of $6001 \times 100/58\,699 = 10.2$ per cent, which is rather low.

Fixed capital	£	£
Stock		
60 maiden gilts at £90	5 400	
3 boars at £250	750	
		6 150
Housing		
Farrowing accommodation	5 000	
Dry sow accommodation	6 000	
360 feeder houses at £50	18 000	
		29 000
Equipment		
Sow feeders, weighers trolley, etc.	1 000	
Mill and mixer	1 500	
		2 500
		£37 650
Working capital		
Food costs	13 712	
Labour costs	4 587	
Other costs	2 750	
		21 049
Total capital		£58 699

Fig. 19.6 Capital required to start 60 sow herd producing baconers

It will be seen from Fig. 19.7 that from the eleventh month current receipts are £5150 and expenses £4434, leaving a cash balance of £716 a month, or £8592 per year. These are, of course, estimates and will be subject to fluctuation. Nevertheless, if the farmer were to borrow some £60 000 to start this enterprise, the profit would be quite inadequate to repay the loan, unless interest rates fall to 10 per cent or less. At 15 per cent, for example

For livestock, say £21 000 @ 15 per cent over 10 years;
repayment per year £ 4 200
For buildings, say £38 000 @ 15 per cent over 20 years;
repayment per year £ 6 080
£10 280

If the farmer has capital to spare, he could almost certainly find another enterprise that would provide a better return than 10 per cent.

Month	1	2	3	4	5	6	7	8	9	10	11	12	13	14	15
	£	£	£	£	£	£	£	£	£	£	£	£	£	£	£
Sows food, Batch 1	100	100	100	100	100	F200	180	100	100	100	100	F200	180	100	100
Sows food, Batch 2		100	100	100	100	100	F200	180	100	100	100	100	F200	180	100
Sows food, Batch 3			100	100	100	100	100	F200	180	100	100	100	100	F200	180
Sows food, Batch 4				100	100	100	100	100	F200	180	100	100	100	100	F200
Sows food, Batch 5					100	100	100	100	100	F200	180	100	100	100	100
Sows food, Batch 6						100	100	100	100	100	F200	180	100	100	100
Boars food	30	30	30	30	30	30	30	30	30	30	30	30	30	30	30
Creep feed						111	222	222	222	222	222	222	222	222	222
Feeders, Batch 1								438	612	788	897	—		438	612
Feeders, Batch 2									438	612	788	897	—		438
Feeders, Batch 3										438	612	788	897	—	
Feeders, Batch 4											438	612	788	897	—
Feeders, Batch 5												438	612	788	897
Feeders, Batch 6													438	612	788
Total food costs	130	230	330	430	530	841	1032	1470	2082	2870	3767	3767	3767	3767	3767
Other costs	250	250	250	250	250	250	250	250	250	250	250	250	250	250	250
Labour	417	417	417	417	417	417	417	417	417	417	417	417	417	417	417
Total payments	797	897	997	1097	1197	1508	1699	2137	2749	3537	4434	4434	4434	4434	4434
Pigs sold												5150	5150	5150	5150
Monthly cash balance (+) or deficit (−)	−797	−897	−997	−1097	−1197	−1508	−1699	−2137	−2749	−3537	−4434	+716	+716	+716	+716
Cumulative deficit (−) = capital invested	−797	−1694	−2691	−3788	−4985	−6493	−8192	−10329	−13078	−16615	−21049	−20333	−19617	−18901	−18185

Notes 10 maiden gilts are purchased monthly for six months. They farrow (F) five months later. Working capital (i.e. Cumulative deficit) reaches a maximum in month 11.

Fig. 19.7 Working capital required by 60 sow herd producing baconers

As in the previous example, there is no single 'correct' answer for the amount of capital required. The amount spent on fixed equipment could be reduced if the farmer already had buildings that could be cheaply converted. With care, the figure of £50 per fat pig for new buildings could be reduced. On the other hand, if inferior buildings raised the food conversion rate, such an economy could be dearly bought. The pigman could probably tend 70 sows if the buildings are well-designed and labour saving. This would reduce the labour costs per pig produced. With home grown barley, the ration might be cheapened. None of these changes, however, will raise the profit to a level that will justify the capital required. With a skilled pigman and above average management it would be possible to produce more pigs with a better food conversion rate. This could double the profit. It would, however, be foolhardy to assume such levels of efficiency in a new and untried enterprise. A farmer who already had pig buildings could continue in business with profits at their present level. But a newcomer would be well advised to reject the plan until conditions improve. Profits from pig production depend heavily on the ratio between pig prices and food costs. A change in this ratio could provide a much more favourable outcome.

Questions

1. Rewrite the farm plans at current prices.
2. Prepare a capital profile for a farm type with which you are familiar.

20 Capital investment

There is a constant need for more capital in farming—to take advantage of new techniques, to intensify production and (all too often) to finance the replacement of stocks whose value has been increased by inflation. Indeed, unless the farmer is careful, investment can become a bottomless pit which continues to absorb a large part of his income. It follows, therefore, that capital expenditure should be incurred only when the cost can be genuinely justified. A large part of this book has been concerned with planning changes on the farm and preparing budgets to show whether the farmer is likely to gain as a result. The criterion has been a simple one—if the change has been carried out, will it increase the farmer's profit? We have still to consider the question of how the change is to be financed. Some changes involve no more than a switch from one crop to another and are easily financed. Others are more fundamental and require substantial amounts of capital. This raises the point of whether the results are likely to justify the capital required.

There are three reasons why project evaluation is important. In the first place, few farmers have the reserves to finance large projects and must borrow at least part of the capital required. If so, the farmer should be able to prepare a convincing case for his bank manager or whoever is lending the money. Secondly, the project should be profitable enough to repay interest and allow the farmer to recover the capital invested during the lifetime of the project. Thirdly, the project should provide a large enough surplus to reward the farmer for the risk and responsibility of managing the new enterprise.

Simple criteria for investment

To show one simple method, let us take an example. Suppose a farmer invests £1000 in a new enterprise and obtains a profit of £250 a year. This is a return of 25 per cent on the capital originally invested. If the farmer had borrowed at 10 per cent, then after paying £100 interest, he would have 15 per cent or £150 a year left. If the income continued unchanged and the loan were not repaid, 'a return of 25 per cent' would be a reasonable assessment of the project.

Unfortunately, cases are seldom as simple as this. The amount invested may vary. The £1000 is the peak investment and as the equipment and buildings deteriorate, the value declines eventually to £500. As the average amount invested is only £750, a return of £250 is 33 per cent compared with 25 per cent on the peak investment.

Another simple criterion is the *pay back period*. In our example, a return of £250 would pay back the £1000 invested in four years. In this case the shorter the period, the better the investment. As a test, it is likely to appeal to a lender whose main interest is the return of his loan. The disadvantage is that it gives no credit for the later stages beyond the pay-back stage. This test will therefore rate a project giving a quick return above another that took longer to become established but gave higher returns in the long run.

Discounted cash flow

For small projects, such criteria may be adequate. But if they are large, more precise standards are required. These take into account considerations which have so far been ignored. For example

(*a*) receipts and payments are seldom spread evenly over the years. Investment may not occur all at once but be spread over a period and overlap the first returns. The return may also vary, rising to a peak after a number of years and then declining;

(*b*) investments tend to have a definite life. Equipment wears out and additional capital may be necessary to replace it. Even if a project could be continued idefinitely, it may eventually become uneconomic for some reason not at present foreseen. The investment should therefore be profitable enough to allow for recovery of capital invested within the life of the project.

These points can be illustrated by means of an example. Suppose that a farmer starts a new enterprise such as a laying flock or a beef herd. He invests £6000 during the first year in housing and stock and a further £1500 in the second year. Revenue begins in the second year (£500) and grows steadily to give a net cash flow of £2000 in the second and third years. In the fourth year, the unit is enlarged and an additional £3500 is invested. Revenue reaches a peak of £3000 in the fifth, sixth, seventh and eighth years and then declines in the ninth year. The enterprise is finally wound-up in the tenth year and the stock and equipment sold for £4000.

The payments and receipts for each year are set out and the difference tabulated as the *cash flow*. No distinction is made between capital and current items. As will be seen later, this is not necessary when we are dealing with the whole life of a project at one time.

	Capital expenditure £	Net* receipts £	Net cash flow £
Year 0	6 000	—	− 6 000
1	1 500	500	−1 000
2	—	2 000	+ 2 000
3	—	2 000	2 000
4	3 500	2 500	− 1 000
5	—	3 000	+ 3 000
6	—	3 000	3 000
7	—	3 000	3 000
8	—	3 000	3 000
9	—	2 000	2 000
10	—	4 000†	4 000
	£11 000	£25 000	£14 000

* Receipts, *less* annual costs (feeding-stuffs, repairs, etc.).
† Salvage value of building and equipment, *plus* sale value of livestock.

How is one to judge the success of this enterprise? The net cash flow has fluctuated from year to year. In three years there was a deficit; in seven years there was a surplus. In all, the farmer has paid out £11 000 and received £25 000, leaving a surplus of £14 000. This alone, however, is not a sufficient criterion of success. In particular, one consideration has so far been ignored—the cost of using capital. The farmer has borrowed money to start this enterprise and this has cost him eight per cent a year. Even if he had owned the capital invested, the farmer could have invested the money quite safely at eight per cent in government stocks. It would thus be reasonable to charge interest at the rate on the amount invested in the business. It would also be reasonable to credit the enterprise with interest on any surpluses that emerge. One way of putting the investments and surpluses from different dates on the same footing would be to carry them forward with interest to the date when the project ended and judge its performance accordingly. But in most cases, the farmer is not holding a post mortem on the past but is framing a plan for the future. He is therefore looking at the project from the starting point when he must decide whether or not to invest. It would, therefore, be more useful to carry the value of investments and returns back to the starting date. But if items are carried back, interest should not be added but deducted. This is known as *discounting*.

The process may be explained as follows. Suppose you own £100 and the interest rate is 10 per cent. If this £100 were invested, it would earn £10 in interest in the next year, making £110 in all. If this £110 were then invested for a second year, it would earn £11 interest making £121 at the end of two years or, to carry the process further, £161 at the end of five years. In other words, if money can be invested at 10 per cent then £100 now is worth £121 in two years and £161 in five years. But if £121 in two years' time is worth £100 now, what is the value of £100 in two years' time? The answer is 100/121 or £82·60. Thus £82·60 is the *discounted value*, at present, of £100 promised or expected in two years' time. Similarly, £100 in five years' time is worth 100/161 or £62·10 now. This is because £62·10 invested now would become with interest £100 in five years' time. To save trouble in calculating this sum, discount tables are published (*see* Appendix 1) which give the *Net present value* (NPV) of £1, at one, two or more years at various rates of interest. For example, £1 in five years' time at eight per cent is worth £0·681 now.

This process of discounting provides a means of assessing the present value of a cash flow at various future dates. The net cash flow in our example has thus been discounted at eight per cent in the following way.

Example 1

	Cash flow £	Discount factor £	Discounted cash flow £
Year 0*	−6 000	×1·000	−6 000
1	−1 000	×0·926	−926
2	2 000	×0·857	1 714
3	2 000	×0·794	1 588
4	−1 000	×0·735	−735
5	3 000	×0·681	2 043
6	3 000	×0·630	1 890
7	3 000	×0·583	1 749
8	3 000	×0·540	1 620
9	2 000	×0·500	1 000
10	4 000	−0·463	1 852
	£14 000		+£5 795

* This assumes that the project starts from the date when the £6000 capital is spent. Year one states the result one year later.

It will be seen that the value of future receipts and expenses dwindle as they recede into the future—in this case down to only 50 per cent in year nine. Discounted in this way, the value of the total cash flow of £14 000 falls to £5795. This means that £5795 in hand now has the same value as £14 000 over the next ten years. This is so because the £1852 given for year ten, if invested now would with interest, be worth £4000 in ten years. This statement could be repeated for all the other sums quoted in column 3 which, if invested now, would by the year quoted amount to the sum in column 1.

The £5795 is in fact the net present value of this enterprise. It represents the surplus the farmer can expect (if the budget is reliable) after allowing for the recovery of capital invested and for the current rate of interest. If there is no surplus, the investment is not worth undertaking. If there is a surplus, it is for the farmer to decide whether it is large enough to compensate for the risk and responsibility entailed.

Internal rate of return

The question now arises of what rate of interest should be used in preparing such budgets? If the capital is borrowed, then the rate charged is an obvious choice. Even if the farmer is using his own capital, he should allow the interest rate he would have obtained if he had not used it for the project concerned. If the money would otherwise have been invested in stocks or shares, he should allow the current rate, say five per cent. If the money would otherwise have been invested in another project on the farm, he should allow the return he gets on tenant's capital on his farm (say 15 per cent).

However, instead of stating the answer as a lump sum after allowing some arbitrary rate of interest (e.g. £1000 after allowing eight per cent), there is some advantage in stating the outcome simply as a percentage rate of return on the capital invested (e.g. 16 per cent). This has the merit of allowing the farmer to compare this rate directly with other projects or investments. The method used is to calculate the *Internal rate of return* (IRR). The procedure is as follows. When the NPV is calculated the size of the surplus depends on the interest rate used. Thus, if a higher rate of interest is used the surplus diminishes. It follows, therefore, that a point will be reached when the surplus disappears. The interest rate at this point is the return or IRR from the enterprise. Finding the proper rate is a matter of trial and error. It is done by trying one rate and, if it is too low, trying another which is just too high (or vice versa). When the answer is bracketed between two rates the actual figure can be estimated.

In this case, the answer is obviously far above eight per cent because there is a large surplus of £5795. For this reason, 20 per cent is tried as a first estimate. As this produces a deficit of £180, this is too high. The calculation is therefore repeated for 15 per cent. This produces a surplus of £1554. It is evident that the rate of return is between 15 per cent and 20 per cent and nearer 20 per cent. The exact rate is estimated by interpolation. If a rise of £1734 (from −£180 to £1554) is produced by a

	Net cash flow £	20% Discount factor	DCF £	15% Discount factor	DCF £
Year 0	−6000	×1·000	−6000	×1·000	−6000
1	−1000	×0·833	−833	×0·870	−870
2	2000	×0·694	1388	×0·756	1512
3	2000	×0·579	1158	×0·658	1316
4	−1000	×0·482	−482	×0·572	−572
5	3000	×0·402	1206	×0·497	1491
6	3000	×0·335	1005	×0·432	1296
7	3000	×0·279	837	×0·376	1128
8	3000	×0·233	699	×0·327	981
9	1000	×0·194	194	×0·284	284
10	4000	×0·162	648	×0·247	988
			−£180		+£1554

change of five per cent (from 20 per cent to 15 per cent) then a rise of £180 would be produced by $5 \times 180/1734 = 0.5\%$. The IRR is thus $20\% - 0.5\% = 19.5\%$. This return of 19½ per cent is reasonably satisfactory and somewhat above the average return on tenant's capital. If money has to be borrowed at eight per cent, there is a margin of 11½ per cent as a reward for risk and enterprise. On the whole, the farmer should probably not embark on an enterprise giving less than 15 per cent and if he is really short of capital, not less than 18 to 20 per cent. If the return falls below these levels, he should try to devise another plan that is more profitable.

Preparing a DCF budget

In drawing-up estimates of Discounted Cash Flow, the question arises of the number of years that should be included in the budget. Some enterprises have predictable lives. An apple orchard, for example, might start bearing in seven years, rise to a peak in eighteen years and be ready for grubbing in forty years. In the case of livestock, however, it is more difficult to set a limit. The farmer should be able to budget the costs and returns for establishing a new herd for the first two or three years with a fair degree of accuracy. By that time, the net cash flow will have levelled out and will presumably remain at that level, at least so far as can be foreseen. Even if the farmer hopes that his new enterprise will continue indefinitely, he would be wise to set a time limit. With new buildings, this could be 10 or at the most 15 years. The buildings will no doubt last longer, but as new techniques are introduced, the farmer will almost certainly wish to make alterations that will require more capital.

Quite apart from this, economic conditions can change and dairy cows or pigs that seem so successful now may no longer be profitable on that farm. It follows, therefore, that the farmer should budget to recover capital sunk in fixed assets within a reasonable period. For this reason, specialized equipment should be valued at the final date at no more than its scrap value. In the case of buildings this might be a nominal value for storage. Livestock are less of a problem because they are saleable and the capital sunk in them can usually be recovered. They can, therefore, be treated as if sold at valuation in the final year.

When dealing with an enterprise in which the cash flow remains constant for some years, time can be saved by using an annuity table (*see* Appendix 2) to calculate the discounted return for a group of years. Suppose, for example, a farmer intends to build up a pig herd with money borrowed at eight per cent

	Cash flow	Discount factor @ 8%	DCF
Year 0	−£5000	×1·000	−£5000
1	+500	×0·926	463
2 to 9*	+1000	×5·320	5320
10	+3000	×0·463	1389
		NPV	+£2172

* Annuity of £1 per year @ eight per cent for nine years (£6·246), *less* year one (£0·926).

When dealing with machinery and equipment, a shorter period than ten years may be prudent. A farmer offered a contract for some new crop (e.g. vegetables for freezing) would have to buy special harvesting or processing machinery. If this equipment has a life of eight years the budget should write off the value in this time. It might also be wise to repeat the calculation using five years in case the farmer might want to withdraw after that time.

Choosing between projects

So far, discussion has centred round whether or not an investment is justified. Sometimes a farmer may be faced with a choice between two enterprises that are mutually exclusive—either because they would occupy the same land or buildings or because there is not enough capital to finance them both.

The two criteria already described, net present value (NPV) or internal rate of return (IRR), can be used to rank enterprises in order of priority. If the enterprise requires nearly the same amount of capital, these two criteria will usually rank them in the same order. But if one enterprise is much larger than another, this may not be so.

To take an example, assume that a farmer has to choose between two projects giving the following returns

	Project A cash flow	Project B cash flow
Year 0	−£1000	−£3000
1	+200	+300
2–9	300	600
10	400	1600
IRR	25%	15%
NPV (discounted @ 8%)	£966	£1211

In this case Project A gives a higher return on capital: 25 per cent, compared to 15 per cent for Project B. On the other hand, Project B gives a larger NPV (£1211 compared to £966). Which test should be used? In fact, these two tests measure different qualities. The productivity per unit of capital is measured by IRR. Thus, if one project gives a return of 15 per cent and another gives 20 per cent, then the latter makes better use of each unit of capital. The IRR does not, however, measure the size of the contribution that each scheme is expected to make to the profit of the farm as a whole. By contrast, NPV measures the size of the contribution but ignores the amount of capital. This means that if the NPV is used the farmer will choose a large project giving a large NPV in preference to a small one with a smaller NPV even if the latter has a higher percentage return on capital. One justification for ignoring the amount of capital involved is that if the money has been borrowed it does not belong to the farmer. His responsibility is to pay the interest and, having done so, he need not be concerned with the amount involved. On the other hand, if things go wrong, the farmer would soon find the repayment of a large sum more of a burden than a small one. On the whole, the author is inclined to favour IRR.

In the present case, it is easy to see that Project B has no great advantage over A because it needs £2000 extra capital to produce an extra £245 NPV (£1211 *less* £966), which means a poor return. This conclusion can be proved formally by deducting the returns of A from B and discounting the difference.

	Cash flow B–A	Discount factor @ 10%	DCF
Year 0	−£2000	×1·000	−£2000
1	+100	×0·909	+91
2–9	300	×4·849	1455
10	1200	×0·386	463
			+£9

It is obvious that the return from the extra £2000 is only 10 per cent. This is hardly enough. It would thus be advisable to choose Project A and (if the farmer wished to invest an additional £2000) increase the size of Project A or look for some other project with a better return than 10 per cent. There are other occasions when the conclusion is not so obvious, especially if the projects are of different lengths. For this reason, we need a method of comparison such as that given above.

In choosing between projects, some consideration should also be given to the risk involved. The farmer should look for a higher IRR from a risky enterprise than from a safe one.

Capital gearing

Another point worth mention is the case where the farmer has the choice of starting a new venture on a small scale with his own capital or on a larger scale with borrowed capital. Suppose the farmer has prepared a budget for a new livestock enterprise. The estimated results are as follows, using his own capital of £5000

	Cash flow	Discount factor @ 20%	DCF
Year 0	−£5000	×1·000	−£5000
1–9	+1100	×4·031	+4434
10	3000	×0·162	486
			−£80

The IRR is 20 per cent and the enterprise seems quite a desirable one. The farmer considers that, with an extra £5000, he could double the size of the enterprise and the returns from it. Half the capital required is for new buildings. He could, therefore, borrow an extra £5000 for the buildings on a 10-year mortgage at, say, eight per cent or £745 a year. What is the return on this larger enterprise? The IRR on the whole £10 000 is also, of course, 20 per cent. But half the capital is costing the farmer only eight per cent. The extra profit (£355, i.e. £1100 *less* £745 mortgage) could thus be said to accrue to the farmer and to the £5000 of capital he has invested. The larger enterprise can thus be presented as follows (including only the farmer's capital and treating the mortgage as an expense):

	Cash flow
Year 0	−£5000
1–9	+1455
10	5255*

* (£3000 × 2) − £745

This yields a return of 29 per cent, which is even more attractive than 20 per cent. It will be appreciated that such a calculation is for the farmer's own information. The lender would be interested only in the 20 per cent return for the whole venture which appears to provide ample cover for the eight per cent he expects. The fact that the farmer is providing half the capital would also reassure him. He might think, 'even if the return on the whole enterprise falls by two thirds, there will be almost enough to repay my loan'. (In this eventuality the unfortunate farmer would be left with no return.)

The device of using borrowed capital at a fixed interest rate to augment the return on capital owned by the business is known as *gearing*. If the return from the whole business is well above the cost of the borrowed capital, the return on the capital provided by the business is greatly increased. Indeed, the higher the ratio of borrowed capital the higher the gearing and the greater the return on the capital owned by the business. Working on borrowed capital is, of course, risky and the higher the gearing, the greater the risk. If profits fall *below* the cost of borrowed capital, losses are also geared-up and exaggerated. Used with discretion, however, by a farmer confident of his ability to make profits, it is a legitimate way to accelerate the growth of a business.

Example 2: Calculation of NPV and IRR: a case in detail

Having dealt with farm planning, cash flow and project appraisal, it now remains to put these techniques together in a single example. Let us assume that a farmer already has a mixed farm and would like to start a new livestock enterprise (say a pig or beef herd). He has prepared a budget of the enterprise as it should appear when fully in operation.

Preliminary budgets

Year 2 and later

	£		£
Opening valuation	4000	Sales	5000
Purchases (food, etc.)	3000	Closing valuation	4000
Depreciation of buildings	500		
Estimated profit	1500		
	£9000		£9000

The capital expenditure at the beginning will be

	£
Buildings (net of grant)	5000
Livestock	3000
	£8000

The purchase of livestock is shown as

	Year 0		
Purchase (stock)	£3000	Closing valuation	£3000

During the first year, the herd will become established. It should increase in value to £4000, and some stock will have been sold before the end of the year.

	Year 1		
	£		£
Opening valuation	3000	Sales	1500
Purchases (food, etc.)	2000	Closing valuation	4000
Depreciation of buildings	500		
	£5500		£5500

At first sight, an enterprise that requires £8000 of capital and provides an annual profit of £1500 seems reasonably attractive. If the farmer had savings of £8000 to invest he could be earning an extra £1500 a year in cash within two years. Unfortunately, his capital is already committed in the farm and he must borrow. He visits his bank manager, who is sympathetic but asks for a feasibility study to show how large an overdraft will be required and how long repayment will take. The first attempt (Fig. 20.1) shows the cash flow and trading accounts for the first 12 years. The appraisal is made, however, on the cautious assumption that the project lasts only ten years. The marginal rate of tax is 30 per cent. (This is the rate paid on the last of the present profits and will also apply to any additional profits from this enterprise.) The interest on the overdraft is 10 per cent.

The procedure is as follows (see Fig. 20.1).

(1) Fill in receipts, payments and valuations in the cash flow statements and the trading account from the preliminary budgets already given.

(2) Under Income Tax rules, the building can be written off in ten equal instalments. Enter £500 depreciation in the trading account years one to ten.

(3) In each year, complete first the cash flow and then the trading account.

(4) The balance in the cash flow is the closing overdraft. This is also the opening overdraft next year and from it is calculated the interest.

(5) Each trading account gives a profit or loss. Income Tax (30 per cent of the profit) is paid the next year and is entered in the cash flow. The loss in year one reduces tax from other sources and is entered as a credit in the cash flow year two.

The following points should be noted

(a) The bank overdraft which starts at £8000 rises to £9300 at the end of year one. This is due to interest (£800) and the fact that expenditure (£2000) exceeded income (£1500) by £500.

(b) At the end of year two, the overdraft (£7990) is still nearly as high

Year

Cash flow	0	1	2	3	4	5	6	7	8	9	10	11	12
	£	£	£	£	£	£	£	£	£	£	£	£	£
In													
Receipts	—	1 500	5 000	5 000	5 000	5 000	5 000	5 000	5 000	5 000	5 000	5 000	5 000
Income Tax (rebates)	—	—	240	—	—	—	—	—	—	—	—	—	—
Overdraft (at end)	8 000	9 300	7 990	6 960	5 866	4 694	3 437	2 090	646	—	—	—	—
	8 000	10 800	13 230	11 960	10 866	9 694	8 437	7 090	5 646	5 000	5 000	5 000	5 000
Out													
Overdraft (at beginning)	—	8 000	9 300	7 990	6 960	5 866	4 694	3 437	2 090	646	—	—	—
Expenditure	8 000	2 000	3 000	3 000	3 000	3 000	3 000	3 000	3 000	3 000	3 000	3 000	3 000
Interest (to bank)	—	800	930	799	696	587	469	344	209	65	—	—	—
Income Tax paid	—	—	—	171	210	241	274	309	347	387	430	450	600
Cash withdrawn	—	—	—	—	—	—	—	—	—	902	1 570	1 550	1 400
	8 000	10 800	13 230	11 960	10 866	9 694	8 437	7 090	5 646	5 000	5 000	5 000	5 000

		Year											
	0	1	2	3	4	5	6	7	8	9	10	11	12
	£	£	£	£	£	£	£	£	£	£	£	£	£
Trading account													
Sales and receipts	—	1 500	5 000	5 000	5 000	5 000	5 000	5 000	5 000	5 000	5 000	5 000	5 000
Closing valuation	3 000	4 000	4 000	4 000	4 000	4 000	4 000	4 000	4 000	4 000	4 000	4 000	4 000
Net loss	—	800	—	—	—	—	—	—	—	—	—	—	—
	3 000	6 300	9 000	9 000	9 000	9 000	9 000	9 000	9 000	9 000	9 000	9 000	9 000
Purchases and expenses	3 000	2 000	3 000	3 000	3 000	3 000	3 000	3 000	3 000	3 000	3 000	3 000	3 000
Interest (bank)	—	800	930	799	696	587	469	344	209	65	—	—	—
Depreciation	—	500	500	500	500	500	500	500	500	500	500	—	—
Opening valuation	—	3 000	4 000	4 000	4 000	4 000	4 000	4 000	4 000	4 000	4 000	4 000	4 000
Net profit	—	—	570	701	804	913	1 031	1 156	1 291	1 435	1 500	2 000	2 000
	3 000	6 300	9 000	9 000	9 000	9 000	9 000	9 000	9 000	9 000	9 000	9 000	9 000

Fig. 20.1 Feasibility study no. 1 for new livestock enterprise financed by bank overdraft

as at the beginning. Thereafter, it falls slowly until it disappears during year nine.

(c) The profit in year two is only £570 compared to £1500 in the preliminary budget. It has been reduced by the cost of interest. As the overdraft falls, the profit rises slowly to £1500 in year ten and then to £2000 in year eleven after the buildings have finally been written-off.

(d) As the overdraft is extinguished, a cash surplus emerges in year nine. This can be used to enlarge the enterprise. It is assumed, however, that it is withdrawn for private consumption or investment elsewhere.

(e) Year twelve shows the long-term result which will continue indefinitely so long as the buildings are satisfactory. The farmer might, of course, wish at some point to reorganize the enterprise and inject more capital.

The next task is to calculate the IRR and NPV.

	Expenditure £	Receipts £	Net cash flow £	Discount factor @ 10%	NPV £
Year 0	−8000	—	−8000	×1·000	−8000
1	−2000	+1500	−500	×0·909	−455
2–9	−3000	+5000	+2000	×4·849	+9698
10	−3000	+9000	+6000	×0·386	+2316
				Net present value:	£3559

The NPV is £3559 and the IRR is 17·2 per cent. These are satisfactory results and are easily calculated.

Some business consultants, however, prefer to use NPV net of tax. The justification is that different methods of financing an operation might incur different amounts of tax and the return net of tax might reveal the effect. If income tax is deducted from the net cash flow given above, the result is as shown on facing page.

The NPV at 10 per cent is now £2356 and the IRR is almost exactly 15 per cent. It may seem surprising that the deduction of tax at 30 per cent makes so little difference and reduces the return only from 17·2 per cent to 15 per cent. The reason is that in this case, there is a large amount of interest to pay. For this reason, profits (and the income tax paid on them) are quite low.

	Net cash flow (less tax) £	NPV @ 10% £	NPV @ 15% £
Year 0	−8000	−8000	−8000
1	−500	−454	−435
2	+2240	+1850	+1693
3	1829	1373	1203
4	1790	1223	1024
5	1759	1092	874
6	1726	973	746
7	1691	867	636
8	1653	772	541
9	1613	684	458
10	5120*	1976	1265
		£2356	+£5

* £2000, *less* £880 (tax on years nine and ten), *plus* stock sold for £4000. Buildings are written-off.

The appraisal

The next point is to decide whether a return of 17·2 per cent can be regarded as satisfactory. It can be compared with the cost of capital (10 per cent), the return on equities (say seven per cent), government bonds (say twelve per cent) or the return on tenant's capital on the rest of the farm (say 15 per cent). If the IRR of 15 per cent (net of tax) is used instead, it must of course be compared with other returns net of tax at the same rate as the farmer pays. Deducting tax at 30 per cent, the cost of borrowing capital is seven per cent, the return on equities 5 per cent, on bonds 8½ per cent, and on tenant's capital in the rest of the farm 10½ per cent.

It is understandable that large companies should wish to deduct levies such as Corporation Tax before calculating the IRR, but the benefit of deducting income tax from farming projects is rather less obvious. The return without deducting tax is simple to calculate and easier to compare with other rates which are usually quoted without deduction of tax.* Whatever the merits of deducting tax, it is not customary to deduct

* One anomaly caused by deducting tax is the following. A farmer who borrows heavily will pay more interest and less tax than another who is debt-free. As tax is deducted for any given project, but interest is not, a farmer heavily in debt would show a higher IRR than one who was not.

interest or depreciation when calculating NPV or IRR. Depreciation is not included, because it is allowed for in the salvage value of buildings and equipment included at the end of the project. Interest is not deducted, because this would confuse the picture. It is best to calculate the rate of return, e.g. 20 per cent, and compare this with the cost of borrowing (say eight per cent) or alternative uses (say 15 per cent). If interest were deducted first, such clear-cut comparisons would be difficult to make.

When the budget was completed, the farmer took it to his bank manager. The latter agreed that a return of 17 per cent seemed reasonable and would cover the cost of borrowing (10 per cent) by a slim but (if all went well) an adequate margin. He objected, however, to the size of the loan and the eight years required to repay it. Bankers prefer short-term loans and like to see the sum borrowed covered by new assets that can easily be realized. In this case, the peak overdraft of £9300 is far above the £4000 that could be realized by selling the livestock. If the farmer has other assets such as title deeds, there should be ample security. Nonetheless, the banker would like to see this debt paid off reasonably soon because the farmer is quite likely in a year or two to ask for a loan for some other improvement not at present foreseen. The bank manager would also prefer to see the farmer investing some savings of his own in the venture.

The bank manager, therefore, suggested that the farmer should obtain a mortgage for the buildings (£5000) using the title deeds of the farm as security. This would reduce the maximum overdraft to just over £4600. The overdraft, however, would still last for seven years. The farmer then offered to save £500 a year from his income from the rest of the farm and use this to reduce the overdraft more quickly. The new budget is shown in Fig. 20.2.

A revised budget

Two new items have been introduced. The annual mortgage repayment of £815 includes both interest and repayment of capital. In the early years, the repayment is mainly interest and in later years, it is mainly capital (*see* Appendix 1). The interest (which is chargeable against profits) is entered in the trading account. The whole of the repayment (£815) is entered in the cash flow. The £500 a year which the farmer intends to save is also entered there. These savings reduce the maximum overdraft to £4115 and it disappears entirely in the fourth year. This proposition satisfies the bank manager.

One point should be noted. The paying in of £500 a year does not change the amount of capital invested, because the money put in by the farmer is balanced by a withdrawal of a similar amount by the bank. The NPV and IRR are the same as those already calculated.

It now remains to appraise the project from the point of view of the farmer. In theory, the new herd produces an extra profit of £1500 a year from year two. In fact, the farmer will have his income reduced by £500 a year for four years and after that will see it increased in cash by only about £800 a year until year eleven. There can be little doubt that the accumulation of capital out of profits can be a slow and painful process. On the other hand, the farmer has acquired substantial assets—stock worth £4000 and buildings that should have enhanced the value of the farm. As a precautionary measure, the buildings have been written off after ten years, but if the farmer keeps the herd, they will undoubtedly have some value after that date.

The real difficulty is that the farmer is borrowing at 10 per cent and making only 17 per cent. This does not leave much margin from which to pay off a large loan. With lower rates of interest, the picture would be quite different. If money could be borrowed at seven per cent, the overdraft would be cleared in about five years without any extra savings. With loans at 10 per cent, the proposition is marginal and if conditions are less favourable than was assumed, the new enterprise could be a liability. Before embarking on it the farmer should consider whether there is any way in which capital costs could be reduced. Buildings, for example, are often unnecessarily massive and expensive and may in fact impede alterations at a later date. The returns can also be improved by having better stock or a better system, because the rate of return depends on the efficiency of production. Quite a modest improvement in the food conversion rate could increase the IRR from 17 per cent to 20 per cent or more. A fall in the interest rate (which at the time of writing is at peak levels) could reduce the burden of repayments. If there is a sharp fall in interest rates in two or three years' time, it might be worth repaying the balance of the mortgage and taking out a newer one at the lower rate. Such a change will cost a fee but might well be worthwhile.

When a project is somewhat marginal, the decision is apt to depend on temperament. If pride of possession is the motive, the plan is quite feasible and the farmer can have his new herd at not too great a personal cost. If, however, a higher standard of living is his motive, then he must be prepared for a long wait, or he must find a more profitable alternative.

					Year								
	0	1	2	3	4	5	6	7	8	9	10	11	12
	£	£	£	£	£	£	£	£	£	£	£	£	£
Cash flow													
In													
Receipts	—	1500	5000	5000	5000	5000	5000	5000	5000	5000	5000	5000	5000
Income Tax (rebate)	—	—	240	—	—	—	—	—	—	—	—	—	—
Overdraft (at end)	3000	4115	2602	1362	54	—	—	—	—	—	—	—	—
Cash paid in	—	500	500	500	500	—	—	—	—	—	—	—	—
	3000	6115	8342	6862	5554	5000	5000	5000	5000	5000	5000	5000	5000
Out													
Overdraft (at beginning)	—	3000	4115	2602	1362	54	—	—	—	—	—	—	—
Expenditure	3000	2000	3000	3000	3000	3000	3000	3000	3000	3000	3000	3000	3000
Interest (bank)	—	300	412	260	136	5	—	—	—	—	—	—	—
Mortgage	—	815	815	815	815	815	815	815	815	815	815	—	—
Income Tax	—	—	—	185	241	291	342	357	372	390	408	428	600
Cash withdrawn	—	—	—	—	—	835	843	828	813	795	777	1572	1400
	3000	6115	8342	6862	5554	5000	5000	5000	5000	5000	5000	5000	5000

Trading account		Year												
		0	1	2	3	4	5	6	7	8	9	10	11	12
		£	£	£	£	£	£	£	£	£	£	£	£	£
Sales and receipts		—	1500	5000	5000	5000	5000	5000	5000	5000	5000	5000	5000	5000
Closing valuation		3000	4000	4000	4000	4000	4000	4000	4000	4000	4000	4000	4000	4000
Net loss		—	800	—	—	—	—	—	—	—	—	—	—	—
		3000	6300	9000	9000	9000	9000	9000	9000	9000	9000	9000	9000	9000
Purchases and expenses		3000	2000	3000	3000	3000	3000	3000	3000	3000	3000	3000	3000	3000
Interest (bank)		—	300	412	260	136	5	—	—	—	—	—	—	—
Interest (mortgage)		—	500	470	435	395	355	310	260	200	140	75	—	—
Depreciation		—	500	500	500	500	500	500	500	500	500	500	—	—
Opening valuation		—	3000	4000	4000	4000	4000	4000	4000	4000	4000	4000	4000	4000
Net profit		—	—	618	805	969	1140	1190	1240	1300	1360	1425	2000	2000
		3000	6300	9000	9000	9000	9000	9000	9000	9000	9000	9000	9000	9000

Fig. 20.2 Feasibility study no. 2 of new livestock enterprise financed by bank overdraft, mortgage and current savings

The scope for capital appraisals

One final comment should be made on the reliability of the results. All budgets dealing with the future are liable to error and this applies particularly to estimates of returns in eight or ten years' time. Discounting does nevertheless reduce the importance of estimates of results some years ahead. In consequence, they bear much less weight in the final result than estimates of the immediate future which should be fairly firm.

It will be appreciated, moreover, that capital budgets are not in fact a forecast of the future. This is not possible. Their purpose is simply to estimate the outcome of a particular plan. The results are therefore only as reliable as the assumptions on which they are based. These assumptions, particularly about the level of efficiency to be expected, depend on the judgment of the farmer (or his adviser) and on whether he has the skill to carry out the project as planned. There are other uncertainties, particularly about prices, which are beyond the power of the farmer to influence. But as one of the professed aims of agricultural policy is to help to stabilize prices, the risk of sharp fluctuations should not be too great, at least for the main farm products.

There is, however, another hazard that can be the most crippling of all—the lack of finance to complete a project already begun. Borrowing on the basis of optimistic plans without adequate preparation can easily lead a farmer into undertaking more than he can accomplish and promising repayment when this is plainly impossible. Even if the enterprise is successful, the farmer short of funds may be driven to short-term expedients to raise cash such as selling-off stock or equipment at a loss. Worse still, he may find repayment almost impossible and be left with a burden that takes a lifetime to repay. This is a hazard than can be largely avoided by the means described in this chapter. If a plan appears to be feasible and profitable with a reasonable margin for contingencies, the odds are in favour of success unless conditions are much less favourable than could reasonably be expected. On the other hand, if it fails on either count (of profitability or feasibility) then the odds are against success unless conditions are unusually favourable. In an uncertain world, this is as much as the farmer can expect and it should enable him to plan ahead with a reasonable degree of confidence.

These in outline are the chief methods used in assessing a capital investment. Similar methods are employed in business for large industrial projects. They are also used by developing countries to justify international loans (e.g. from the World Bank) for irrigation and reclamation schemes. In such cases, other considerations such as the social cost of labour and the effect on the balance of payments have to be introduced, but in principle, the methods are the same.

Inflation and project appraisal

So far, in this chapter, inflation has been ignored. The usual justification for doing so is to suggest that during a period of inflation, costs, receipts and profit margins probably increase at about the same rate even if the farmer is left with an apparently enlarged profit paid in depreciated pounds. It could thus be argued that inflation has no real effect on the viability of a project. In Example 2, we were considering a return of 17 per cent on funds borrowed at 10 per cent. If inflation raised these two figures to 25 per cent and 18 per cent, the conclusions would probably still be valid.

This argument is, however, a slight oversimplification. In practice, high interest rates tend to discourage investments—partly because it may not be easy to find projects that will give a return of 25 per cent or more.

There are, however, farmers prepared to take a risk and invest at lower rates than those quoted. The justification would be somewhat as follows. Money can be borrowed on two bases.

(1) flexible rate of interest. The rate of interest on a bank overdraft varies with the market. The Agricultural Mortgage Corporation also gives loans at flexible rates (somewhat higher than the fixed rate). Suppose that a project was expected to yield 20 per cent and money could be borrowed at 18 per cent. There would be hardly any margin to repay the loan and the former would have to live on income from the rest of the farm. The farmer might argue that if Government policy reduced the rate of inflation, interest should fall to 10 or 12 per cent within two or three years. Even if it does not, inflation will erode the cost of the loan;

(2) fixed rate of interest. This would apply to a mortgage from AMC or elsewhere. In this case, the farmer must count on inflation lasting long enough to erode the real cost of the loan. Suppose that annual inflation rates over the next five years were say 18 per cent, 15 per cent, 13 per cent, 11 per cent, 10 per cent. In these conditions the cost of living would have doubled in this time and if farm incomes had kept pace, the cost of repaying the loan would have halved.

These two strategies are plausible and if conditions are as stated, they could be successful.

There is of course an element of risk. If inflation decreased rapidly, then a fixed interest loan would become a much greater burden. If inflation increased, the flexible loan interest would increase and could cause difficulties.

In periods of uncertainty, appraisal of plans becomes more speculative. Financial estimates, however, become even more necessary. The crucial period is the first two or three years. Hardly any surplus over expenses is expected and if conditions change for the worse, the farmer could have a cash deficit large enough to cause serious difficulties. The moral is

(1) prepare an appraisal, ignoring inflation to decide if the scheme is likely to be successful in the long run;
(2) draw up a detailed cash flow statement for the first two or three years. Try the effect of temporary set-backs—a rise in interest rates when a fall was expected, delays in starting the project, disappointing yields in the early stages and consider the measures that could be taken to tide the project over until conditions improved. If the project is sound and the farmer can weather the first two or three years, all should be well—at least one hopes so.

Tests of financial solvency

To conduct a business successfully, it is not enough to make a profit—the capital position must be sound so that the business remains solvent and able to meet its liabilities as they arise. A number of tests employed in business and industry are sometimes used in farming—particularly in large companies and partnerships. The tests are mostly based on the balance sheets and the net profit. These are a few.

Liquidity ratio: ratio of liquid assets (cash and debtors expected to pay soon) to current liabilities (creditors, short-term loans, bank overdraft). This shows whether there is enough ready cash to pay short-term debts.

Current ratio: similar, but includes easily realizable assets such as crops and livestock for sale.

Capital gearing: ratio of long-term loans to net capital. This shows the extent to which the business is operating on borrowed capital.

Return on capital: net profit as percentage of net capital. With high gearing this return is much greater than if calculated on total assets.

Ratio of net capital to total assets: this shows the proportion of the capital that belongs to the farmer. (The remainder is debts and loans.) If net capital falls to zero, the business is insolvent.

Ratio of fixed assets to total assets: This shows the proportion of the capital tied up in equipment, buildings, land, etc. that cannot quickly be turned into cash.

Such tests can be useful to someone examining a business from the outside, e.g. a sleeping partner or a possible purchaser of a business. He should note if any ratios are deteriorating from year to year. This might indicate that the business is getting into difficulties. They are of less interest to the farmer who operates on his own without many debts or loans.

Questions

1. Assuming that you have only a limited amount of capital, which project (A or B) would you prefer?

	Cash flow	
	A	B
	£	£
Year 0	−3000	−3000
1	+300	+2000
2	700	1500
3	1000	1000
4	1500	700
5	2000	500

You intend to borrow the capital at twelve per cent.
Both projects cease after year five.

2. If the projects in Question 1 continue until year ten with the same cash flow as in year five, which project would you prefer?

3. In Example I in this chapter, extra capital was invested in year four. Assume that this is a separate investment. Compare the returns from this and the original project.

4. Recalculate Example 2 on the assumption that money can be borrowed for eight per cent. With use of farm labour, you can reduce the cost of buildings by £1000. Prepare an assessment.

5. Prepare an assessment of the capital invested in the pig herd described in Example 3, Chapter 19.

6. Assume that you already have a 300 hectare farm and are considering whether to rent in addition the 160 hectare arable farm described in Example I, Chapter 19. Prepare an assessment for one of the following situations (a) the farm is next door. You will need only one extra man and £16 000 of additional machinery;

(*b*) the farm is 50 miles away and you will need to employ a manager;

(*c*) you can buy the farm at £5000 a hectare. If you expect land values to increase by three per cent a year, would this change your assessment?

7. You wish to tender a rent for the 160 hectare farm as described in Question 6(*a*). Giving yourself a reasonable return on capital, how much rent could you afford to offer?

8. Prepare a budget to justify the expenditure of capital to introduce one of the following on a mixed farm

(*a*) a laying flock of 10 000 poultry (using either purchased or home-grown food);

(*b*) a barley beef unit;

(*c*) a contract for 25 hectares of vining peas.

If you had to choose one of these projects which would you prefer?

21 Farm planning in the tropics

So far, farm planning has been studied in a temperate climate. Many of the readers of this book are, however, located in the tropics and for their benefit a brief indication will be given of the way in which the techniques described can be adapted to suit warmer climates. As might be expected, the principles of successful farm organization are the same throughout the world, but their application in practice is, however, rather different.

Let us look first of all at some of the problems that have to be taken into account.

(1) There are approximately 2000 million people in the developing countries. In the majority of these, 50 to 80 per cent of the population live off the land compared to less than 10 per cent in most developed countries. The population is growing at about $2\frac{1}{2}$ per cent a year and in spite of migration to the towns, the rural population is still growing at about two per cent a year. In the developed countries, the farm population is declining and, as farm production is static or increasing, this means more output per man and a higher standard of living for those left. In developing countries the standard of living in rural areas could decline unless output is increased substantially.

(2) A large proportion of the rural people are arable farmers growing crops to feed their families. As cultivation is by hand the area a family can cultivate is only one to three hectares—depending on the size of the family.

(3) Most of these farmers now grow some cash crops which they sell to pay for clothing and other necessities.

(4) The standard of living varies enormously, but for many it is not much above subsistence level.

On the whole, family farmers tend to be very conservative and view innovations with suspicion. Some Advisory Officers who have tried unsuccessfully to persuade farmers to change their ways would say that they are ignorant and stubborn. Such an attitude betrays a lack of appreciation of the farmers' point of view. Their present system of farming was evolved over the centuries and was well adapted to the environment. Within these limitations the farmers' methods were successful and did fulfil the primary objective of supporting their families. This is not to say that these methods could not be improved under modern conditions. But before altering them, the Advisory Officer should make sure that he appreciates the advantages of the present system before he attempts to replace it. The farmer's reluctance to adopt new methods is in fact quite understandable. A man at subsistence level cannot afford to take risks—if the innovation is successful, he may be able to buy a few luxuries, but these are not essential. On the other hand if the innovation fails, his family might starve.

Methods of increasing farm production

In the old days, when the population was smaller and there was land to spare, food supply was less of a problem. When a young couple got married, they were given a plot from the tribal land which they cleared and used to grow food. In these circumstances, the output of food matched the increase in population.

Unfortunately there is no longer a reservoir of unused land in every neighbourhood to provide for increasing population. Governments therefore feel impelled to intervene to secure additional supplies of food. This means that the advisory or extension services of the Ministry of Agriculture usually have to take the initiative in devising schemes to increase production. Many methods can be tried, but from the point of view of organization, they can be broadly classified under the following headings

(1) output from existing holdings can be increased. Crop yields can be raised by the use of improved varieties, fertilizers, pesticides and fungicides. The Advisory Officer will rely on results obtained on experimental stations and will use demonstration plots to show the improved methods to farmers. The farmers, however, will wish to know whether the increased yields will pay for the costs—by a substantial margin that allows for possible failures. This is important because yield responses in the field are often substantially less than on the experimental farm where they receive meticulous care and there is less risk of infection from neighbouring fields;

(2) fragmented holdings can be rationalized by consolidating scattered pieces of land into a single farm. With all his land within one ring fence, the farmer is much more likely to take a personal interest in maintaining fertility and avoiding soil erosion;

(3) shifting cultivation can be replaced. In some areas, the forest is cut down and burnt. The land is cultivated for two or three years until the accumulated fertility is exhausted. The land is then left fallow for ten or 20 years for the forest to grow and the soil to recover. The devising of a system of permanent cultivation is a difficult technical problem, but if it can be solved, the gain can be substantial.

With (2) and (3) above, farm budgets can be given to the farmer to show him the reward that he can expect from adopting new and sometimes quite drastic changes in his system of husbandry;*

(4) new crops can be introduced to provide food for the towns, raw materials for processing factories, or goods for export. But before the farmer will agree to grow the new crop, he must be convinced he will obtain an adequate reward for his trouble.

To persuade the farmer, cost estimates are sometimes produced including not only seeds, fertilizers, pesticides, etc., but also family labour at the local wage rate. If receipts exceed costs, the crop is supposed to be 'profitable' and recommended to the farmer.

As readers of this book will realize this is a naive and misleading conclusion. The farmer does not wish to know merely whether the crop is profitable, but whether it pays better than the crop he already grows. This means trying the effect of introducing the new crop into a budget representative of typical farms in the area. If the gross margin of the new crop exceeds the crop displaced, the farmer's income will be increased by the *difference* between the two gross margins.

On the other hand if the farmer can enlarge his holding and grow the crop on new land, then the net gain is the *whole* gross margin of the new crop. One important proviso must be made. Additional land means more work. If the farmer can hire casual labour this solves the problem. But if the family must do all the work, care should be taken that they are not overtaxed or neglect existing crops. Estimates should therefore be made of the peak seasonal labour requirement of the new plan, particularly for sowing, weeding, and harvesting.

The introduction of a new plantation crop is a special case, because the farmer will have to wait until the trees or bushes come into bearing. This point will be dealt with later.

(5) New settlements can be made on virgin land reclaimed from forests or from desert land that is irrigated. The farmers may be allowed to farm in their traditional way or they may be introduced to a new system that will provide a better family income. The latter calls for

---

* A good example is Kenya.

careful planning of the size of holding a family can manage and the capital required.

Mechanization

If a British farm worker can deal with 50 hectares of crops and an African farmer with only two hectares, the productivity of the former appears to be 20 times as great as the latter. Most of this is due to mechanization. Why, it may be asked, not use mechanization to increase the output and income of the African farmer to the same level of his European counterpart? There are two difficulties.

(1) Mechanization is intended to save labour. It pays to use it in Britain because machines cost less than man power. In Africa, the position is reversed. Farm machinery and spare parts are imported and expensive whereas labour is comparatively cheap. The replacement of men by machines is thus less attractive. Indeed, on large mechanized arable farms in the tropics costs can be higher than with hand cultivation.

(2) To bring costs to a reasonable level a tractor must be used to cultivate at least 20 hectares—i.e. about ten times the area of an average arable holding.

Even if a family farmer cannot afford to own a tractor he may be glad to use the services of a contractor to ease work at a busy season, e.g. to enable him to cultivate and plant more crops at the beginning of the wet season. The contractor may of course be a farmer who works for neighbours when his own cultivations are completed.

Mixed crops

In some areas (e.g. West Africa) three or four crops are planted in mixtures at the beginning of the wet season. Mixtures of course are only suitable for hand cultivation. Each of the crops is harvested as it becomes mature, usually leaving cassava to be harvested as required during the dry season. How are we to value this mixture? We could attempt to split the costs and returns between the individual crops but the answer is not particularly useful. A more practical solution is to treat each type of mixture as a crop. Some advisory officers are apt to despise mixtures but in practice the gross margins of mixtures often exceed those of pure stands of the crops of which they consist.

Fixed and variable costs

If we are dealing with *existing* holdings, gross margin analysis can be carried out on the lines described in the earlier part of this book. One difference is that on small family farms, there are hardly any fixed or common costs. Nearly all the expenses (including casual labour) are *variable costs*. The family income is thus the sum of the gross margins with hardly any deductions.

On the other hand, the number of man days of work the family can supply can be treated as a fixed asset and it is this that governs the size of holding they can operate.

Farm planning

In the examples that follow, emphasis has been given to situations not dealt with in earlier chapters—in particular land settlement and commercial plantations. Other topics include decisions on the size of holding, the assessment of capital requirements, and the financing of loans. The treatment is necessarily brief and we can deal with only a limited range of circumstances. The examples could, however, be rewritten for other crops and other conditions within the framework suggested.

Of the four schemes considered, three (1, 2, and 4) include settlement schemes for family farmers. The fourth (3) is a commercial plantation.

(1) Family farms growing annual cash crops including two crop and three crop rotations.

(2) Family farmers introduced to plantation crops.

(3) Large commercial plantation.

(4) Large plantation designed for division into family farms.

Size of holding

A major consideration in land settlement is the determination of a suitable size of holding. Essentially, there are two criteria that can be used. The aim can be either

(1) to provide the *maximum income* for a farm family. In practice, this means designing the largest holding the family can manage. To take a simple example, if the net return per hectare is A500, and a family can cultivate two hectares, then a 'maximum' holding would provide them with a comfortable living of A1000. The disadvantage is that maximum holdings are expensive to create and require a large supply of land. But if there is no shortage of land and funds are available, this is the ideal solution. ('A' stands for an anonymous local currency).

(2) To settle the *maximum number* of families on the land available. This may be necessary in over-populated areas where land for settlement is scarce. In this case, the minimum size is the smallest size that will provide a family with a subsistence living just above the poverty

line. To put the matter in simple form, if the net return from one hectare is A500 and the minimum income on which a family can live is A250 then a minimum holding will be half a hectare. The farm planner should, however, try to avoid the creation of subsistence holdings as small as that. Even if they provide a quick solution to an unemployment problem, they tend in the long run to become a rural slum as the standard of living rises elsewhere in the country. In practice, settlement agencies compromise between these two extremes. Much as they would prefer large holdings, they usually prefer to spread their funds over a large number of moderate-sized holdings.

So far we have been discussing small farms operated by family labour. We could, however, have larger commercial holdings operated by paid labour. Indeed, if the farmer has the capital and the ability to manage paid labour, there is no limit to the size of holding he can operate. The transition from a family farm to a larger commercial farm is, however, a big step and the number of farmers so far able to operate larger units is still limited in most parts of the tropics. A case can, however, be made for including a few larger holdings in any settlement scheme to give scope for farmers able to operate them.

Family farm with annual crops

Let us assume that plant breeders have produced a new maize variety which with fertilizer gives substantially higher yields than indigenous seed. Before advocating its use the first step is to decide how it will fit into the present farming system. A survey shows that the typical farm in the locality is 2 hectares in size, the area a family can cultivate by hand. A simplified budget for the farm is given in Fig 21.1.

Ground nuts	0·6 ha @ A600 GM	A360
Maize	0·7 ha @ A200 GM	140
Sorghum	0·7 ha @ A160 GM	112
	Family income	A612

Fig. 21.1 Budget of 2 ha holding before improvement. (Some of the output is consumed on the farm, the rest is sold).

Variable costs for seed, fertilizer etc. are quite small and as fixed costs are negligible, total GM is equal to family income. The new maize variety tested locally has an output of A350, variable costs of A50 and a gross margin of A300. As the local maize has a GM of only A200, it would pay to substitute the new variety. The increase in family income would be $0.7 \times 100 = $ A70 or 11 per cent. Could reorganization be taken further? Substitute maize for sorghum? This would mean growing two maize crops in succession and might lead to lower yields. Grow more ground nuts with a GM of A600? The constraint might be risk of disease or possibly lack of labour to harvest more than the present area. The increase in income is however worthwhile and the new variety can be advocated.

Suppose that we have a different problem of resettling farmers. Their land is being flooded by a new dam and they are to be moved to reclaimed jungle. The cost of clearing the bush and taking anti-erosion measures is to be paid from the dam project. Let us assume that Fig. 21.1 shows the system of farming at the old site. As the climate is similar and the soil is good, the farmers can continue to grow the crops with which they are familiar. The opportunity is taken however to improve the farmer's incomes as some compensation for losing their old homes. The new maize is an obvious choice and the advisory services are also recommending improved varieties of groundnuts and sorghum.

What size of holding should be recommended? The farmers can manage 2 ha but would like rather more. The chief labour bottleneck is the beginning of the rainy season when the land must be cultivated and the crops sown promptly. Any delay results in loss of yield. If however the settlement agency can provide tractor ploughing on contract the average family might be able to manage 2·4 ha. Fig. 21.2 shows a budget for the new site.

Ground nuts	0·8 ha @ A750 GM	A 600
Maize	0·8 ha @ A300 GM	240
Sorghum	0·8 ha @ A200 GM	160
	Total gross margin	1000
	Ploughing, say	100
	Family income	A 900

Fig. 21.2 Budget for 3 ha holding after resettlement.

If correct there is a potential increase in income of A288 or 80 per cent. This is due to more land, higher yields or to better prices because a new road will give better access to the market.

In many areas, the cropping is more complex than has been shown so far. Much of the produce is consumed on the farm. Small farmers remote from a market tend to be self sufficient in case a drought or other misfortune makes food scarce and expensive, and they are unable to buy any when they need it. On large farms near towns, farmers sell more and buy most of the food they require. In planning holdings, the farmer's wishes must however be respected and provision made for growing a variety of vegetables and fruits.

In assessing the income and standard of living of holdings, it is best to include produce consumed at home at farm gate prices or market price less transport.

The example given in Fig. 21.1 was of a 2 ha holding. To be more exact this was the area cultivated. On fertile soil with permanent cultivation 2 ha is all that the farmer requires. In many parts of Africa and elsewhere, the yields of crops under continuous cultivation decline, and fertility can be restored only by adding a fallow period to the rotation. Thus if the land is cropped for three or five years then fallowed for a similar period, the farmer must have the use of at least 4 ha. If cropping and fallow are three and six years, he must have the use of 6 ha. In the examples given however the gross margins are calculated on the area (2 ha or $2\frac{1}{2}$ ha) in cultivation at any one time. The use of a fallow need not affect the analysis.

As mentioned earlier, many farmers grow crop mixtures. Maize for example might be accompanied by groundnuts, cassava or yams. Observation by the author in Ghana showed that although the yield of the principal crop might be less than if grown alone, this was more than compensated by the output of the subsidiary crops. It would therefore be pointless to advise the farmer to substitute a pure crop of improved maize with a GM of A300 per hectare for a maize mixture totalling, say A400 per ha. Improved maize in the mixture with fertilizer that also benefited the other crops might of course raise the total GM to A450 or more. But without testing, that is speculation. Pure crops do however lend themselves to mechanical cultivation and are therefore preferred on larger holdings.

In the example given earlier, the innovation was an improved variety of maize, a crop the farmers already knew. The innovation might however be a novel crop of which they had no previous experience. If, for example, a factory is built to process sugar cane or can tomatoes or pineapple, neighbouring farmers must be persuaded to grow it. Once again budgets should be prepared to show whether, at the prices offered, the gross margin of the new crop exceeded the crops likely to be displaced. Indeed, the increase in income should be large enough to compensate the farmer for the effort of learning to grow a strange and possibly risky crop.

How much reliance can be placed on budgets of the kind recommended here? This depends on two factors

(1) The accuracy of the estimates of inputs and outputs that have been used. These in turn depend on thorough testing not only in experimental plots but also in farmer's fields. Attention should be given to the possibility of a long term decline in soil fertility.

(2) The willingness of farmers to carry out the practices recommended. Farmers often have a shrewd grasp of the financial implications of making a change, and when they can see the benefits, will adopt new practices if it pays them to do so. For this reason, the advisory officer armed with realistic budgets will find his advice much more palatable to the farmer.

A warning should be given against over elaborate plans that depend on strict adherence to complicated rules that the settlers may neither understand nor appreciate. In practice such schemes are apt to fail. In the long run farmers will make their own choice of crops. While some will be unsuccessful, others will do better than expected and may take advantage of opportunities not foreseen when the scheme was introduced. In the meantime, the advisory officer has provided guidance that the farmer can follow with a reasonable prospect of success.

Plantations

The alternative to cash crops is plantation crops. Figure 21.3 gives the comparative returns per hectare for the chief plantation crops.*

| | Per hectare | | Per family | |
	Man days	Gross margin	Size† (hectares)	Income
		A		A
Cocoa	100	750	5·0	3750
Oil palm	80	640	6·25	4000
Coffee	155	1280	3·22	4122
Coconut	43	340	11·63	3954
Rubber	112	530	4·46	2364

† Assuming 500 man days, the equivalent of two adults, per family.

Fig. 21.3 Profitability of plantation crops

* These five plantation crops are not necessarily all suitable for the same site. The Planning Officer might well have a choice of sites for his settlement—site A (best sort for coconuts) and site B (best sort for cocoa). An economic comparison would thus be useful.

Coffee is to be the most profitable with the highest return both per hectare and per family (A4122). Cocoa has the second highest return per hectare but as more labour is required, it is fourth in income per family (A3750). Coconuts have a low return per hectare but with a lower labour input, a family can manage 11·63 hectares giving a family income of A3954. The least profitable is rubber (A2364).

The returns shown are the average per hectare over the whole life of the plantation including establishment. The estimates assume average fertility and soil suitable for the crop concerned. When climate and conditions are suitable for plantation crops, they are usually more profitable than the annual cash crops already described. Plantation crops have other advantages—on the whole they suffer less from drought or heavy rain and they require much less soil cultivation. The disadvantage is the long waiting period until the crop is established.

Family farm with plantation crops

Annual crops such as maize or ground nuts are sown and harvested within a few months. Working capital invested in them can therefore be recovered within a year. Plantation crops are, however, quite a different matter because young trees may take three or four years to come into bearing. A farmer must therefore be prepared to wait for several years before he obtains an adequate return. The accumulated total of expenditure during this period constitutes the substantial amount of capital required. This factor may present no difficulty to a commercial firm that can raise the necessary capital but a family farmer short of cash could find it a substantial handicap. Once the trees come into bearing, however, the family farmer should have no difficulty in financing tree crops because current receipts can pay for current expenses. For this reason, governments frequently provide loans to help family farmers wishing to grow plantation crops to make a start.

Capital required

It is now necessary to estimate the capital required for such crops and the period over which the farmer could be expected to repay a loan. This can be assessed by constructing a cash flow profile. The crop chosen as an example is coffee and it is assumed that the farmer also has a small area of cash and food crops on which the family can live until the coffee is established. Costs and returns for one hectare of coffee have been estimated by the loan officer as shown in Fig. 21.4. Initial costs include A313 to a contractor to clear the land from secondary jungle and a drying floor in the third year. The annual costs include plants in the first year and materials such as fertilizers and insecticides. Returns begin in the fourth year, increase until the ninth year and remain at about this level for 20 years or more.

Year	Costs Estab- lishment	Annual	Receipts	Surplus or deficit	Loan	Repay- ment of loan	Net cash return
1	313	560	—	−873	873	—	—
2	—	108	—	−108	108	—	—
3	250	185	—	−435	435	—	—
4	—	367	350	−17	—	—	−17
5	—	367	700	+333	—	200	+133
6	—	367	1050	+683	—	493	+190
7	—	367	1400	+1033	—	493	+540
8	—	367	1750	+1383	—	493	+890
9	—	367	2100	+1733	—	493	+1240
10	—	367	2100	+1733	—	—	+1733

Fig. 21.4 Repayment of loan for coffee on family farm

There are large deficits in the first three years and to cover this the Ministry will provide a loan. Interest is charged at eight per cent and is calculated from the amount owing at the beginning of each year.

Year	1	2	3	4	5
Brought forward	—	873	1051	1570	1696
Interest (8%)	—	70	84	126	136
Loan	873	108	435	—	−200 (repaid)
Carried forward	873	1051	1570	1696	1632

The farmer can repay nothing in the first four years and only A200 in the fifth year. The debt is then A1632 and the farmer agrees to repay this in four equal instalments. Looking up a mortgage table, a loan of A1000 at eight per cent is repaid by A302 per year for four years. On A1632 this is equivalent to A493 per year. This is inserted in Fig. 21.4. It can be seen that the farmer has to wait seven years before the plantation gives him an income of more than A200 and ten years before he obtains the full benefit of an extra A1733 net cash return per year.

With interest, the farmer has repaid a total of A2172 or 53 per cent more than A1416 borrowed. This is quite logical but it might be consided unfair that he should pay interest on the whole period. In some schemes, therefore, the farmer is given a period of grace, interest free, before repayments begin. It is important to remember that the collection of debts from farmers can be difficult and expensive, especially in the early stages when the farmer is expected to hand over most of his receipts. It is of course easier to collect instalments if the farmer sells his produce through a co-operative or official agency, but even then, he might be tempted to evade repayment by selling produce to a merchant. Care should therefore be taken to avoid burdening the farmer with a load of debt that will tempt him to default. Repayments should therefore leave the farmer with enough cash to provide an incentive and allow for unexpected difficulties. On the other hand, if the repayments are likely to be burdensome or last a very long time, the plan should be rejected. If the authorities are particularly anxious to implement the scheme to alleviate local poverty or increase exports, they should be prepared to subsidize it to some extent, e.g. by charging less interest.

Year	1	2	3	4	5	6	7	8
Establishing plantation	A							
Clearing jungle	31 250							
Roads, etc.	35 000							
Field equipment	50 000						50 000	
Plant				25 000				
Housing	33 000							
	149 250			25 000			50 000	
Overhead costs								
Salaries	17 000	17 000	17 000	17 000	17 000	17 000	17 000	17 000
Administration	3 000	3 000	3 000	3 000	3 000	3 000	3 000	3 000
Maintenance	2 000	5 000	8 000	11 000	14 000	14 000	14 000	14 000
	22 000	25 000	28 000	31 000	34 000	34 000	34 000	34 000
Variable costs and labour								
Labour	31 125	28 250	22 500	27 500	30 250	34 000	37 750	41 500
Materials	43 500	9 750	16 750	33 375	33 375	33 375	33 375	33 375
	74 625	38 000	39 250	60 875	63 625	67 375	71 125	74 875
Sub-total	245 875	63 000	67 250	116 875	97 625	101 375	155 125	108 875
Contingencies (10%)	24 587	6 300	6 725	11 687	9 762	10 137	15 512	10 887
Total cost	270 462	69 300	73 975	128 562	107 387	111 512	170 637	119 762
Receipts				49 000	98 000	147 000	196 000	245 000
Surplus						35 488	25 363	125 238
Deficit	270 462	69 300	73 975	79 562	9 387			
Cumulative deficit = capital invested	270 462	339 762	413 737	493 299	502 686	467 198	441 835	316 597

Notes: 1. In practice, a whole plantation would not be cleared in one year—parts would be renewed each year to give a continuous flow of supplies from year to year. 2. Capital invested reaches a peak in year 5. Capital invested is recovered by year 11.

Fig. 21.5 Costs and returns from 100 hectare plantation

Commercial plantation estates

The economics of production on a large plantation differ from those of a small family farm. This can be illustrated by taking an example. Similar data are used but for 100 hectares. The cash flow for establishing such a plantation is shown in Fig. 21.5. Fixed assets include internal roads, field drains, an office and houses for the manager and foreman. The tractor, Land Rover, and field equipment is renewed every six years. A processing plant is erected in the fourth year as the crop comes into bearing. Expenses include paid labour and a contingency allowance of 10 per cent to allow for unforeseen expenditure.

Receipts begin to exceed expenses in year six. The annual surplus reaches a plateau in year nine and continues at this level for 20 years. Yields then begin to decline and the plantation is cleared when receipts fall below the level of costs in year 33. Under good conditions, the trees might be worth cropping for 30 or 40 years, but when making estimates it is prudent to be conservative. (In fact, discounted returns more than

9	10	11		28	29	30	31	32	33
							50 000		
							50 000		
17 000	17 000	17 000	Repeat years	17 000	17 000	17 000	17 000	17 000	17 000
3 000	3 000	3 000		3 000	3 000	3 000	3 000	3 000	3 000
14 000	14 000	14 000	12 to 27	14 000	14 000	14 000	14 000	14 000	14 000
34 000	34 000	34 000		34 000	34 000	34 000	34 000	34 000	34 000
45 250	45 250	45 250		45 250	43 000	40 750	38 500	36 250	34 000
33 375	33 375	33 375		33 375	33 375	33 375	33 375	33 375	33 375
78 625	78 625	78 625		78 625	76 375	74 125	71 875	69 625	67 375
112 625	112 625	112 265		112 625	110 375	108 125	155 875	103 625	101 375
11 262	11 262	11 262		11 262	11 037	10 812	15 587	10 362	10 137
123 887	123 887	123 887		123 887	124 412	118 937	171 462	113 987	111 512
294 000	294 000	294 000		294 000	264 600	235 200	205 800	176 400	147 000
170 113	170 113	170 113		170 113	143 188	116 263	34 338	62 413	35 488
	Surplus								
146 484	+23 629	+193 742							

from establishment to clearing the land after a life of 33 years

30 years ahead have little value and an extra five or even ten years would have little effect on the final result.)

It will be seen that the cumulative cash deficit in Fig. 21.5 reaches a peak of A502 686 in year 5. This is the amount of capital necessary to finance the establishment of the plantation. A manager should therefore be able to finance it with credits of A350 000 in the first year and further amounts of A100 000 in the third and fourth years.

It will be noted that the large plantation has substantial costs for management and office expenses that the family farmer escapes. It also has investment in roads, housing and field equipment.

The question therefore arises, if the large plantation has higher costs and smaller profit margins, how can it compete with the family farm? The answer is that the manager of a large plantation has some advantages. He has access to the latest technology and the education to apply it. He has the funds to acquire improved crop varieties, pesticides and fertilizers. He can control the quality of the product and take care to satisfy the market. He may also undertake much of the processing and sell the produce for a higher price. All of these tend to increase output per hectare. He can employ machinery to reduce labour costs, although this is less important for plantation crops where harvesting is still done by hand. When the advantages are set beside the additional costs of a large plantation in the example given, the return per hectare, when the enterprises are fully in operation, is A1700 both on the family farm and on the large plantation.

It is thus evident that so long as the manager of a large plantation can keep a step ahead of the family farmer in production techniques, he can offset his higher overhead costs. But, in time, the family farmer can also acquire these advantages.

The net present value for this example is A341 774 and the financial internal rate of return on capital is 15·5 per cent. If we accept 10 per cent as the minimum return necessary to justify a project, the project is worth implementation.

Before accepting this verdict, it is prudent to prepare a *Sensitivity analysis*. The results obtained depend on the accuracy of the assumptions and some may prove to be incorrect. Agriculture is always faced with uncertainties and no one can foretell the future. What is possible is to examine the effect of changing some of the assumptions. Of these, the most important are the yield per hectare and the price of the product. In fact with a fall in receipts of 30 per cent (due to lower prices or lower yields or a combination of both) the project still shows a profit and a return on capital of 7·3 per cent. This would be a disappointing result but the enterprise would still be viable.

Over a short period prices could fall even more drastically. The effect can be gauged by considering only the annual costs and returns after the business is established. Even if the receipts fell by 50 per cent, they would still cover current costs. At that level, there would be hardly any margin to pay for renewals of plant or equipment but the business could survive for two or three years—in the hope that markets would eventually improve. Many tropical products for export do in fact suffer from price fluctuations of that order. Hence the pressure for international agreements to stabilize prices.

It is not customary in such estimates to allow for the effect of inflation. On the whole, costs and prices tend to rise in unison and insofar as this is true, increases in cost should, *in the long run*, be compensated for by higher prices.

Land settlement on plantation estates

We have dealt with the family farmer that adds one hectare of plantation crop to his holding. It also assumes that he knows the crop well enough to cultivate it on his own. But if the crop is a new one, local farmers may be reluctant to start growing it. The initiative in introducing the crop can be left to the large commercial plantations that can recruit skilled staff and raise enough capital to establish the new industry. Another alternative is to set up a *Government agency* to establish plantations, importing skilled managers and technicians as necessary. The local population employed on the plantation will acquire skill in dealing with the crop and eventually the plantation can be divided into small farms. An example will now be given to show how this can be organized. In the first stages, the cash flow will be closely similar to that of the commercial plantation. Instead, however, of merely showing a profit, the Agency will have two other objectives.

(1) To provide family farms that will earn the settlers a satisfactory income.

(2) To recover from the settlers a reasonable proportion of the capital invested which can then be used for other projects.

Suppose, for example, that the 100 hectare plantation already described is eventually to be divided into 40 holdings of $2\frac{1}{2}$ hectares with individual houses. If the houses are placed on the individual holdings, each farmer will be close to his land. On the other hand, the provision of amenities such as electricity, water, internal roads and drainage will be expensive. It is therefore intended to establish a compact village of 40 houses costing A5000 each.

The items that the settlers are expected to repay are

	A
Roads, etc.	35 000
Clearing jungle	31 250
Settlers' houses	200 000
	A266 250

A simple solution is to reserve to the Agency the right to manage the plantation for up to 15 years. The cash flow (Fig. 21.6) suggests that if all goes well the capital should have been recovered by year 11.

Year	Profit	Loan repayment (50% of profit)	Cash to settlers (10% of profit until debt is paid then 60%)	
			Total	Per family
	A	A	A	A
6	25 488	12 744	2 549	64
7	65 363	32 682	6 536	163
8	115 238	57 619	11 524	288
9	160 113	80 057	16 011	400
10	160 113	80 057	16 011	400
11	160 113	3 091	92 977	2 324
12	160 113	—	96 068	2 402
Total	846 541	266 250	241 676	6 041

Fig. 21.6 Repayment of loan—settlers on large estates

The settlers will, however, have had to wait a very long time. They could be allowed to participate at an earlier stage by giving them a share of profits in addition to their wages. The Agency could, for example, retain 40 per cent of the profits as a contribution towards overhead costs. Of the 60 per cent due to the settlers, 50 per cent could be reserved to pay off loans and 10 per cent distributed in cash. The profit is defined for this purpose as the cash surplus less A10 000 per year for depreciation of houses. (The Agency would buy the tractors, and field equipment.)

Repayment per settler $\dfrac{266\,250}{40}$ = A6656.

If the estimates of costs and returns are correct, the settler's debt to the Agency will have been paid off by year 11. In the meantime they will have received a bonus, in addition to wages, of A64 in year 6 rising to A400 in year 10 and A2402 in year 12. Wages would be tapered off—say from year 10.

The Agency should also have covered the capital investment and part of the administrative costs. As a commercial undertaking the plantation should have had a cumulative surplus of A533 968 at the end of year 13 after paying all administrative costs at project level. This is more than enough to pay the A200 000 for settlers' houses and the A241 676 cash bonus to the settlers.

There is an element of subsidy in the scheme. No interest has been charged and the Agency headquarters has incurred costs for supervision which are not included. It is not usual, however, to expect settlers to pay for such items.

At the appointed time, the Agency can divide the plantation into $2\frac{1}{2}$ hectare plots and hand them over to the settlers.

It might seem to be a pity to break up the organization of the plantation in this way. Some settlers might neglect their holdings and their pests and diseases could be a nuisance to others. Produce sold in small quantities and of varying quality could increase costs and reduce receipts. Some of these disadvantages could be overcome if the settlers formed a cooperative to deal with marketing and any processing necessary.

Another alternative would be to retain the plantation as a single unit. Tasks such as pest control or marketing could then be organized for the whole colony. Some form of management would, however, be necessary to organize joint operations. The Agency could hand over to a committee of settlers and if the committee had the ability to manage and the settlers obeyed the rules, the organization could work well. Otherwise, disputes are likely to arise. One solution would be for the Agency to continue to take an interest in the plantation and appoint a manager, at least for a few years.

Schemes prepared by the Land Settlement Agency would probably be submitted to the Ministry of Finance for approval. The report would also contain other background material, e.g.,

(1) The reasons for choosing the locality and the crops to be grown;
(2) An assessment of the demand for the product and probable prices;
(3) An estimate of the improvement in standard of living of the settlers;
(4) The source of the funds to finance the scheme.

If the scheme were to be submitted to the World Bank or another donor country, the figures would probably be adjusted to allow for accounting or 'shadow' prices. This would show the effect of the scheme on the national economy.

22 Taxation

Income Tax

A tax on income has been imposed in the United Kingdom for more than a hundred years. Until 1939, the farmer was given special treatment and was taxed on the rented value of the farm. This was partly because the farmer seldom kept satisfactory accounts and partly because farm profits were low and the yield in tax would have been small. After the outbreak of war in 1939, the need for increased revenue led to farmers being assessed on profits as shown by a set of properly prepared accounts.

According to source, incomes are taxed by different sets of rules or schedules. Schedule A is mainly a landlords' tax and refers to rents from houses and land. (Pieces of land let by a farmer are more likely to come under Schedule D with the farm profits.) Schedule B was formerly the farmers' special schedule but now applies to some commercial woodlands. Schedule C deals with interest and dividends taxed at source. Schedule E deals with wages and salaries and applies to farm workers' salaried managers and directors of farming companies.

Schedule D
Schedule D is the ordinary businessman's tax and includes profits from farming.

The farmer is entitled to prepare his own accounts and submit them for taxation purposes. Unfortunately as the law on taxation becomes more complex, most farmers prefer to leave the matter to a professional accountant. This costs a fee but in return the accountant can use his skill to ensure that his client pays no more tax than is necessary. It is worth noting that although the accountant certifies the accounts, this is on the basis of information submitted to him. The accountant will try to ensure that the accounts are complete but he cannot be held responsible for items omitted altogether. The onus is thus on the farmer to provide the accountant with all the necessary information. The deliberate omission of income is of course heavily penalized.

Tax is levied on profits made during the previous year. The Income Tax year ends on 5 April but accounts ending on other dates during the previous year will normally be accepted.

For the 1981–82 year of assessment (commencing 6 April, 1981) accounts closing on, for example, 28 May or 29 September, 1980 would serve.

For income tax purposes, the following items must not be charged in the trading account.

(1) Interest on the farmer's own capital
(2) Household or private expenses
(3) Income Tax
(4) Salary to the farmer.

There are some items often shared between the farm business and the farmer as a private person. If the following have been charged to the farm, a share (agreed with the Inland Revenue) must be deducted for private use.

(1) Motor car, telephone, electricity.
(2) Farm produce used in the house, e.g. eggs, milk, etc.
(3) Two-thirds of the value of the farmhouse if included in the rent of the farm (the remaining one-third is for the use of part of the house as a farm office).
(4) Farm labour used in the house or garden.

Capital allowances
For taxation purposes, the Inland Revenue draws a careful distinction between capital expenditure and other expenses. Capital expenditure so far as the farmer is concerned, includes the purchases of implements and machinery, buildings and land. Capital expenditure (apart from the concessions mentioned below) is not allowable as an expense when arriving at the profit of the farm. Thus if a farmer spends £20 000 on a new cowhouse he cannot charge it against profit. Once erected he can charge repairs but if he enlarges it or improves it, the cost would again be capital expenditure. The farmer that wishes to erect a building or buy expensive machinery thus has to find the money out of his profits or resources. This fact is recognized and there are now a number of capital allowances that the farmer can set against profits.

Agricultural buildings and works
A tenant or owner who erects new buildings can charge against profits an *initial allowance* of 20 per cent in the first year and also a *capital allowance* of 10 per cent a year for eight years including the first year,

Cowhouse (cost net of grant)	£10 000
Initial allowance 20% of £10 000	2 000
Capital allowance 10% of £10 000	1 000
Total allowances for first year	3 000

for the next seven years, a capital allowance of 10 per cent, i.e., £1000 can be claimed.

Machinery and plant (new or secondhand)

The farmer can now charge the whole cost of buying machinery against profits in the same year. If he wishes he can charge part of the cost in the year of purchase and the rest in succeeding years. This might be an advantage if there was a loss or a very small profit in the first year.

The value of equipment not written off is put into a 'pool' and depreciated 25 per cent a year on a diminishing value basis. This depreciation can of course be charged as an expense. The 'pool' includes equipment bought before 1972 (when the 100 per cent allowance began) and motor cars which are treated separately.

The value of a motor car is written down by 25 per cent a year. If, for example, a farmer buys a car for £4000, it is written down by £1000 in the first year. If the tax inspector agrees that three-quarters of the mileage is for farm use, the farmer can charge £750 in the trading accounts in the first year and a corresponding share in succeeding years. The car must be appropriate to the size of the farm, and the maximum cost allowed is £8000 with a first year allowance of £2000. A share of running expenses can also, of course, be charged.

Averaging profits

The profits of farming vary widely from one year to another due to the weather, disease and other factors over which the farmer has little control. Fluctuating incomes tend however to incur more tax; a farmer earning £40 000 profit in one year and none the next would pay more tax than if he had two profits of £20 000 each. This fact has recently been recognized by the Chancellor of the Exchequer and farmers are now able to average the profits of two successive years, provided that the lower profit is 70 per cent or less of the higher one.

Profit in year 1	£20 000
Profit in year 2	30 000
	£50 000

Assessment for year 1	£25 000 (half of £50 000)
Assessment for year 2	£25 000 (half of £50 000).

Suppose that the profit in year 3 is £15 000

Profit for year 3	£15 000
Assessment for year 2	25 000
	£40 000
Revised assessment for year 2	£20 000
Assessment for year 3	£20 000

Averaging is allowed in this case because the profit in year 1 (£20 000) is only 66 per cent of year 2 (£30 000). The profit in year 3 (£15 000) is only 60 per cent of the assessment for year 2 (£25 000). If the lower profit is between 70 per cent and 75 per cent of the higher, partial spreading is allowed. The first year eligible for averaging was 1977–78.

Losses

Losses can be set against other income in this order—other earnings, investment income, wife's earnings, wife's investment income. Any balance left over can then be carried forward and set against future farm profits.

Corporation Tax

If a farm business is a limited company, Corporation Tax may have to be paid on profits. If profits exceed £200 000 the tax is 52 per cent of the profit. If profits are below £80 000 the rate is 40 per cent. Between £80 000 and £200 000, there are intermediate rates. In calculating the profit liable to tax, fees to directors (which can include the farmer) can be charged. Liability to this tax is one of the disadvantages of turning a farm business into a limited company.

Taxes and inflation

Since 1939, costs and prices have increased from year to year— sometimes only by two or three per cent, sometimes by 15 per cent or more. Inflation can distort accounts and produce misleading estimates of farm profits. A simple example will make this clear. Suppose that a farmer spends £10 000 producing crops and livestock that he expects to sell a year later for £13 000 leaving a profit of £3000. In the meantime, however, prices have increased and he sells the produce for £15 000. The accounts then show a 'profit' of £5000 or £2000 more than he expected. When the farmer sees this he is delighted at the higher profits and decides that he can afford a new tractor or even a holiday in Spain. The tax inspector meantime demands £2000 in tax instead of the £1000 the farmer expected on a profit of £3000. A further difficulty is that with rising costs the farmer has to spend £12 000 (instead of the £10 000 he expected) to finance the next year's production. Thus, instead of having an extra £2000 profit to spend as the account seemed to indicate, he is short of cash to pay current expenses.

This is, of course, a simplified example but it does illustrate the fact that in a period of inflation, the higher profits that the accounts show could encourage the farmer to embark on over optimistic expenditure leading in due course to severe cash flow difficulties and higher taxes.*

This result suggests that profits should be defined in a different way. If in the example given we had set the £15 000 sales against the cost of inputs *at the same date* (£12 000) we should have shown a profit of £3000.

The effects of inflation on profits have now been recognized and proposals have been made to revise accounting methods to overcome them. One simple method, called *Current Purchasing Power* or CPP, is to use the official cost of living index which measures the shrinking value of money. Thus, if the index increases by 10 per cent, this indicates a fall of 10 per cent in the value of the £. This index could thus be used to adjust costs and returns during the year to one price level. One difficulty is that changes in the prices of individual inputs and outputs do not necessarily keep in step with one single index.

A more detailed method, normally called *Current Cost Accounting* or CCA, is to adjust items individually to agree with changes in the cost of replacing them. One difficulty is that goods and services change in character and replacements available after a period may no longer be the same as the original.† No single method has yet met with general acceptance but the official Sandilands Committee produced a report that on the whole favoured CCA. An agreed procedure, acceptable to the accountancy profession will no doubt be adopted.

In the meantime, the Chancellor of the Exchequer has introduced measures which reduce some of the difficulties caused by inflation.

Depreciation of machinery

When a machine is purchased the orthodox method is to charge a share of the cost each year as depreciation. This allows the farmer to charge the whole cost of the machine over its life. If prices were stable this

---

* The same problems can arise in large industries where inflated profits can encourage dividends that are not strictly justified and demands for higher wages from workers who believe that firms can afford them.

† Two alternatives have been suggested—sale value and 'value in use'. The latter is theoretically desirable but difficult to define in practice.

allowance would also be sufficient to pay for replacing it. If prices are rising, however, a depreciation allowance based on the purchase price five or ten years previously, when prices were lower, is not sufficient to pay for a replacement.

A recent Cambridge survey showed that the written-down value of machinery was only 40 per cent of the cost of replacing it—even at second-hand prices. If this is so it means that depreciation based on historic costs covered only 40 per cent of the cost of replacing the machinery when it was finally worn out. However, this problem has been alleviated by the fact that machinery can now be written off in the year of purchase.

The herd basis

If livestock are included in the opening and closing valuations as 'stock in trade' then any increase or decrease in their value will affect the profit. In a period of inflation a dairy herd valued at market prices could give rise to large paper profits. If the price of cows increased from £200 to £300, a herd of 100 cows would increase in value by £10 000 and this would be taxed as profit. This would be misleading because the cows are part of the equipment of a dairy farm, kept not for sale but to produce milk. Old cows are eventually sold but these are merely a by-product.

To avoid such paper profits a dairy farmer can elect to have the dairy herd treated on the 'herd basis'. If so, adult cows are omitted from the opening and closing valuations in the trading account. Thus if the price of cows rises or falls the profit is unaffected. The following points should be noted.

(1) The cost of replacing animals in the herd can be charged as an expense e.g. if a farmer buys a cow for £400 to replace an old one sold for £250, he can charge £150 for replacing one cow. If the replacement is a home bred heifer the cost of rearing will already have appeared in the trading account and the only additional entry needed is to credit the proceeds of the sale of the old cow.

(2) If the farmer buys cows and increases the size of the herd, the cost is capital expenditure and cannot be entered in the trading account. If the herd is enlarged with home-bred stock, the heifers are entered in the trading account as a 'sale' when they enter the dairy herd. The cost of rearing them has already appeared in the trading account.

(3) If the herd is sold, the proceeds do not appear in the trading account as a receipt. This concession applies only if at least a fifth of the herd is sold during the year and is in effect lost if there is a replacement within five years.

(4) A farmer starting in business can choose the herd basis but having made his choice, he must normally adhere to it.

(5) Although generally used for milking cows the herd basis can be used for other breeding stock, i.e. pigs, sheep and poultry. It does not apply to flying flocks of cattle or sheep (even if they calve or lamb while on the farm) or young stock (except hill sheep where replacements are reared on the farm).

Stock relief

Stock relief was introduced in 1975 to assist companies to counteract the effect of inflation in increasing valuations. It was later extended to cover farmers and other trades and professions. If the value of stock increases, the excess can, in certain cases, be deducted from the profit. Stock in this case includes the normal valuation in the trading account (omitting machinery and livestock on the herd basis).

Starting a farm

As already mentioned Income Tax during any one tax year is normally levied on the profit made in the previous year. In the first year of farming, there is no 'previous' year. For this reason there are special rules for the first and second year. The normal rule is

1st year—taxed on profits between date of entry and 5 April following
2nd year—taxed on first complete year
3rd and later years—taxed on profits of previous year (or to be more exact, on the profit shown in a set of accounts finishing during the previous year).

Suppose that a farmer starts farming in September 1980. His accounts in the first three years show the following profits

Year ending 30 September 1981	£2 000
Year ending 30 September 1982	£6 000
Year ending 30 September 1983	£10 000

The tax year ends in April each year. The assessments for taxation would thus be as follows

1st assessment—tax year 1980–1 (ending April 1981). Taxed on profit made up to April 1981. At that date he has been farming for six months. As he made £2000 in the first 12 months he is presumed to have made £1000 by April. Assessment £1000.

2nd assessment—tax year 1981–2 (ending April 1982). Taxed on profit in first complete year ending September 1981.

Assessment £2000

3rd assessment—tax year 1982–3 (ending April 1983). Taxed on profit shown in accounts finishing during the previous year, i.e. year ending September 1981.

Assessment £2000

4th assessment—tax year 1983–4 (ending April 1984). Taxed on profits in accounts finishing during the previous year, i.e. year ending September 1982.

Assessment £6000.

It will be seen that, in this case, the accounts for the year ending September 1981 appeared in three different assessments. It follows therefore, that if (as is likely) the profit in the first year is a modest one, the farmer will pay very little tax for the first three years. He can, however, choose in the second and third years to be assessed on the actual profits made during the tax year (April to April). In this case

2nd assessment—tax year 1981–2, ending April 1982
April 1981 to September 1981 half of £2000	£1000
September 1981 to April 1982 half of £6000	3000
	£4000

3rd assessment—tax year 1982–3, ending April 1983
April 1982 to September 1982 half of £6000	£3000
September 1982 to April 1983 half of £10 000	5000
	£8000

In this case, the second alternative is less favourable to the farmer than the first. If, however, the farmer had made a larger profit in the first year and a poorer one in the second or third year, the second alternative might have been preferable.

Giving up farming
It will be noticed that when one is starting a farm, parts of the first financial year are assessed two or three times. When a farmer is giving up, the process is reversed and a period is never effectively taxed. The choice of whether the farmer is assessed on the previous year or on the profits made in the tax year rests, however, with the Inland Revenue.

Personal taxation

We have shown how business profits are assessed for taxation. These, together with other forms of income such as dividends, fees, salaries, wages and in the case of married men, his wife's income give the taxpayer's total income on which tax is levied. There are, however, certain allowances of which the following are the most important, the rates being those current after the Finance Act 1981.

Married man	£2145
Single man	1375
Life assurance premiums	
(subject to certain rules)	15%

There are also official allowances for old age, a housekeeper for a widow or a widower, dependent relative, etc. Until recently there were deductions for children. In most cases this has been replaced by child benefit, a weekly payment of £5.25 per child.

After deducting these allowances, income is taxed at the following rates.

30%	0–11 250
40%	11 251–13 250
45%	13 251–16 750
50%	16 751–22 250
55%	22 251–27 750
60%	Over £27 250

There is an additional levy of 15 per cent on investment income (e.g. dividends from shares) exceeding £5500. The maximum rate on earned income (e.g. from farm profits) is thus 60 per cent and on investment income 75 per cent. These rates may seem high but until April 1979, the maximum was 83 per cent on earned income and 98 per cent on investment income. The following are examples of the way in which Income Tax is calculated.

(1) Mr White is a bachelor and has a small farm. His accounts show a net profit of £9000.

Assessment under Schedule D		£9 000
Less single allowance		1 375
Taxable income		£7 625
£7 625 @ 30%	£2 287	
Tax payable	£2 287	

(2) Mr Black has a large farm. His accounts show a net profit of £30 000. His wife has an investment income of £6500.

Assessment under Schedule D	£30 000
Investment income	6 500
	36 500
Less married allowance	2 145
Taxable income	£34 355

11 250 @ 30%	3 375
2 000 @ 40%	800
3 500 @ 45%	1 575
5 500 @ 50%	2 750
5 500 @ 55%	3 025
6 605 @ 60%	3 963
34 355	£15 488

Investment income surcharge
£6500−£5500 = £100 @ 15%   150
Total tax payable   £15 638

Normally the incomes of husband and wife are treated as one—the husband claims the allowances and pays the taxes. A wife that prefers to deal with her own affairs can, however, ask for a separate assessment and pay her own tax. A farmer's wife who does the farm accounts can be paid a reasonable salary which can be included as a farm expense. The wife can claim a single person's tax-free allowance (in addition to the married allowance claimed by the husband).

Pay As You Earn

Farm workers like other wage earners must pay tax if their incomes are high enough. The farmer is responsible for deducting tax from the workers' pay packet and for sending the money to the Inland Revenue. Assume for example, that John Smith is a farm worker. His earnings (including overtime, bonuses, piece work and holiday pay, but omitting payments in kind such as free milk, cottage or board) are £80 in the first week, £85 in the second, etc. The Inland Revenue has notified the farmer that Smith's code number is 181H. (This denotes his personal allowances; in this case £1810 as a married man with no children.)

Each week the farmer enters details on a deduction card (Fig. 22.1). Gross pay is entered in column 2 and total pay to date in column 3. The farmer then looks up the Free Pay Table (supplied by the Inland Revenue) and notes that in week 1 (April 6–12) a man with code no. 181 is entitled to £35 free of tax. This is entered (column 4) and deducted from £80, leaving £45 taxable (column 5). The farmer then looks up the taxable pay table for week 1 and notes that the tax on £45 is £13·50 (column 6). This is deducted from his pay packet. In week 2, Smith is paid £85, making £165 to date. After deducting £70 free pay, £28·50 tax is due on the £95 taxable pay to date. As Mr Smith has already paid £13·50, the balance of £15 (column 7) is deducted from his pay packet. It is thus evident that Smith is paying tax not on his earnings in the week but on the cumulative total to date. The reason for this complication is to ensure that men with fluctuating incomes do not pay an undue amount of tax when earnings are high in any one week.

One consequence of this system is evident in week 4 when Smith was off ill. As he had no earnings, this reduced his average earnings and he was due a refund of £10·50.

1 Week no.	2 Pay in week or month	3 Total pay to date	4 Total free pay to date as shown Table A	5 Total taxable pay to date	6 Total tax due to date as shown by taxable pay tables	7 Tax deducted or refunded in the week or month (mark refunds R)
	£	£	£	£	£	£
1	80	80	35	45	13·50	13·50
2	85	165	70	95	28·50	15·00
3	82	247	105	142	42·60	14·10
4	—	247	140	107	32·10	10·50R
5	80	327	175	152	45·60	13·50
6	80	407	210	197	59·10	13·50

National Insurance contributions are also entered on the deduction card and the workers share is deducted from his pay packet. Pensions for retirement, widowhood and invalidity are no longer on a flat rate but include an addition related to the employee's earnings.

Value Added Tax

Value Added Tax (VAT) is a widely based tax levied on most goods and services sold in this country. All the countries of the EEC have such a tax and part of the proceeds is used to finance the EEC budget.

The way in which VAT is levied can be illustrated by taking a simple example. Suppose that the levy is 10 per cent.

(1) A manufacturer makes a product and sells it for £100. He adds 10 per cent VAT to the bill and sends the tax to the Customs and Excise.

Most goods pass through two or more hands before they reach the customer. At each stage, the product or output of one business becomes the raw material or input of the next. At each step, the price rises and the value added is taxed. This is done in the following way.

(2) Suppose that the product mentioned in (1) above is manufactured in two steps and then sold by a retailer, e.g. Manufacturer A makes a

product which he sells to Manufacturer B for £50 adding £5 VAT. The tax is sent to the Customs and Excise. B completes the manufacture and sells it to the retailer for £80, adding £8 VAT to the bill. Before sending this sum to the tax authority, he deducts the £5 VAT he paid to Manufacturer A: he therefore sends £3 (£8 less £5) to the Customs and Excise. This is of course 10 per cent of the £30 increase in value (£50 to £80).

The retailer then sells the product for £100, adding £10 VAT. He deducts the £8 VAT paid to B and sends £2 to the Customs and Excise. The final consumer pays £110, including £10 VAT.

The Customs and Excise has collected £10 tax in three stages, £5 from A, £3 from B and £2 from the retailer.

At present there are two rates of tax. A zero rate is levied on items such as food, books, medicines, newspapers and children's clothing. Most other goods and services bear a standard rate of 15 per cent.

The farmer is thus in a special position because nearly all his products—cereals, sugar-beet, vegetables and livestock are zero rated. He thus charges no VAT on his sales. On the other hand, he pays VAT on many of his purchases such as fertilizer or spray materials, and this can be recovered. He can also recover VAT on a reasonable proportion of items such as telephone or petrol shared between the farm and the farmer's household. Seeds and feeding stuffs are zero rated.

On balance therefore, the farmer normally receives repayments from the Customs and Excise. The only sales on which he would have to collect VAT are items such as wool, flowers, bulbs, nursery stock or contract work.

So far as book-keeping is concerned, the farmer should ensure that the bills he pays state the amount of VAT included. It is advisable to insert a column for VAT charges in the cash analysis book. Every three months (or monthly if preferred) the farmer sends a return to the Customs and Excise stating the amount of VAT collected and paid. Inspectors make occasional random checks to see that the VAT regulations are being obeyed. Records should therefore clearly show the name of firms and the materials purchased or sold and should be retained for at least three years.

All businesses with a taxable turnover of more than £15 000 must be registered. This would therefore include all but quite small farm enterprises. A business that is exempted collects no VAT—on the other hand, it cannot reclaim VAT on its inputs. For this reason a farmer with a small business might ask to be registered and, if suitable, he will be accepted.

Some types of business are entirely exempt from VAT. These include insurance, finance, betting, education, health and burial.

Taxes on capital: Capital transfer tax

For many years there has been a tax on inherited wealth. Until 1975, this was Estate Duty or, in common parlance, 'death duties'. As the rates were heavy, it is not surprising that property owners tried to avoid this levy on their heirs. One easy way was to give away some property, usually to their wives or children during their lifetime. In consequence, the tax was extended to cover gifts up to seven years before the death of the property owner. As it was still possible to avoid the tax by gifts made in good time, Estate Duty was replaced in 1975 by Capital Transfer Tax which levied a tax on gifts of property throughout the donor's life.

Two concessions were made however—gifts between husband and wife were exempted and gifts during the donor's lifetime were taxed on a reduced scale.

The effect of these changes was that the tax could no longer be avoided altogether by making gifts. It was nevertheless evident that the withdrawal of large amounts of capital could cripple the finances of a family business such as farming. In the 1981 Finance Act therefore, two further concessions were made. Gifts more than ten years before death were exempted and the scale for lifetime gifts on larger estates was reduced. It is thus once again possible to avoid this tax on gifts made more than ten years before the death of the property owner. A farmer could do this by taking his son into partnership in good time and passing part of the property over to him.

The present rates of CTT are given as follows.

Slice of capital exceeding	And up to	Legacy at death (1)	Lifetime gifts (2)
—	£50 000	Nil	Nil
£50 000	60 000	30%	15%
60 000	70 000	35%	17½%
70 000	90 000	40%	20%
90 000	110 000	45%	22½%
110 000	130 000	50%	25%
130 000	160 000	55%	30%
160 000	510 000	60%	35%
510 000	1 010 000	65%	40%
1 010 000	2 010 000	70%	45%
2 010 000	And over	75%	50%

(1) Estate at death plus gifts within 3 years of death
(2) Gifts between 3 and 10 years of death. Over 10 years—no CTT.

If the owner of property dies, the first £50 000 is free of tax. The next slice up to £60 000, pays 30%. Thus if the estate is £60 000, £50 000 pays no tax and the remaining £10 000 pays 30% or £3 000. The rate levied on each additional slice increases steadily until the excess over £2 010 000 pays 75 per cent. These rates also apply to gifts within three years of death.

The tax on gifts between three and ten years of death is at lower rates varying from 15 to 50 per cent. No CTT is payable on gifts made more than ten years before death. No tax is levied on

(1) the first £50 000 of the estate;
(2) gifts or legacies between husband and wife;
(3) the first £3000 of gifts in any one year;
(4) small gifts of up to £250 to any one person;
(5) wedding gifts up to £5000 for a child, £2500 for a grandchild or great grandchild and £1000 for most other people;
(6) gifts to charities and political parties, (only £200 000 at death or within one year of death);
(7) gifts out of income forming part of the donor's normal expenditure.

In spite of concessions, the rates of tax are very high. Public opinion may have little sympathy for a young man who inherits wealth and lives off the proceeds for the rest of his life without doing any work, but when wealth represents the capital required to conduct a business, the payment of CTT could cripple it. In recent years, the value of land has increased dramatically and so also has the liability to CTT. Thus while the proceeds after tax may provide a comfortable living for a childless farmer who sells out on retirement and lives on the proceeds, it is hard on a son who inherits and wishes to continue the farm business. He may find that to pay the CTT he is saddled with large debts or compelled to sell some land and this could reduce the efficiency of a well-planned unit.

In recognition of these facts the transfer of property by a working farmer is reduced in value by one half (the 'working farmer' must have occupied the property for the two previous years and derived 75 per cent of his income from agriculture).

This reduction in value of 50 per cent applies to owner occupiers and to agricultural land and buildings up to 1000 acres (six acres of rough grazing count as one acre) or if preferred £250 000 in value. The value of land let is reduced by 20 per cent. As tenanted land is worth perhaps 30–40 per cent less than land with vacant possession, this brings the value down to about half.

There is a parallel concession for business property that could be used as an alternative. A farmer (or farmer and wife) who own or have a controlling interest in a farm business can have the value of the property reduced by 50 per cent. This could cover land in excess of 1000 acres or business property such as livestock or machinery not covered by the agricultural concession. Lower reliefs apply in certain cases—20 per cent reduction for minority shares in a business and 30 per cent for assets used in a business but owned by a partner or controlling shareholder (e.g. land let by a farmer to his company or partnership).

Example

An owner occupier has agricultural property worth £600 000 reduced for CTT to £300 000.

(1) He dies leaving £200 000 to his wife (exempt from tax) and £400 000 to his son.

The son's share is reduced to £200 000, taxed as follows

			£
Up to £50 000	50 000	zero	—
50– 60 000	10 000 @ 30%		3 000
60– 70 000	10 000 @ 35%		3 500
70– 90 000	20 000 @ 40%		8 000
90–110 000	20 000 @ 45%		9 000
110–130 000	20 000 @ 50%		10 000
130–160 000	30 000 @ 55%		16 500
160–200 000	40 000 @ 60%		24 000
Total tax on	£200 000		£74 000

The son thus pays £74 000 on the £400 000 inherited. (He will also have to pay tax on his mother's estate if she dies leaving it to him.)

(2) Suppose instead that during his lifetime the farmer had given £80 000 to his wife (exempt) and £200 000 to his son. The latter, reduced to £100 000 is taxed as follows

			£
Up to £50 000	50 000	zero	—
50–60 000	10 000 @ 15%		1 500
60–70 000	10 000 @ 17½%		1 750
70–90 000	20 000 @ 20%		4 000
90–100 000	10 000 @ 22½%		2 250
Total tax on	£100 000		£9 500

Twelve years later, the farmer dies leaving £120 000 to his wife (exempt) and £200 000 to his son. The latter reduced to £100 000 is taxed as follows

			£
Up to £50 000	50 000	zero	—
50– 60 000	10 000 @	30%	3 000
60– 70 000	10 000 @	35%	3 500
70– 90 000	20 000 @	40%	8 000
90–100 000	10 000 @	45%	4 500
Total tax on	£100 000		£19 000

The total duty paid was thus £9500 plus £19 000 = £28 500 which is much less of a burden. In this case, the farmer had carefully retained more than half the property in his own hands. If he had been prepared to give away more at an earlier date, the tax could have been reduced further. (The farmer could also have given another £3000 a year to his son free of tax, but this has been omitted to simplify the example.)

If, by contrast, the farmer had made no gifts in his lifetime and had died a widower, the tax on his estate would have been £134 000.

Although tax might be saved, it is easy to understand why a farmer might hesitate to pass over most of his property to others, even to members of his own family, if it meant losing control of the farm business. Indeed, if he gave his property to his son and the latter died first, the farmer might find his son's wife and children less accommodating than his son, and they might wish to withdraw their money at an awkward moment. A farmer wishing to retain control should therefore retain a majority interest in his own hands.

Capital Transfer Tax on land and agricultural property can be paid in eight yearly instalments, normally free of interest.

Capital Gains Tax

If property is purchased and sold some years later for a higher price, the increase in value is liable to Capital Gains Tax (CGT). Property in this case includes land, buildings and investments. The first £3000 of gain each year is free of tax. The remaining gain is subject to a tax of 30 per cent. There are a number of exemptions—motor cars, dwelling house, national savings certificates, government stocks held for at least one year, winnings from gambling or the pools and chattels such as jewellry or furniture where the proceeds are less than £2000. The tax applies only to increases in value after 6 April, 1965. If the property was acquired before that date the capital gain is apportioned as from 1965. Alternatively, the taxpayer can ask for it to be based on the market value in 1965.

If a farmer has sold a farm, he can postpone the payment of tax if he reinvests the proceeds in another farm. This is called 'rolling over' and applies only if the new asset is acquired within 12 months before and three years after the disposal of the old asset. The liability to tax still exists however and will arise if the second farm is sold out at a later date. CGT is not, however, payable on death. Tax retirement relief is available (up to £50 000 at 65) on retirement.

Development Land Tax

When land is developed or sold for development, any profit is subject to tax at a rate of 60 per cent. The first £50 000 is normally exempt from Development Land Tax (DLT) (but not from CGT) for each year (husband and wife each qualify separately). Rules exist to prevent double taxation and a gain taxed under DLT is not charged to CGT.

Final comment

The law on taxation is very complex. When rates are high, wealthy men devise ingenious schemes to avoid tax and the Chancellor of the Exchequer has to introduce counter measures to plug loopholes. For this reason, a farmer would be well advised to consult his accountant and his solicitor who can give professional advice on what is a specialized subject. A farmer should, however, aquire a general knowledge of the subject so that he can appreciate the implications of the advice he receives.

There is one final comment. Farmers and accountants are sometimes inclined to regard the trading account merely as a statement prepared to satisfy the Inspector of Taxes. The aim of this book is to show that its main purpose should be to provide the farmer with the information necessary to improve the efficiency of his farm and maximize his income. The farmer should therefore ensure that his accountant does provide the details he requires for this purpose. This can usually be done at the time with very little extra trouble or expense. If the farmer has to pay fees to an accountant, he should at least ensure that he obtains full value for his money.

National insurance   A levy on wages (8·75 per cent from employees, 13·7 per cent from employers, lower rates for widows, married men etc.) to help pay for social benefits.

Collection is as for PAYE.

23 The microcomputer on the far

An interesting new development is the use of small computers as an aid to farm accountancy and management. Large commercial firms have been using computers for a number of years but until recently the cost was far beyond the reach of the farmer. The introduction of the microcomputer has, however, greatly reduced the cost.

When first invented, a computer processing unit would have filled a large room. Now it has been steadily reduced to a silicon chip only two or three centimetres long. This has made possible the production of small microcomputers. Such machines cannot perform the mathematical feats of the large main frame installations found in government and university research departments but they are quite adequate for the tasks described in this chapter.

The chief credit for introducing microcomputers into farming practice belongs to a few large farming companies that bought equipment and hired professional programmers to write programs suitable for their business. This was an expensive operation but having produced workable systems, some of them set up businesses to sell their expertise to other farmers. In cooperation with equipment manufacturers, they market a 'package deal' including programs (*software*) and a suitable computer (*hardware*). So far, the field has been left almost entirely to private enterprise. The government advisory services are, however, prepared to give advice to firms offering computer services as well as to individual farmers.

Computer hardware

As can be seen from Fig. 23.1, the equipment includes a central processor, a keyboard, an external memory, a visual display unit and a printer.

Central processing unit The central processing unit includes a microprocessor (silicon chip) which performs the calculations and controls the peripheral equipment. It is surrounded by supporting circuits and

Fig. 23.1 A microcomputer with keyboard, display unit and two disc drives. The operator is inserting a floppy disc. A printer would be a useful addition. (Photograph: Microsense Computers Ltd)

includes an internal memory used while the computer is in operation. The memory capacity is measured in *bytes* (a byte is roughly one letter or a number) and a microcomputer usually has up to 64 000 bytes (64K). If too small, the computer cannot handle complex problems.

Keyboard   The keyboard resembles a typewriter.

External memory   Information and instructions for any particular program are usually stored on *floppy discs* that resemble gramophone records. When in use, these are inserted into disc drives. One disc carries general instructions about the program and the other contains the data for the farm concerned. If we are dealing with the accounts, for example, one disc would contain instruction about preparing items such as the trading account, lists of debtors and creditors, cashflow, comparisons with the previous year, etc. The other disc would contain details of purchases, sales and other items and would be brought up to date, say once a week.

As an alternative, information can be stored on magnetic tape, but the location of items of information is slower than on a disc. Cards and punched tape are used on other types of computer but are less suitable for the purposes described here.

Display unit   This resembles a television set.

Printer   This enables the farmer to make a record on paper of information displayed on the television screen.

Language   To shorten the process of preparing programs, certain conventions are used. These form a *language*. There are several languages in use—Cobol, Fortran, Algol, and Basic. Most microcomputers use Basic although there are many dialects. A program prepared in one language or dialect cannot usually be used on a computer programmed for a different language.

Uses of the microcomputer

There are two main uses for the microcomputer on the farm. The first and most popular is to handle the accounts. The second is to analyze individual enterprises, especially dairy cows, pigs and cash crops. Similar programs could be prepared to deal with fattening cattle, broiler fattening and egg production.

Farm accounts

When purchases and sales are keyed in, code numbers are used to indicate their nature (e.g. feeding-stuffs), the supplier or customer (e.g. Smith & Co.) the enterprise concerned (e.g. dairy cows) and other details (e.g. VAT, quantity, date, etc.). This enables the computer to sort the information in any way required, e.g. cost of feeding-stuffs fed to cows last month or the same month last year.

In the *Cash analysis system* described earlier in this book, purchases and sales were entered only when paid or the money was received. The same procedure can be followed here. It is, however, an easy matter to go one stage further and enter purchases and sales on credit as they occur. One advantage is that the total for any item is the net amount and needs no further adjustment for debtors or creditors. The system thus becomes virtually double entry although it is not necessary to learn orthodox double entry book-keeping.

The farmer can get a print out of unpaid bills at the end of each month ready for cheques to be written. If the farmer is short of cash, he can decide which he can afford to pay and which can be postponed.

If the farmer has a cash flow problem, he can prepare a budget beforehand and compare it month by month with the actual results to ensure that he does not exceed the overdraft agreed with his bank.

Pay Roll

A program can be included to calculate wages and print pay slips with details of tax, overtime, etc.

Report trail*

The following report trail shows how a farmer might use the computer to examine his accounts without waiting until the end of the year. If any item seems anomalous, the farmer can trace it back stage by stage to the original transactions.

When the accounts program is switched on the options available are displayed as a *menu* on the screen, for example

(1) profit and loss account;
(2) financial summary (management accounts);
(3) enterprise analysis;
(6) supplier/customer ledgers;
(7) transaction analysis;
(8) inspector;
(9) report query.

Suppose that the farmer choses option (1). Profit and Loss account. He presses key no. 1 and Fig. 23.2 comes up on the screen. The date is early June and the figures produced are for the last complete month— May. Alongside appears the cumulative total since the beginning of the year, i.e. April and May. The *profit* for one month is not by itself necessarily very meaningful (in this case because the crop expenses are yet not matched by crop sales) but the individual costs are of interest. Suppose that the farmer decided to examine the dairy enterprise. He chooses option (3) and Fig. 23.3 comes on the screen. In this case the receipts and variable costs are set against the budget previously prepared by the farmer. It wil be seen that the gross margin for May is well below the budget. Although less milk was sold than expected, substantially more 'Feed–Other' was used. The farmer can then call for the details (Fig. 23.4). This shows the invoices in detail and the farmer can examine the reasons for the large quantities of feed used.

Dairy herd

In a large herd, the cowman cannot be expected to remember details about each individual cow. For this reason, dairy herd programs include *action lists*, to draw the attention to events requiring attention in the

* This is a shortened version of an example kindly supplied by Farmplan.

Profit and Loss Account

Code	May	Year to date
Sales	£	£
01 Milk	7 629·98	16 470·18
10 Calves	61·00	61·00
12 Fat cattle	2 586·00	2 627·44
20 Grain	0·00	0·00
25 Val change	−2 500·00	−2 500·00
	7 776·98	16 658·62
Variable costs		
55 Feed-concentrates	1 158·91	2 786·10
57 Feed-other	2 338·38	2 831·59
60 Vet + AI	256·04	417·15
62 Dairy + sundries	209·69	309·63
70 Fertilizer	1 526·10	1 526·10
71 Seed	324·00	534·00
72 Chemicals	564·00	930·50
85 Misc	160·81	453·31
	6 537·93	9 788·38
Common costs		
2200 Labour	1 540·75	2 709·33
2400 Machinery	1 152·78	1 559·46
Other overheads*	442·67	1 160·27
	3 136·20	5 429·06
Net profit/loss	−£1 897·15	£1 441·18

* condensed

Fig. 23.2 Profit and loss account for month of May. Cumulative total since April 1 given for comparison

next few days. A print out can therefore be handed to the cowman once a week giving, lists of

(1) cows due to calve;
(2) cows due to be dried off;
(3) cows that have missed service;
(4) cows to be pregnancy tested, etc.

The lists can include other details about the cows on the lists, e.g. difficulty in calving, mastitis, etc.

Tables can be displayed at any time giving details for each cow, e.g.

Dairy

	Enterprise Analysis					
	May			Accumulated		
Sales	Amount	Budget	Difference	Amount	Budget	Difference
Milk	7 629·98	8 000·00	370·02	16 470·18	17 000·00	529·82
Calves	61·00	100·00	39·00	61·00	100·00	39·00
Fat cattle	2 586·00	2 500·00	−86·00	2 627·44	2 500·00	−127·44
Transfers out	—	—	—	—	—	—
Val diff	−2 500·00	−2 500·00	—	−2 500·00	−2 500·00	—
	7 776·98	8 100·00	323·02	16 658·62	17 100·00	441·38
Purchases						
Livestock	—	—	—	—	—	—
Transfers in						
Feed-conc	1 127·91	1 000·00	−127·91	2 692·10	2 250·00	−442·10
Feed-other	2 338·38	1 750·00	−588·38	2 831·59	2 350·00	−481·59
Vet + AI	230·04	250·00	19·96	370·85	450·00	79·15
Sundries	158·20	—	−158·20	215·62	100·00	−115·62
Bedding	51·49	25·00	−26·49	94·01	100·00	5·99
Misc	109·81	50·00	−59·81	109·81	100·00	−9·81
	4 015·83	3 075·00	−940·83	6 313·98	5 350·00	−963·98
Gross margin	3 761·15	5 025·00	1 263·85	10 344·64	11 750·00	1 405·36

Fig. 23.3 Dairy enterprise account for May and total since 1 April. Budget prepared beforehand given for comparison

Invoice 0061	42T Brewers Grains	£769·50
Invoice 0074	20 bags High Mag Mix	123·48
Invoice 0104	80T Brewers Grains	1445·40
	Total	2338·38
	Budget	1750·00
	Difference	£558·38
	Excess	33%

Fig. 23.4 Details of feeding-stuffs/other used in May

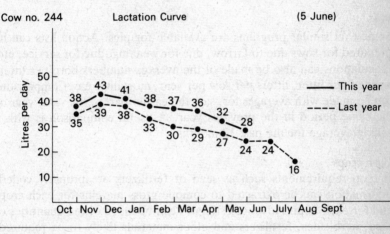

Cow no. 244   Lactation Curve   (5 June)

Other details

Lactation	3rd	
Calving index	348	
Last service	13/12/79	
Days since last service	175	
Service dates	19/11/80	13/12/80
Calving to conception, days	67	
Days since calving	242	
Pregnancy diagnosed	Yes	
Date last calved	7/10/79	
Date due to calve	19/9/80	
Yield to date (kg)	8603	
Peak recording	43	
Change on last recording	−12%	
Yield over 305 days	(incomplete)	
ditto last year (kg)	8702	etc.

Fig. 23.5 Lactation curve and other details for an individual cow (Farmplan)

yield per day over the past three weeks, with a star to draw attention to any yields that have fallen by more than 10 per cent.

It is also possible to call for further details of individual cows (Fig. 23.5).

Some packages include a system for checking food rations. The farmer can enter details of the ration he intends to feed and a table showing the energy, protein, mineral content, etc. will appear on the screen and can be compared with requirements. If not satisfactory, he can then change the quantity of any ingredient or substitute one food for another in order to bring the total closer to requirements or to reduce the cost of the ration. Calculations can also be made of the food cost per cow or per litre of milk and of the margin over food costs.

Pigs

Somewhat similar programs are available for pigs. Action lists can be prepared for sows due to farrow, due for weaning, due for service, etc. Calculations can also be made of the average numbers born per litter, weaned per litter, litters per sow per year, mortality, etc. Comparisons can be made with averages for, say, the earlier part of the same year or the same period in the previous year. A useful comparison is with a rolling average for the past 12 months.

Cash crops

If crop requirements such as seed or fertilizers are properly coded, information can be extracted to compile gross margins for each crop, and for each field. Advance estimates can be made of the quantities of seed, herbicides, fertilizers and other materials likely to be required. These can be useful for placing orders or compiling budgets.

Field histories can be compiled giving details of previous crops grown, yields obtained, fertilizer applied, etc. If the farm is large and there are many fields, this information may be useful in deciding on the treatment to be given to any particular field.

Scope for microcomputers

It will be seen that the tasks accomplished by the microcomputer systems are closely similar to those described elsewhere in this book. The same results could be calculated by the farmer with the aid of a pocket calculator. The machine, however, can retrieve information, make calculations and display results in a few seconds that would require many hours of clerical work.

Packages designed for the farm business including hardware and software are available for about £3000 to £6000. More elaborate installations for large farm companies with sub-offices linked to a head office might cost £10 000 or more. As the preparation and testing of a sophisticated program might take months of work the copyright is carefully preserved. A standard package would probably include a program for accounts and one or two others. Additional programs might cost from £100 up to £500 and substantially more for one tailored to a farmer's special requirements. Programs vary greatly in quality. Some of the cheaper ones can do simple tasks but are limited in scope. Those of better quality are more flexible and comprehensive and include built-in checks that draw attention to errors in the data keyed in.

The cost of an outfit is thus about half that of a tractor. What size of farm would justify this expense? The answer depends on the complexity of the organization rather than on the number of hectares. The following types would probably justify a microcomputer.

(1) A farm with a herd of over 200 cows or 250 sows. The continuous monitoring of breeding and the efficient utilization of feeding-stuffs could produce worthwhile savings—especially if the farmer had to leave the day-to-day management to the stockman.

(2) A farm with 100 hectares of mixed fruit or vegetables marketed throughout the year.

(3) A large company with several farms under separate management. A computer in the head office would enable the general manager to keep close control over the finances and to compare the efficiency of the different managers.

On the other hand, a 500 hectare cereal farmer with no livestock might have hardly enough transactions to justify a machine.

In attempting to justify a purchase, it might be prudent to write-off the cost in three or four years. The equipment would last longer but as improved models and programs appear, the farmer might be tempted to buy one.

Annual costs (excluding interest on any loan necessary) might be estimated as follows

Cost of equipment say £5000, write-off over 4 years	£1250
Maintenance 10% of £5000	500
Updating of programs	250
Stationery, discs, etc.	200
	£2200

On a big farm with two or three clerks in the office, savings on dealing with accounts might allow the farmer to dispense with one of the staff. This alone would pay for the equipment. The farmer would also get additional information about his enterprises as a bonus.

If the farmer had one secretary/typist, he might hesitate to dispense with her services unless he can spend in the office several hours a week that might be better spent on the farm. If he retains his secretary, the computer cost would have to be justified by savings due to closer monitoring and improved efficiency. In practice, the benefit would depend on the farmer's temperament. If he is keenly interested in costings and efficiency, and is prepared to act on the results the computer could become an invaluable aid to management. Otherwise, it would be an unnecessary luxury.

Instead of having a microcomputer on every farm, data could be processed centrally. In the USA, Land Grant Colleges provide such a service and farmers send data to the computer by telephone. In Great Britain a telephone would probably be too expensive for this purpose unless the farms were close to the centre. Data can, however, be sent by post and this alternative is already in operation in a few cases. The disadvantage is that the farmer cannot manipulate the machine himself but must accept the analysis provided by the centre. The advantage is that the farmer does not have to invest capital in equipment.

The MAFF have suggested that the microcomputer is justified on about five per cent of the largest farm businesses. This may be true now but as equipment improves it may become cheaper. Programs will certainly become more sophisticated and available at a modest price. This should bring small computers within the reach of a larger proportion of farmers than this estimate suggests.

Acknowledgements
The author is indebted to the following for supplying information on their systems:

Farmplan Computer Systems Ltd, Ross-on-Wye, Herefordshire.
Farmfax Ltd, Stockbridge, Hampshire.
Daisy Dairy Information System, University of Reading.
Pigtales Ltd, Great Hatfield, North Humberside.
Farm Systems, Bar Hill, Cambridgeshire.
Agricultural Computer Services, Thurming, Norfolk.
Upthorpe Computer Programs, Didcot, Oxfordshire.

Appendix 1

Gross margins

Whenever possible, local standards should be used. The following gross margins per hectare are, however, given as an indication of the levels to be expected (1980).

Crops	Yield	Output £	Seeds, fertilizer sprays, etc. £	Gross margin Average	Low	High
Winter wheat	5 tonnes	550	150	400	350	520
Spring wheat	4 tonnes	440	120	320	250	400
Winter barley	4·5 tonnes	480	110	370	270	450
Spring barley	4 tonnes	400	100	300	250	400
Spring oats	4 tonnes	400	100	300	250	350
Field beans	3 tonnes	400	100	300	220	380
Field peas	3 tonnes	480	160	320	220	450
Potatoes	30 tonnes	1500	750	750	350	1400
Sugar-beet	35 tonnes	950	300	650	480	800
Winter rape	2·5 tonnes	580	180	400	320	500

Livestock:		
	Dairy cows (average)	£500–£650 per hectare
	Young dairy stock and store cattle	£150–£250 per hectare
	Cattle (more intensive)	£100–£200 per hectare
	Sheep (lowland)	£150–£250 per hectare

Casual labour (e.g. for harvesting potatoes) has not been charged. As some farmers use it and others do not, this is best when comparing farms. When using gross margins for planning an individual farm, casual labour and contract charges should be deducted.

The returns per hectare from grazing livestock depend on the quality of grazing and management and are much more variable than for crops (*see* Chapter 17). Some intensive forms of cattle rearing apparently show very high returns 'per hectare' because (apart from a little hay) very little of their food is coming from the land.

	Stocking density
Grazing livestock units	
Dairy cow	1·0 unit
Beef cows, other cattle over 2 years	0·8 unit
Cattle 1–2 years	0·6 unit
Cattle under 1 year	0·4 unit
Lowland ewe (plus lambs)	0·2 unit
Hill ewe (plus lambs)	0·1 unit
Other sheep over 6 months	0·1 unit

Forage hectares: pasture, silage, hay, kale and other fodder (but not grain crops)

$$\text{Stocking density} = \frac{\text{Forage, hectares}}{\text{Grazing livestock units}}$$

A reasonable average is about 0·6 hectares per livestock unit. If the figure is high, it indicates under-stocking or poor quality grazing or fodder. A low figure may indicate very productive grazing and fodder. It may, however, mean that the farmer is depending heavily on the use of concentrates. For this reason, some authorities prefer 'feed hectares per grazing livestock unit'. Feed hectares are forage hectares plus an allowance for purchased and home-grown concentrates and cereals.

Work units

A work unit is the average amount accomplished in one man day of eight hours.

Work units attempt to measure the *physical* labour required to operate a farm. Crops and livestock are therefore weighted according to the average amount of labour required for each. Unlike output per £100 labour, this measure is not affected by differences in yields or prices which have no very direct line with labour requirements. The aim of this factor is to measure the amount of productive work accomplished by each man employed.

Divide work units by number of men employed (including an allowance for casuals and farmer's manual work). The average is about 275, but on a well-organized farm should be well over 300. The standards are suited to a mixed farm. Some specialized units (e.g. poultry) use much less labour than these standards imply.

	Per hectare		Per head
Work units			
Wheat, barley	1·5	Dairy cows, cow shed	8
Oats, beans, oilseed rape	2	Dairy cows, parlour	5
Potatoes	14	Beef cows, heifers in calf	2·5
Sugar-beet	6	Other cattle and calves	2·5
Mangolds	30	Lowland ewes	0·5
Turnips, swedes	12	Other sheep	0·3
Kale, cut	12	Hill ewes	0·3
Kale, grazed	2·5	Sows, gilts, boars	3·0
Hay/silage 1 cut	3	Fattening pigs	0·6
Hay/silage 2 cuts	5	Laying hens	0·05
Pasture	1	Pullets	0·025
Peas, can or freeze	4		

An alternative method that requires rather more arithmetic is

(*a*) add 15 per cent (for general maintenance, time lost in bad weather, etc.) to the productive work units calculated above to give 'work units required';

(*b*) multiply the number of workers by 275 (300 for stockmen) to give 'work units used'.

$$\text{Man work index} = \frac{\text{work units required} \times 100}{\text{work units used}}$$

An index of 100 or more indicates good utilization of labour.

Machinery rates of work

The following is a brief list of typical implements to assist in compiling budgets as an exercise. It will be appreciated that specifications and prices vary greatly from one model to another. The reader should not hesitate to substitute other models at current prices to suit particular purposes.

Tractors

30 kW	£8 000
40 kW	£9 000
45 kW	£10 000
55 kW	£11 000
90 kW (4 wheel)	£24 000
135 kW (4 wheel)	£30 000

1. Small Farm (80 hectare arable)

	Width m	Tractor kW	Price £	Speed km/hour	Day (hours)	Time operating %	Ha per day (effective)
Plough, 3-furrow	1	50	1 200	6	7	57	2·4
Cultivator	3	45	800	6	7	57	7·2
Discs	3	40	1 000	6	7	57	7·2
Harrows	4	40	200	10	7	57	16·0
Inter-row cultivator	2·5	40	850	4	7	57	4·0
Rolls	2·5	40	500	4	7	57	4·0
Corn drill	3	40	2 400	10	6	47	8·5
Potato planter, 2-row	1·5	45	2 000	4	6	47	1·7
Sugar-beet drill	2	30	950	4	6	47	2·3
Sprayer	8	30	600	6·	6	37	10·7
Fertilizer distributor	6	40	500	10	6	47	16·9
Combine harvester, SP		(50)	15 000	5T per hour	8		3·8
Potato harvester* (elevator)		45	4 200		6		0·6–1·0
Sugar-beet harvester		45	4 300		7		1·0

* About 10 casuals to pick up the potatoes.

Effective rate of work of a variety of implements suitable for smaller farms. Man hours per hectare makes allowance for time lost in adjustments, turning, cultivating headlands, changing fields and other contingencies. Field size 8–10 hectares. Small farmers often buy larger implements second-hand.

288

2. Medium Farm (200 hectare arable)

	Width m	Tractor kW	Price £	Speed km/hour	Day (hours)	Time operating %	Ha per day (effective)
Plough, 5-furrow	1·5	90	2 100	6	7	60	3·8
Cultivator	3·5	55	1 200	6	7	60	8·8
Discs	3·5	50	1 250	6	7	60	8·8
Harrows	5	45	350	10	7	60	21·0
Inter-row cultivator	2·5	40	850	4	7	60	4·2
Rolls	6	40	1 400	4	7	60	10·1
Corn drill	4	45	3 000	10	6	50	12·0
Potato planter, 2-row	1·5	45	2 000	4	6	50	1·8
Sugar-beet drill	2	30	950	4	6	50	2·4
Sprayer	12	30	1 100	6	6	40	17·3
Fertilizer distributor	6	40	500	10	6	50	18·0
Combine harvester, SP		(70)	22 000	8T per hour	8		6·4
Potato harvester*		45	9 000		6		0·9
Sugar-beet harvester		45	4 300		7		1·1

* 1 or 2 casuals may be required on the machine.

Effective rate of work of a variety of implements suitable for a medium-sized farm. The tractors quoted are the minimum size required (1 kW = 1⅓ HP). There is, of course, a wide range of implements available at varying prices. Prices quoted were typical in 1980. Field size 15 to 20 hectares.

3. Very Large Farm (800 hectare arable)

	Width m	Tractor kW	Price £	Speed km/hour	Day hours	Time operating %	Ha per day (effective)
Plough, 7-furrow	2·5	135	4 000	6	7	65	6·8
Cultivator	5·5	135	1 700	10	7	65	25·0
Discs	4	55	1 500	6	7	65	10·9
Harrows	6	55	400	10	7	65	27·3
Inter-row cultivator	5	40	1 500	4	7	65	9·1
Rolls	7·5	40	2 000	4	7	65	13·7
Corn drill	6	55	5 400	10	6	55	19·8
Potato planter, 4-row	3	50	5 000	4	6	55	4·0
Sugar-beet drill	2·5	30	1 350	4	6	55	3·3
Sprayer	12	45	3 000	6	6	45	19·4
Fertilizer distributor	8	55	1 500	10	6	55	26·4
Combine harvester		(130)	40 000	12T per hour	8		10·6
Potato harvester*		45	9 000		6		1·0
Sugar-beet harvester		SP	22 000		7		2·3

* 1 or 2 casuals may be required on the machine.

Effective rate of work of implements suitable for a very large farm. Fields 25 hectares or more. Larger tractors and cultivators may sometimes be justified to cultivate (or subsoil) heavy land quickly to increase the area of autumn-sown crops.

Appendix 2

Net Present Values

Discount factors for computing the present value of £1 in n years from now

Year	Percentage (r)													
n	5	6	7	8	9	10	12	15	20	25	30	40	50	60
1	0·952	0·943	0·935	0·926	0·917	0·909	0·893	0·870	0·833	0·800	0·769	0·714	0·667	0·625
2	0·907	0·890	0·873	0·857	0·842	0·826	0·797	0·756	0·694	0·640	0·592	0·510	0·444	0·391
3	0·864	0·840	0·816	0·794	0·772	0·751	0·712	0·658	0·579	0·512	0·455	0·364	0·296	0·244
4	0·823	0·792	0·763	0·735	0·708	0·683	0·636	0·572	0·482	0·410	0·350	0·260	0·198	0·153
5	0·784	0·747	0·713	0·681	0·650	0·621	0·567	0·497	0·402	0·328	0·269	0·186	0·132	0·095
6	0·746	0·705	0·666	0·630	0·596	0·564	0·507	0·432	0·335	0·262	0·207	0·133	0·088	0·060
7	0·711	0·665	0·623	0·583	0·547	0·513	0·452	0·376	0·279	0·210	0·159	0·095	0·059	0·037
8	0·677	0·627	0·582	0·540	0·502	0·467	0·404	0·327	0·233	0·168	0·123	0·068	0·039	0·023
9	0·645	0·592	0·544	0·500	0·460	0·424	0·361	0·284	0·194	0·134	0·094	0·048	0·026	0·015
10	0·614	0·558	0·508	0·463	0·422	0·386	0·322	0·247	0·162	0·107	0·073	0·035	0·017	0·009
11	0·585	0·527	0·475	0·429	0·388	0·350	0·287	0·215	0·135	0·086	0·056	0·025	0·012	0·006
12	0·557	0·497	0·444	0·397	0·356	0·319	0·257	0·187	0·112	0·069	0·043	0·018	0·008	0·004
13	0·530	0·469	0·415	0·368	0·326	0·290	0·229	0·163	0·093	0·055	0·033	0·013	0·005	0·002
14	0·505	0·442	0·388	0·340	0·299	0·263	0·205	0·141	0·078	0·044	0·025	0·009	0·003	0·001
15	0·481	0·417	0·362	0·315	0·275	0·239	0·183	0·123	0·065	0·035	0·020	0·006	0·002	0·001

For the general case, the discount factor is given by $\dfrac{1}{(1 + r)^n}$

Example: if interest is 12 per cent, a promise to pay £100, 10 years from now, is worth at present £100 × 0·322 = £32·2

Annuity Tables

Discount factors for computing the present value of a future annuity

Year							Percentage (r)							
n	5	6	7	8	9	10	12	15	20	25	30	40	50	60
1	0·952	0·943	0·935	0·926	0·917	0·909	0·893	0·870	0·833	0·800	0·769	0·714	0·667	0·625
2	1·859	1·833	1·808	1·783	1·759	1·735	1·690	1·626	1·527	1·440	1·361	1·224	1·111	1·016
3	2·723	2·673	2·624	2·577	2·531	2·486	2·402	2·284	2·106	1·952	1·816	1·588	1·407	1·260
4	3·546	3·465	3·387	3·312	3·239	3·169	3·038	2·856	2·588	2·362	2·166	1·848	1·605	1·413
5	4·330	4·212	4·100	3·993	3·889	3·790	3·605	3·353	2·990	2·690	2·435	2·034	1·737	1·508
6	5·076	4·917	4·766	4·623	4·485	4·354	4·112	3·785	3·325	2·952	2·642	2·167	1·825	1·568
7	5·787	5·582	5·389	5·206	5·032	4·867	4·564	4·161	3·604	3·162	2·801	2·262	1·884	1·605
8	6·464	6·209	5·971	5·746	5·534	5·334	4·968	4·488	3·837	3·330	2·924	2·330	1·923	1·628
9	7·109	6·801	6·515	6·246	5·994	5·758	5·329	4·772	4·031	3·464	3·018	2·378	1·949	1·643
10	7·723	7·359	7·023	6·709	6·416	6·144	5·651	5·019	4·193	3·571	3·091	2·413	1·966	1·652
11	8·308	7·886	7·498	7·138	6·804	6·494	5·938	5·234	4·328	3·657	3·147	2·438	1·978	1·658
12	8·865	8·383	7·942	7·535	7·160	6·813	6·195	5·421	4·440	3·726	3·190	2·456	1·986	1·662
13	9·395	8·852	8·357	7·903	7·486	7·103	6·424	5·584	4·533	3·781	3·223	2·469	1·991	1·664
14	9·900	9·294	8·745	8·243	7·785	7·366	6·629	5·725	4·611	3·825	3·248	2·478	1·994	1·665
15	10·381	9·711	9·107	8·558	8·060	7·605	6·812	5·848	4·676	3·860	3·268	2·484	1·996	1·666

For the general case, the discount factor is given by $\dfrac{1 - (1 + r)^{-n}}{r}$ where r = rate of discounting, n = year of cash flow

Example: if interest is 15 per cent, a promise to pay £1 a year for 10 years is now worth £5·019

Annual Mortgage Repayment
Annual repayment per £1000 borrowed (including interest and repayment of loan)

Years	Rate of Interest (r)								
n	7	8	9	10	11	12	15	18	20
1	1070	1080	1090	1100	1110	1120	1150	1180	1200
2	553	562	569	576	584	592	617	639	658
3	381	388	395	403	409	417	439	460	476
4	296	302	309	316	322	330	351	372	388
5	244	251	257	264	271	278	299	320	334
6	210	216	223	230	237	243	265	286	301
7	186	192	199	206	212	219	240	262	278
8	168	174	181	188	194	202	223	245	261
9	154	160	167	174	181	188	210	232	248
10	142	149	156	163	170	177	200	223	239
11	134	140	147	154	161	169	191	215	231
12	126	133	140	147	154	162	185	209	226
13	120	127	134	141	148	156	179	204	221
14	114	121	129	136	143	151	175	200	217
15	110	117	124	132	139	147	171	196	214
20	94	102	110	117	126	134	160	187	205
30	81	89	97	106	113	124	152	181	202
40	75	84	93	102	111	121	150	180	200

For the general case, the annual charge is given by $\dfrac{Cr(1 + r)^n}{(1 + r)^n - 1}$

where C = capital investment
$\quad r$ = rate of interest
$\quad n$ = years of repayment

Example: if you borrow £1000 at 12 per cent for 20 years, you repay £134 each year for 20 years

Mortgage Repayment Data

Breakdown of repayment per £1000 borrowed: I = Interest; R = Repayment of loan; L = Loan outstanding

Loan through 10 years	6%			8%			10%			12%			15%			20%		
	I	R	L	I	R	L	I	R	L	I	R	L	I	R	L	I	R	L
1	60	76	924	80	69	931	100	63	937	120	57	943	150	50	950	200	39	961
2	55	80	844	74	75	856	94	69	868	113	64	879	143	57	893	192	46	915
3	51	85	758	69	81	776	87	76	792	106	71	808	134	66	827	183	55	860
4	46	90	668	62	87	689	79	84	709	97	80	728	124	76	751	172	67	793
5	40	96	572	55	94	595	71	92	617	87	90	638	113	87	664	159	80	713
6	34	102	471	48	101	494	62	101	516	77	100	538	100	100	564	143	96	617
7	28	108	363	39	110	384	52	111	405	65	112	425	85	115	449	123	115	502
8	22	114	249	31	118	266	40	122	282	51	126	299	67	133	316	100	138	364
9	15	121	128	21	128	138	28	134	148	36	141	158	47	153	163	73	166	199
10	8	128	0	11	138	0	15	148	0	19	158	0	24	163	0	40	199	0

Loan through 30 years	6%			8%			10%			12%			15%			20%		
	I	R	L	I	R	L	I	R	L	I	R	L	I	R	L	I	R	L
1	60	13	987	80	9	991	100	6	994	120	4	996	150	2	998	200	1	999
5	57	16	929	77	12	948	97	9	963	118	7	974	149	3	987	199	2	994
10	51	21	833	71	18	872	92	14	903	113	11	927	145	7	960	196	4	978
15	44	29	706	63	26	760	83	23	807	104	20	846	138	14	906	190	11	939
20	34	38	535	51	38	596	69	37	652	88	36	701	124	28	799	174	27	842
25	21	51	306	33	56	355	46	60	402	61	63	448	94	58	553	134	67	601
30	4	69	0	7	82	0	10	96	0	13	111	0	20	132	0	33	167	0

Example: if you borrow £1000 for 30 years at 15 per cent, you will repay £152 a year, including (in first year) £150 interest and £2 repayment of capital and (in 30th year) £20 interest and £132 capital. Interest is usually chargeable for Income Tax, capital repayment is not.

Index